Strategic Uses of Alternative Media

Strategic Uses of Alternative Media

Just the Essentials

Robyn Blakeman

M.E.Sharpe
Armonk, New York
London, England

Library of Congress Cataloging-in-Publication Data

Blakeman, Robyn, 1958–
  Strategic uses of alternative media : just the essentials / by Robyn Blakeman.
     p. cm.
  Includes bibliographical references and index.
  ISBN 978-0-7656-2555-7 (hbk. : alk. paper)— ISBN 0-7656-2556-4 (pbk. : alk. paper)
  1. Marketing. 2. Advertising. 3. Alternative mass media. 4. Social media. I. Title.

HF5415.B4557 2011
658.8′72—dc22   2010054315

Printed in the United States of America

The paper used in this publication meets the minimum requirements of
American National Standard for Information Sciences
Permanence of Paper for Printed Library Materials,
ANSI Z 39.48-1984.

∞

| EB (c) | 10 | 9 | 8 | 7 | 6 | 5 | 4 | 3 | 2 | 1 |
| EB (p) | 10 | 9 | 8 | 7 | 6 | 5 | 4 | 3 | 2 | 1 |

Contents

Introduction

Strategic Uses of Alternative Media: Just the Essentials is an in-depth, yet simply stated discussion of alternative media, its use, and the role it plays in advertising. My step-by-step approach focuses exclusively on alternative media as a strategic and often more targeted way to deliver a product's or service's message.

The use of alternative media is more than a passing trend. The way consumers view and use advertising is forcing marketers to reexamine how they reach and interact with the intended target. Because targets are inundated with thousands of advertising messages each day, it is critical to find delivery methods that are guaranteed to reach them, where they are, with an attention-stopping message that interests them. Whether the client chooses to "wow" with guerrilla marketing or quickly and inexpensively text the target, alternative media vehicles offer creative, convenient, and unique ways to deliver often-personalized messages of indeterminate length. These messages can often be delivered globally, used to camouflage economic limitations on the part of the advertiser and the target, and/or reflect cultural diversity. Strategy—and issues surrounding strategic campaign and media development—is critical to understanding today's ever-changing advertising climate.

Alternative media is still a developing educational topic. Few books on the market go beyond an introductory examination of new media in general or its journalism-based technological, social, cultural, and political uses. Some texts look at alternative media options from simply a specific media point of view. Research into this area reveals a significant number of books on alternative or new media, but none that (1) focuses exclusively on advertising, (2) looks at specific media options, or (3) concentrates on the strategic, creative, or targeted and economical use of such media in advertising.

My distinct approach helps readers determine when it is best to use traditional media, when to abandon traditional strategies altogether, and when it is appropriate to employ a strategic mix of both traditional and alternative media in a product- or service-oriented campaign. Additionally, rather than dissecting only a small sample of the varied types of alternative media, my examination looks at the remarkable assortment of alternative media available and how it is being used now, how it will be used in the future, and how it will change the overall visual/verbal message delivered to the targeted audience. Discussions deal solely with the field of advertising and the effects alternative media have on the economy, society, and the move toward global advertising, as well as the strategic development of the advertised message. Topics should ignite practical discussion across the diverse disciplines that make up advertising, marketing, and even public relations by offering both business and creative solutions.

The information-packed chapters in this book are organized into three specific areas. The first takes an in-depth look at how and why marketers and advertisers employ alternative media and how agencies are finding more inexpensive and targeted ways to work within a tight economy. The second examines the strategic implementation of alternative media into the promotional mix, and how the use of alternative media can affect the budget, strategy, and development of the creative message. The third breaks down the multitude of alternative media vehicles available to today's advertiser by dissecting the varied choices and uses for such media—one topic at a time—creating an invaluable research tool that students, professors, and small business professionals alike will refer to time and again.

Student examples of traditional media options appear throughout the text, challenging the reader to see beyond the safety of traditional print and broadcast media. Putting an alternative spin on traditional options makes advertising more interactive, creative, and memorable, while setting the product or service apart from other competitors within the brand category.

Part I

Understanding Alternative Choices

1

Alternative Media Is Changing the Way Businesses Reach Their Target

Figure 1.1 **Sample Ad: Band-Aid**

Source: Created by Chelsa Bowen, The University of Tennessee, Knoxville.

Defining Alternative, New, or Emerging Media

Alternative media, new media, and emerging media are all terms used to describe a diverse array of media vehicles that are often used to support more traditional vehicles such as print (newspaper and magazine), broadcast (radio and television), and even out-of-home and direct marketing.

The term *alternative media* describes a vehicle(s) that cannot be labeled as traditional; *new media,* on the other hand, implies the vehicle(s) have never been used before, and *emerging media* suggests the vehicle(s) is standing out and away from the pack. So which is the most accurate description in the field of advertising? The correct response depends on the proposed media vehicle, how it will be used, and the element of personal preference. Arguably, there are very few—if any—new media vehicles that advertisers have not already thought of or utilized at one time or another. It could be further argued that the Internet and mobile marketing, for example, are new, but both fall more into the emerging category than new media. The least debatable moniker encompasses new, unknown, and emerging vehicles under the all-purpose heading of "alternative media."

PQ Media, the industry-leading media tracker, defines alternative media as "media buying strategies that attempt to bypass the clutter of traditional advertising and marketing in an effort to reach target audiences, primarily through new media such as the Internet, but also by using alternative means through traditional media such as product placement in broadcast television."

No matter what you call it, these very creative promotions and ads look for a highly visible venue that will reach the target and combine it with a creative, tantalizing, and possibly shocking message that is both memorable and viral. Nontraditional surfaces can surprise and reach the target wherever they are, often when they least expect it.

A media vehicle is considered alternative if it has a large, small, round, flat, stationary or moving, edible or nonedible surface that will hold a message and ensure the targeted consumer will come in contact with it. Often placed in unusual or unconventional places, these highly targeted, creative, and sometimes interactive vehicles are excellent at delivering both a meaningful and memorable ad more effectively than traditional media vehicles. And, unlike most other vehicles, they cannot be clicked out of, turned off, zapped, or deleted.

Opting for Alternative Media

Advertisers employ alternative media when traditional vehicles are unsuccessful at reaching the target. The diversity of these vehicles assures the message will reach the target wherever they are and whether they consciously choose to receive the message or not. Like traditional advertising, alternative media is constantly evolving and experimenting with new ways to reach potential consumers with a message that will attract and hold their attention.

To do this effectively, alternative media substitutes the traditional mass message sent to a mass audience with a personalized message sent to a specific niche of targeted individuals. This strategy makes it one of the best ways to advertise a brand, attract attention, increase traffic to a website, and gain equity creatively within a brand category. More and more advertisers are looking at alternative media as a viable way of reaching their targeted audience because of the following trends: (1) the target is becoming more fractured; (2) traditional media is not reaching the target; (3) it takes more to get and hold the target's attention; and (4) advertisers are looking more at behavior than reach and frequency.

Products and services employing alternative media most often include general retail, clothing, music, books, children's products, home and garden, financial services, office materials, health and fitness, and charitable organizations, to name just a few.

Typically, the choice of advertising vehicle depends largely on where it is used in the purchase process. For example, traditional advertising is especially good for attracting and launching new products and soliciting new customers. Alternative media vehicles, on the other hand, are great for conducting research and developing and maintaining a positive customer relationship. Campaigns that employ a mixture of both traditional and nontraditional media vehicles are more successful at developing a lasting relationship with the target while building both brand awareness and brand image.

Most alternative media vehicles have little to say but are extremely effective at: (1) directing offline consumers to a website; (2) encouraging online sales; (3) encouraging additional inquiries; (4) successfully reaching the elusive and highly coveted 18- to 34-year-old target group; and (5) tracking online and offline return on investment (ROI), or whether the marketer or client made more than was spent on advertising.

Spending on these new media vehicles has a short history, but available data show growth each year since the economic downtown that began in December of 2007. They are a great choice for businesses looking to interact with their target and create buzz at the same time. Smaller advertisers find the niche markets and narrow reach of alternative media especially attractive; larger or more urban-based businesses find it a great way to reach a multicultural audience in busy areas.

Because interactivity is an important component in grabbing attention and creating memorable encounters, messages must speak to the target in diverse ways—both visual and verbal. Some are thought provoking, others funny, and still others shocking, but all of them work to invoke curiosity and generate excitement with their highly creative approaches.

One of the most exciting aspects of alternative media is its ability to captivate the public's imagination with its visual/verbal voice. As marketers become more aware of the new media's effectiveness, they are adopting it more often in order to attract consumer attention. There are hundreds if not thousands of forms of alternative media that can be incorporated into any event or program or placed on any shaped surface. Here is a list of options:

- 3-D Catalogs
- 3-D Out-of-Home (Extreme Out-of-Home)
- ATM Machine Advertising
- Advergaming
- Aerial Advertising
- Airport Advertising
- Augmented Reality
- Automated Shelf and Aisle Advertising
- Banners
- Bathroom Advertising
- Bilingual Street Teams
- Blogs
- Body Billboards
- Branded Vinyl Stickers (Postering)
- Bubble Clouds
- Buses (Inside and Out)
- Bus Shelters
- Bus/Train/Subway Terminals
- Bus Wraps
- Business Card Backs
- Buzz Advertising
- CDs
- Card Deck Mailings (Poly Packs)
- Catalog Bind-Ins/Blow-Ins
- Chairs/Benches
- Chopstick Advertising
- Cinema Advertising
- Coffee Cup Sleeves
- Consumer Generated Advertising (Social Media)
- Co-op Mailings
- Coupons
- DVR Advertising
- Digital Out-of-Home
- Direct Marketing/Relationship Marketing
  * Direct Mail
- Doggie Bag Advertising
- Door-to-Door Advertising
- Downloadable Videos
- Drive-In Advertising
- E-direct marketing
- E-zines
- E-mail
- Endorsements
- Escalator Handrail and Steps
- Event Graffiti Performances (Wallscapes)
- Event Sponsorships
- Exercise Equipment
- Faxes
- Flyers (Traditional/Suction Cups)
- Free Standing Inserts (FSI)
- Fruits and Vegetables
- Gaming
- Gas Pump Top Advertising
- Gas Pump Nozzles

- Grocery Cart Advertising
- Guerrilla Marketing
- Hand Stamp Advertising
- Home Video Advertising
- Influencer Marketing
- Inserts
- Interactive TV
- iPods
- Issue Advertising
- Live Mobile Billboards
- Manhole Covers
- Milk Cartons
- Mobile Advertising
- Mobile Billboards
- Mobile Video
- Mobile Video Cubes
- Movie Promotions
- Moving Walkways
- Newsletters
- On-Cart Advertising
  * Grocery
  * Golf
- Online Classifieds
- Online Video Advertising
- Out-of-Home
- Package Inserts (PIP)
- Parking Garage Advertising
  (Entrance/Exit Gates)
- Parking Garage Ticket Backs
- Parking Meters
- Payroll/Credit Card Stuffers
- Pedicabs (Pedal-Powered Taxis)
- Podcasts
- Point of Purchase Displays
  (POP)
- Police Cars
- Pop-Up Brand Experiences
- Postering Campaigns
  * Splash Campaigns
  * Blanket Campaigns
- Product Placement

- Projection Advertising
- RSS (Web-Feed Format)
- Ride Alongs
- Rip-Away Posters
- Search Advertising
- Sampling Programs (Product/
  Brand Sampling)
  * Event-Based Sampling
  * Flash Mob Brand Sampling
  * Guerrilla Street Team
    Sampling
  * Fill Concept Brand Sampling
  * Point of Use Product
    Sampling
  * Nightlife Product Sampling
  * Covert Product Sampling
  * In-Venue Brand Sampling
  * Van Product Sampling
  * Intercept Brand Sampling
- Satellite Radio
- Scaffolding
- Search Engine Advertising
- Shopping Bags
- Snappable Ads
- Sports Marketing
- Statement Stuffers
- Street Art (Sidewalks and
  Streets)
- Stickers
- Supermarket Shelf Advertising
- Supermarket Shelf Talkers
- Sweepstakes/Contests
- Take-a-ways
- Taxi Cabs (Inside/Outside)
- Telemarketing
- Texting
- Ticket Jackets (Airline, Rail,
  Bus)
- Tissue Packs
- Toilet Seats
- Toilet Stalls

- Tradeshows
- Trucks
- Vacant Storefront Windows
- Valet Parking Tickets/Parking Permits
- Vehicle Wraps
- Videogame/Online Gaming
- Video Projection
- Vinyl Stickers
- Viral Marketing
- Wall Murals
- Webisodes
- Websites
- Wild Posting
  * Rip-Away Wild Postings
  * Snipe Media Wild Postings
  * Sidewalk Chalkings
  * Sidewalk Decals
  * Static-Cling Wild Postings
  * Urban Street Pole Postings
  * Reverse Graffiti and Clean Graffiti
  * Creative Outdoor Poster Billboards
- Word-of-Mouth Marketing
- Workout Equipment

As a support vehicle, alternative media is highly effective at building brand awareness, launching a new product, reinforcing an existing brand image, or reminding the target about a mature or reinvented brand. Its flexibility and variety make it a great choice for local, national, or internationally advertised products, services, and charities. How it is incorporated into a campaign depends largely on the target, the creativity of the vehicle(s) employed, and the quality of the message.

The use of alternative media is on the rise because it is hard for consumers to avoid it. Traditional media vehicles can no longer reach a fractionalized target audience effectively; alternative media brings the message directly to the target and gets them to talk about it. The goal is to create interest thorough interaction with the product or service, thereby encouraging feedback. It is also attractive to marketers because its unexpected nature and in-your-face tactics have been successful in connecting with that all-important target audience composed of buyers in their late teens to mid-thirties. This is the group most resistant to traditional advertising techniques and the most likely to generate additional buzz.

The diversity of vehicles makes it very difficult to define the overall visual/verbal voice of a "typical" alternative vehicle. This is made doubly hard, since few vehicles are actually considered "typical." What is known is that the majority of alternative vehicles rely on a powerful visual/verbal message and creative placement in an unexpected location to get their point across. Copy-light, like out-of-home, such a message never contains more than one or two sentences plus a logo, slogan, or tagline.

As mentioned earlier, alternative media vehicles function well as support vehicles when using more traditional advertising. They are most often confined to showcasing a logo, a slogan or tagline, a color scheme, or—if large enough—a spokesperson or character representative. When possible, resurrect colors, typefaces, headline styles, spokespersons or character representatives, slogans or taglines, a unique layout style, or photographic, illustrative, or graphic images to ensure campaign compatibility.

Reaching the Target in Alternative Ways

Reaching consumers is harder than ever before. With thousands of messages directed at them every day, it has become increasingly important to reach targets where they are, with a message they are sure to see and react to. Today's consumers do not rely on a single media vehicle for information; instead, they employ varying resources to receive information and comparison-shop before purchasing. This multiple use of resources is known as *media multitasking,* the main source of target fractionalization. Reaching the intended target with the right message in the right media requires considerable research, frequent message repetition, smart interactive options, and creative ingenuity.

The choice of media is as important as the development of the creative message. It should advance the brand and use an assortment of old or *brand-centric* and new or *consumer-centric* media vehicles. Visual/verbal messages that are unique and offer some type of interactive and/or viral component can incorporate the use of both.

Since most alternative media—guerrilla marketing among them—play a supportive role in the majority of advertising campaigns, it is difficult to determine their precise ROI. It is important, then, that inquiries be tracked back to varied vehicles by incorporating different promotional or marketing codes for each vehicle used in the campaign.

This very interactive and consumer-focused form of advertising is a concrete way to create dialogue, build a relationship, and obtain feedback, making consumers feel a part of the brand's success.

Understanding Alternative Media's Strengths and Weaknesses

Let's take a look at what the varying types of alternative media vehicles can and cannot bring to the media mix.

Strengths

1. Reach. Messages are received because the target has opted in to receive them, making this a great relationship-building device. These

Figure 1.2   **Sample Ad: Sharpie**

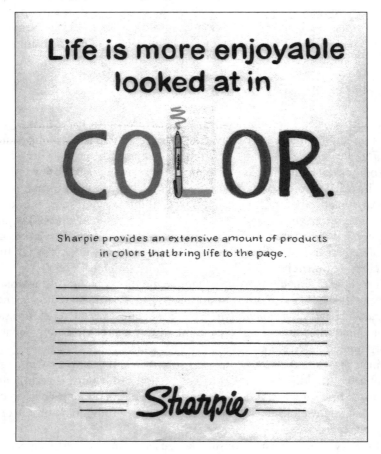

Source: Created by Claire Stephens, The University of Tennessee, Knoxville.

diverse vehicles are also a great way to reach the target where and
when they least (or most) expect it.

2. Unconventional. The unique and often unconventional tactics
used with alternative media often stop consumers in their tracks,
encourage word-of-mouth exchanges, and/or create a great viral
opportunity.

3. Targetable. Many vehicles are highly targetable or permission
based.

4. Creative and Interactive. Vehicles that are both engaging and interactive are always more memorable.

5. Expense. Some alternative vehicles require little or no cost to deliver.

Weaknesses

1. Ineffective. Alternative media by itself will not reach the target. To be effective, it must be woven seamlessly into a traditional media campaign.
2. Ethics. It is important that all methods (especially guerrilla methods) be clearly exposed as advertising so as not to be labeled misleading, deceptive, or unethical.
3. Expense. Not all alternative media options are inexpensive. Guerrilla marketing can not only be expensive but a public relations disaster if not carried out correctly.
4. Word of Mouth. Buzz is only as good as the product, the event, or the visual/verbal message.

Alternative Media in Action

Let's take a look at a few examples of how corporations and charitable organizations have employed alternative media.

The human rights group Witness Against Torture used elevator doors as their canvas to campaign for the closing of the Guantanamo Bay detention camp. From the outside, observers could see a man's hands, apparently attempting to wedge the door open from the inside. Once viewers stepped inside the elevator, they saw the back of that same man in prison garb and leg-cuffs. The copy read, "More than 90% of Guantanamo detainees are held without charge and in extreme isolation. Help stop the abuse. Visit witnesstorture.org."

VIP Gym strongly suggested that people work out a little after that big dinner. To get consumers out of their dinner chairs and running, they covered the backs of chairs in local restaurants with images of flabby, out-of–shape, flattened, naked bottoms, symbolizing the sitters' rear ends: The idea was to let diners know in a not-so-subtle way that they might be a bit bigger than they think. Copy read, "VIP GYM. Get up and run."

To bring attention to the plight of starving children in Africa, Feed South Africa placed pictures of undernourished children sitting in the bottom of grocery carts with their hands outstretched. Any items placed in the cart gave the illusion they were going directly into the hands of the very children who needed them most.

An Australian campaign for water safety placed life-sized posters on the bottom of swimming pools; the graphic depicted a child in swimming trunks lying facedown and motionless. This awareness campaign by Watch Around Water provided a startlingly realistic view of a drowning child from above. Copy read, "Where's Your Child? WATCH AROUND WATER."

Another successful campaign, this one for the National Aquarium in Baltimore, caught people's attention coming and going. Marketers used the entrance and exit gates at a local parking garage to advertise the aquarium's shark exhibit. This creative use of alternative space placed a shark on the gates into and out of the garage, so anyone passing through was exposed to the visual image.

Alternative Media and Cultural, Social, and Global Issues

Alternative media vehicles are especially suited to global marketing because of their adaptability and diversity of media options. The Internet and social media sites make it easy to reach a global audience and customize a product or service to meet the target's particular needs. One of the largest vehicles in the alternative media toolbox—the Internet—has no global boundaries, making it possible for small businesses to compete against their larger, more financially powerful, competitors. Deciding whether or not to advertise globally depends on the brand and the campaign's overall objectives.

Once embedded in the culture, products and services can adapt their message and manner of delivery to strategically reach the target audience where they are, with a message they will understand. Success relies on individualized and culturally adaptive tactics.

Many experts believe that globalized advertising has homogenized consumers' needs and wants, successfully altering many long-standing social and cultural lifestyle practices. Advertising has infected the international community with Westernized ideals and habits: international audiences are eating more fast food products than ever before, adopting a less formal mode of dress, recognizing their love of electronic gadgets, and heightening their awareness of personal hygiene.

Simply put, global marketing is the selling of products and services to an international market. No multicultural target audience is the same. Each interprets visual and verbal stimuli differently. Marketers must be aware of any and all cultural differences (language nuances, social values, literacy levels, media availability, culinary preferences, religious leanings, socioeconomic levels, and government regulations, among others) that can affect the way members of the target audience respond to a message. Each of these factors, in turn, can be further influenced by regional differences within a single country.

Care must be taken to attract, not offend, foreign consumers: changes to packaging may be necessary, along with alterations in color, the overall visual/verbal message, and quite possibly the brand itself in order to adapt to different cultures. In particular, language translations should be monitored for discrepancies in meaning. Even within a given country, the implications of regional dialects have to be addressed. Great copy or slogans used in one language may not be as appealing in another. For example, when translated into Spanish, the popular and long-running slogan "Got Milk?" used by the American Dairy Association means "Are You Lactating?" "Finger-lickin' good," the well-known Kentucky Fried Chicken slogan, is translated into Chinese as "Eat your fingers off."

Slang can also be a problem. Scandinavian-produced Electrolux vacuums suffered a blow after realizing that their slogan—when translated into English—morphed into the rather offensive saying, "Nothing sucks like an Electrolux." On the same note, be careful when using any type of analogy. An analogy compares one thing to another based on similarities; for example, Walt Disney World Resort described itself as "roughly half the size of Rhode Island." Such a reference may be helpful if you live in the United States, but it means very little to an international audience. So if you must use some type of comparison, be sure it has some relevance to the target. When Walt Disney World ran the same ad in the United Kingdom, the theme park's advertising copy reported it was "roughly the size of greater Manchester."

Along with language, cultural differences must be considered to avoid appearing disrespectful or generally out of touch with the target audience. Some of the most common issues involve the interpretation of colors, symbols, levels of brand acceptance and/or preferences, and visual relationships.

Colors carry entirely different meanings to various cultural and social groups. Red in many Western cultures, for example, means hot or dangerous; in China, however, it is often associated with happiness and used prominently in weddings. In tropical regions, green represents danger rather than an environmentally safe product. White in many Asian cultures is often associated with death, whereas many Western cultures equate it with purity.

Having a good understanding of the relevance of color can determine a product's ultimate success or failure in the marketplace. For example, brand loyalty among Pepsi drinkers in Southeast Asia dropped when the company changed their vending machines from a deep rich blue to a light icy blue. Consumers found the new color choice unappetizing, since the lighter shade is associated with mourning and death in that region of the world.

Cultural anomalies are common across the globe and play a huge role in how a brand is marketed and ultimately accepted in different locations. Brands that ignore cultural differences do so at their own peril and expense. Hiring local translators and/or consultants can expose little-known laws and cultural beliefs, such as Malaysia's prohibited use of foreign models in any advertising efforts, Japan's view of images that depict sexual intimacy as offensive, and Saudi Arabia's strict laws against such images.

Consequently, every visual/verbal element must be scrutinized and tested before adoption or transference from one culture into another. Take the introduction of Gerber Baby Food in Africa: It is standard advertising practice in non-English-speaking parts of Africa to depict the contents of a food container on its label. A can of beans, then, would bear a label with an image of the type of beans consumers could expect to find inside the can. In a particularly unfortunate (and revolting) example of the importance of country-specific advertising savvy, the cute little Gerber Baby logo featured on every jar of food implied that each jar contained a concoction made from baby parts!

Sometimes it's not just the packaging that needs changing; the brand itself might need to change in order to achieve international acceptance. Kraft found this out when promoting Oreo cookies in China. The initial introduction of the popular American cookie received a somewhat lukewarm reception from Chinese consumers. Further research revealed that Oreos were considered too sweet for most Chinese tastes. In addition, the Oreo brand was missing out on China's large population of milk drinkers. This data helped Kraft reinvent the Oreo to coincide with consumer needs and wants—and introduced the practice of "dunking" to the Chinese cookie-eating segment.

China's version of the Oreo cookie is thinner, tubular in shape, and less sweet than the original recipe; it features four crispy wafer layers filled with vanilla and chocolate cream and coated in layers of chocolate. To promote the reinvented Oreo, Kraft used street teams to hand out product samples on the streets of Beijing, followed by additional advertising on television and at local events that launched its new taste and look and demonstrated proper dunking techniques.

Research into the likes and dislikes of the international consumer has also helped Kraft tap into Europe's love of dark chocolate and Russia's penchant for premium instant coffees. The more the advertiser knows about the target and their lifestyle, the easier it is to choose the best mix of media vehicles to reach them. Information can also assist the account and creative teams in how to reposition an existing product, introduce new products, and determine the most appropriate visual/verbal message to attract the target's attention in a way that does not alienate or offend.

Not all international advertising is fraught with problems, rules, and regulations. McDonald's has effectively navigated the murky visual/verbal international waters for years with the standardized motto "I'm lovin' it" and the internationally recognized golden arches. Celebrities with a global following can also successfully cross international boundaries, as can product placement in popular movies. For decades, James Bond films have successfully featured BMW, Ford, Sony electronics, and Omega watches, to name just a few. Additional media options available to global marketers include search engine marketing, e-mail campaigns, the placement of links on sites with a similar target audience, websites and banner ads offered in multiple languages, or the use of local trade shows or events to promote trial.

In a global economy, one size does not fit all messages. Meticulous research can help capture attention and encourage some type of action on the part of the target, such as a visit to a website or a brick-and-mortar store for more information or to make a purchase. Let's take a quick look at how research can help define an advertising direction.

Research Is the Foundation for a Successful Campaign

For most creative teams, dealing with research is not the most interesting aspect of advertising: it can be tedious, lengthy, and dry. Without it however, marketers and their advertising agencies would never be able to develop a business plan of attack or an idea that really speaks to the target. They could not define that one characteristic that will attract the target's attention or enable them to accomplish the objectives laid out in that plan.

Initial research is most often gathered by the client and goes through considerable analysis before being used to imagine a creative solution that meets both the client and target's unique needs.

Research will help both the advertising account and creative teams to understand varied cultural anomalies and employ the correct visual/verbal solution in the best media vehicle(s).The answers to any questions about message direction can be found in research results. Additional information can be garnered from focus groups or varied types of surveys. The goal is to build or maintain a unique brand image, challenge competitors' claims, and answer the target's question, What can this product or service do for me?

The data help the account and creative teams get inside the target's head, with a particular focus on avoiding any replication of competitors' advertising efforts or making any cultural, social, or political mistakes. Findings can suggest the best way to solve the target's problem, whether it is through the use of demonstrations or testimonials or copy-heavy informational ads. Research results also confirm the level of knowledge the target has with the brand, what it will take to get them to switch brands, or how to get them to take a second look at a reinvented brand. Research educates the teams so they can seduce the target with statistics; these statistics, however, are camouflaged as a creative idea that not only attracts buyers' attention, but creates a buzz as well.

This plethora of new and existing data improves the dynamic between visual/verbal vehicles, ensuring they are clear and concise—and never simply implied. Creative that is not thoroughly grounded in research findings will be

Figure 1.3   **Sample Ad: GNC**

Source: Created by Jared Thigpen, The University of Tennessee, Knoxville.

ignored by or even offend the target. Incorrectly targeted or vague messages will lead the target to seek out competing brands that more precisely meet their needs, wants, lifestyles, and cultural beliefs. A "clever" message may be more interesting from a creative standpoint, but if it doesn't ultimately reach the target and make a sale, it will fail.

What Is Marketing Research?

The AMA defines marketing research as "the function that links the consumer, customer, and public to the marketer through information. [This] information [can be] used to identify and define marketing opportunities and problems; generate, refine, and evaluate marketing actions; monitor marketing performance; and improve understanding of marketing as a process." Marketing research is all about providing multiple ways to implement, collect, and analyze data. This data will eventually point the way to a visual/verbal solution to the client's advertising problem.

Understanding Qualitative and Quantitative Research

Most research gathered by the client is used to define a marketing strategy for the promotion of their product or service. Very simply, a marketing strategy defines the target, outlines the product, and defines its place among the competition. This data will be used in the development of the marketing plan and influence what information appears in the creative brief. Data can be compiled using either quantitative or qualitative methods.

Quantitative (or primary) *research* refers to new data and involves collecting relevant information in order to find an answer to a particular set of marketing needs. Quantitative data are very specific: such research often employs the use of controlled response surveys, where participants choose the best answer from a finite number of responses. There are two types of surveys available to researchers: formal and informal. *Formal surveys* include closed-ended questions that ask participants to choose from a predetermined set of responses such as "strongly agree," "agree," "disagree," and "strongly disagree," or from a set of multiple-choice answers. *Informal surveys* feature open-ended questions that allow participants to express their opinions.

Formal surveys are most often employed when the survey taker wants to know how the respondent feels about something or needs responses to be ranked in some kind of categorical order. Informal surveys are great when there is no single definitive answer, or the survey taker wants respondents to give an opinion in their own words. These surveys can often be a rich source of insightful and quotable material.

Additionally, primary data may be gleaned from field tests, market surveys, questionnaires or interviews to study market feedback on a particular product or service. Quantitative research is a particularly good resource when more specific product-focused or service-focused results are needed, or when preparing for new product launches or reinventing brands.

Unlike quantitative research, *qualitative* (or secondary) research often uses a smaller group of representative respondents and does not analyze results using statistical techniques. Qualitative surveys are frequently conducted outside of a controlled environment using a predetermined set of questions, but instead of controlling the type of response given by the target, participants are allowed to express their opinions freely. Several different types of research collection methods, including focus groups, one-on-one interviews, and random sampling, are used to define a problem or understand a respondent's knowledge, attitudes, beliefs, and experiences with the brand. Surveys can be conducted in person, through the mail, via phone, or online. Qualitative research also employs the use of observational research techniques that reveal shopping or TV habits, or show how a product is perceived or used by the target. Primary research should rely on secondary research, or existing data, to understand any changes in the marketplace or identify any emerging trends or opportunities. This critical relationship helps marketers assess the marketplace and gives advertisers a better understanding of the product, its competitors, and the targeted audience most likely to purchase the product or use the service.

Utilizing secondary data involves researching, organizing, and processing data that has already been collected by previous research studies. Abundant materials can be found at many government agencies here and abroad as well as nongovernment agencies such as local libraries, universities, and trade associations, or through the use of existing or prepurchased databases, to name just a few. Secondary research is less expensive than primary research but not always as accurate.

Both types of research are used to uncover information regarding the amount of knowledge the target has about the product or service, including how it is used; how it tastes, smells, or feels; any customer service initiatives; and the target's level of knowledge about competitors' brands.

Employing both primary and secondary research techniques assists marketers and advertising agencies in better understanding the target and their needs and wants. This knowledge will ultimately help define the campaign's creative direction.

Advertising agencies rely on the client to supply the majority of research; however, when searching for the target's opinion on one or more specific topics, agencies will often conduct research using focus groups, pretesting, and posttesting.

Focus groups are usually made up of 10 to 12 representative members of the target audience who will interact with the brand in a controlled environment. Participants are asked to give their overall opinions or impressions of the product or service. Focus groups often participate in *pretesting,* also known as *copy testing.* This type of research tests both the visual and verbal aspects of an idea. Usually conducted using a single ad or a representative sample of the campaign, respondents are asked to record their impressions on creativity, brand awareness, and informational quality of the visual/verbal message. *Posttesting* keeps track of how the brand is performing at regular intervals during the campaign's life cycle or is completed after a campaign ends.

Ultimately, research results must be comprehensive enough to help define the target, the key consumer benefit, the objectives, and the overall strategy and tone of voice to be used in creative executions.

Zeroing In on the Target

Once all the surveys and interviews are over and the analysis is complete, the client will know exactly who is most likely to buy their product or use their service. This important group of individuals is known as the *target audience* or *target market.* For advertising efforts to be more consumer-centric, researchers break the target audience down into four specific categories, including demographic, psychographic, geographic, and behavioristic segments.

Demographics deal with the target's personal characteristics, among them, gender, age, income, ethnicity, educational level, marital status, number of children, and occupation. This type of statistical information allows for a certain amount of speculation about how the targeted group will purchase.

Psychographics deals with lifestyle issues, attitudes, beliefs, activities, and personal interests such as the target's view of foreign products, their political leanings, how they spend their leisure time, and whether or not they are product initiators (also known as "first to own"). Do they typically conduct a great deal of research or engage in hands-on trials before purchasing? Are they active or sedentary? Into entertainment, junk food, or techno wizardry? Environmentally conscious, economically frugal, ethnically or culturally influenced, or security conscious?

Psychographics also plays a big role in where the target lives geographically. A *geographic* profile shows where the target lives by country, region, province, state, city, or zip code. Such information may offer cultural insights into their purchase habits, indicating, for instance, if they are more likely to eat fish over red meat or need warm or cool weather clothing. Geographical profiles are also excellent indicators of the type of media vehicles and events the target will be exposed to most often.

A *behavioristic* profile combines the three previous market segment profiles together to determine why a person buys and how. Are they prone to satisfying their emotional wants or more conservative with their money? Are they brand loyal? Do they look for status products? Are they the first to buy new technologically advanced products?

Profiling is particularly important to brands that are marketed internationally. Messages directed at international audiences will often require a different visual/ verbal approach due to cultural and/or language barriers, as discussed earlier.

These varied target segments can be used in any combination to determine a brand's visual/verbal voice and the best media vehicle(s) to deliver the overall marketing message. Other target segmentation classifications are based on usage patterns, as well as a product's strengths, weaknesses, marketplace opportunities and threats, or any other relevant segment, depending on the product or service's business objectives.

Targeting by ethnic group is yet another way to define the buyer. A target's ethnicity apparently influences buying habits and lifestyle. Of the four main ethnic groups in the United States—White, African American, Hispanic American, and Asian American—each group purchases differently and uses different media vehicles. In many countries the difference between urban and rural communities is based on ethnicity and other regional differences.

Market segmentation personalizes the advertised message and determines the appropriate media vehicle(s) to reach that target, thus eliminating media waste. Messages that appear where the target is, that talk about issues the target is interested in, and that offer multiple ways to seek additional information or initiate purchase help to create a relationship with the target. Advertising without the collection of detailed consumer data is not consumer focused and does not encourage an exchange of information on product performance. Nor does it focus on any additional needs and wants the target may have that can lead to suggestions for product improvements, updates, or additional uses.

Beyond isolating target attributes, data collected will also define how the competition positions itself within the market category and help characterize their message, packaging, media vehicles, and so on. Additionally, it will provide ideas on how the product or service can set itself apart from the competition in some memorable way.

A Closer Look at the Target

There are two classifications of target audiences: primary and secondary. A *primary target audience* includes those individuals who are known to use the brand, have used the brand in the past, or are considered likely to use it in the future. Depending on the product or service, a campaign may have a secondary audience, as well. This audience is usually smaller than the primary audience and includes those who play influential roles in the target's life.

Secondary audiences are composed of people most likely to influence a purchase or those most likely to purchase the product on behalf of the primary audience; examples include family and friends of the primary target and previous users of the product or service. An expensive sneaker purchase, for example, might have been influenced by a celebrity spokesperson but purchased by a grandparent or parent. Although primary targets will receive more attention and marketing dollars because research has determined they are the most likely to initiate the purchase, secondary markets can be profitable as influencers or as purchasers.

When advertising efforts are focused on a small, underserved, narrowly defined group that is not targeted by a competitor, advertisers are said to be pursuing a *niche market*. This market can include a specific ethnic or age group, a particular geographic area, or even some type of specialty industry. Members of niche markets buy products that are either highly specialized or traditional favorites; examples of the market include Polaroid camera buffs, Harley Davidson lovers, or Volkswagen Beetle drivers. Due to the small market share connected with these buyers, the number of competitors in any one category is quite low.

The Internet has created a savvier, more informed target. Before they buy, they can compare products' features and benefits, prices, return policies, and quality of customer service assistance. Nationally and internationally, twenty-first–century buyers have taken control of how they purchase, when they purchase, and where they purchase. It is important, then, that research efforts identify a way to set the brand apart from its competitors, define what media the targeted consumers are sure to see or use, and suggest ways to tailor copy and layout to address their particular interests or concerns.

In the final analysis, whether to use alternative media will depend on (1) the brand; (2) the target audience; (3) the objectives or goals to be accomplished by advertising efforts; (4) the advertising tactics of the brand's closest competitors; (5) the key consumer benefit or that one feature/benefit combination that will attract the target's attention; and (6) the strategy or tactics that will be used to express the key consumer benefit and accomplish the stated objectives.

If the goal is to build or reinforce brand image, build awareness, or unabashedly astound the target, alternative media fits the bill. Unique products will stand out without the use of dazzling stunts or unusual creative ideas. But an item with little or no product differentiation, or one that will be advertised globally, may need creative ingenuity to stand out from a crowded, competitive, or unknown pack. Unique messages delivered in unconventional ways will not only attract the target's attention but also create a memorable experience the target will want to pass on via word of mouth, or virally via e-mail or social sites, thus extending the life of the message.

2

Brands and the Economy

Figure 2.1   **Sample Ad: Knoxville Museum of Art**

Source: Created by Victoria Drew, The University of Tennessee, Knoxville.

Building a Brand Is the First Step Toward Defining Image

Mass marketing to a mass audience is all but extinct. The new world order is all about niche markets and personalized messages delivered on a one-to-one basis, primarily to repeat customers. Digging up new customers is expensive, especially in a down economy, and research indicates that it does not reinforce the brand image, build brand loyalty, or establish brand equity.

Collectively, each stage in the buying process must (1) highlight the product or service, (2) work to build an environment that reinforces quality and service, and (3) lay the foundation for a long and mutually beneficial relationship.

Today, any message that is not individualized is almost sure to fail. Armed with 24/7 access to the Internet, buyers can compare products, shop at their convenience, and avoid pesky salespeople, long lines, and inadequate parking by shopping at a time and a place that is most convenient for them.

To be successful in this technologically driven age of advertising, marketers need to initiate an ongoing two-way dialogue with the target. An individualized approach offers multiple opportunities to engage the target in conversation by offering customizable products or by encouraging feedback on product development, performance, uses, future needs, and/or any customer or technological service issues. Advertising that consistently addresses the target's lifestyle, needs, wants, and special interests can set a product or service apart from competitors and successfully execute the communication strategy. When it's done right, a campaign that focuses a tailor-made message on a specific group of people will build a lasting relationship with the target while strengthening brand equity.

Brand Development

In order to stand out from competing products in the target's mind, every brand must have an identifiable look and personality or image assigned to it through advertising and promotional efforts. The word *brand* in advertising refers to a product or service's name and anything used to represent that name visually or verbally. *Brand awareness* is achieved when the target uses this visual/ verbal identity to recognize one brand over another. Name recognition creates a certain feeling in the target—such as reliability, longevity, pompousness, or cutting-edge technology—every time it is seen or heard. "A brand," writes Robert Blanchard, former Procter & Gamble executive, "is the personification of a product, service, or even entire company" ("Parting Essay," 1999). When creating a brand's image, you give a personality and a visual/verbal voice to the brand. This personality is how the target ultimately perceives the product or service as compared to the competition. The more remarkable the brand's image, the more memorable the brand and its uses will be. Being memorable is good; however, a long-lasting relationship built on service, product quality, and reputation precedes the establishment of brand loyalty, brand equity, or ownership in the product or service's category. When a brand offers every-thing the target needs, it becomes harder for competitors' promotions or peer pressure to entice them to switch to another brand.

What's in a Name?

The brand's name says a lot about a product or service, as does the choice of spokesperson, the representative graphic symbol, and any typographic style and color choices employed in the logo or advertising vehicle. The choice of brand name is often based on a characteristic associated with the brand: its use, the solution to a problem, its reputation, or the perception of trust and reliability associated with the product. There are three basic types of brand names: descriptive, comparative, and independent. Descriptive names hone in on one of the brand's specific features. Comparative brand names describe the brand's use or the outcomes that can be expected based on its use. Inde-pendent brand names have no recognizable ties to the brand.

Consistent product performance and high-quality customer service rep-resentatives are far more important to the target than a clever ad campaign. Perhaps Jerry Della Femina puts it best in his book *From Those Wonderful Folks Who Gave You Pearl Harbor:* "There is a great deal of advertising that is much better than the product. When that happens, all that the good advertising will do is put you out of business faster."

Along with an overall visual/verbal image, a successful brand is defined by promoting its strengths while exploiting the competitors' weaknesses. Advertisers must recognize a brand's weaknesses from the start in order to turn them into possible opportunities that will further engage the target.

Building Brand Image

The next step in the brand-building process is to define the brand's image. According to David Ogilvy, in his book *Ogilvy on Advertising,* one of the most important things the creative team needs to do is "decide what 'image' you want for your brand. Image means *personality.* Products, like people, have personalities, and they can make or break them in the marketplace."

Image can be developed based on a product's reliability, use, longevity, or its innovative positioning in a product category. If a brand has parity with its competitors, it is important to assign it a unique and creative appearance to give it personality. This can be achieved by using visually distinct packaging or logo designs. Assigning a jingle to the product or an interesting spokesperson or inquisitive headline style can also give the brand a personalized voice. Blanchard describes brand image this way: "Like a person, you can respect, like and even love a brand. You can think of it as a deep personal friend, or merely an acquaintance. You can view it as dependable or undependable; principled or opportunistic; caring or capricious. Just as you like to be around certain people and not others, so also do you like to be with certain brands and not others."

The best way to build and maintain a strong brand image is to deliver a product that meets or exceeds the target's needs, purchase after purchase. Additionally, each customer contact point must consistently deliver educated, helpful, and courteous assistance. To be the target's first choice when shopping, a brand must value its image—building it, maintaining it, and periodically tweaking it to ensure it remains top of mind.

A brand's essence is more than just a logo; it is also based upon the target's combined knowledge of and experiences with the brand and must be reinforced during every interaction or touchpoint with the target, including its packaging, customer service, delivery drivers, sales personnel, store ambiance, and so on.

Reputation or brand image does not stop with advertising and promotional events. It also needs to appear on shopping bags, invoices, receipts, trucks, wrapping paper, anywhere the consumer takes the brand's image. It is important to keep in mind that the brand represents the entire customer experience—everything else reinforces it.

A brand will ultimately succeed or fail based on its image or reputation. A carefully developed image gives a brand its personality—one that that sets it apart from competitors even if the brand has no recognizable product differences. Image is not bulletproof, however; it must be monitored and maintained constantly, and strengthened when necessary. If ignored, this hard-won image will be jeopardized. It is very difficult to overcome bad publicity resulting from offensive or misleading advertising efforts, a spokesperson's public scandal, or poisonous viral sharing on social networking sites.

Building Brand Loyalty

Modern-day advertisers realize that the target is inundated with advertised messages, making it harder and harder for a single brand to stand out in a field of indistinguishable competitors. Searching for the right target is an expensive process. Today, marketers realize that the most cost-effective way to advertise is to develop long-term brand loyal consumers. Actually, consumer loyalty has very little to do with advertising and much more to do with product reliability and the quality of customer service efforts. Although advertising first ignites brand awareness and may encourage trial, it cannot overcome inconsistent performance by a brand, or poorly made products, or rude or incompetent customer or technical service representatives.

What does it mean to be brand loyal? A consumer must regularly repurchase the product or use the service without the assistance of advertising, without thought, and without concern for price or competitor promotions.

A brand that consistently delivers on its advertised promise and performs reliably—exactly the same way each time it is used—develops a loyal following of satisfied consumers. So, it could be said that loyalty begins with the satisfaction of an emotional need or want and is maintained by quality products and services. Brand-loyal consumers require less advertising and promotional persuasion to repeatedly repurchase their favorite brand. Brands know that the level of loyalty will be stronger if the target can reach out to customer service representatives anytime, day or night; leave feedback online; actively participate in blogs; and be the first to be informed about any upgrades or additions to the product or service.

In an online article titled "Want Loyalty? Buy a Dog!" Egbert Jan van Bel describes loyalty as "a sense of attachment to or even affection for a company's people, products or services." However, this affection can quickly take a negative turn when:

1. Products do not perform reliably with each purchase.
2. The brand's image is tarnished due to any type of negative publicity.
3. The brand lacks quality or customer service initiatives.
4. A revolving door of employees leads to massive worker turnovers.
5. Negative word of mouth runs rampant.
6. The brand becomes known for its lack of comprehensive return, guarantee, or warranty policies.

Loyalty is measured by the lifetime value a customer brings to a brand. Overall, the cost of acquiring a new customer is anywhere from five to ten times greater than the cost of retaining an existing customer. Therefore, it is important to understand that brand loyalty is more than just a repeat purchase: It is an experience with the brand. If this experience is continually nurtured, a loyal customer will:

1. Spend more money over the long term;
2. Repurchase without the need for additional advertising;
3. Generate educated referrals;
4. Tolerate small mistakes or inconveniences; and
5. Be willing to pay higher prices to obtain a quality product or service that offers them a measurable value.

Because a loyal customer can deliver a big return on investment, the relationship must be cultivated through customer service efforts. The quality of customer contact can build or destroy a relationship.

Maintaining Brand Equity

Brand equity is the brand's value in the mind of the consumer. This "value" is based on the target's repeated experience with a product, word of mouth, and reputation. The more satisfaction the consumer receives with each successive purchase, the more brand loyal they become.

When a brand is easily recognizable for its overall quality and is the consumer's first choice in a brand category, it has achieved *brand equity* or has ownership of its particular brand category. Ownership in any category assures a positive ROI and usually requires little more than an occasional reminder ad to maintain a secure hold on the product category.

Even brands with strong equity need continuous management in today's world of instant messaging, product parity, and economic ups and downs. A good product can go bad fast if social sites are not monitored for rumors or consumer complaints, as Ford Motor Company found out in 2008. Twitter rumors abounded when the blogosphere lit up with claims that Ford was forcing the shutdown of a popular website accused of selling unlicensed products bearing the Ford logo. Legal actions set in motion by Ford called for the site owners to "cease and desist." Luckily, Scott Monty, Ford's social media–savvy PR manager for digital media, addressed the issue quickly and used Twitter and the merchant websites to keep outraged posters updated on both the facts of the case and the progress of its resolution. Monty is credited with strengthening the Ford brand by defusing the situation quickly and diplomatically.

A high level of brand equity in a product category can also have its downside. Sometimes, a brand's name becomes so closely linked and representative of a product category that it becomes a generic label for the entire category; such is the case with using the names Kleenex, Wite Out, or Xerox to describe any kind of tissue, copy correction fluid, or photocopy. Once a product's name becomes a generic marker for any product category, it can lose its trademark or ownership of its name. Consequently, leaders in these categories must use their relationship with the target and alert consumers to the differences that set them apart from their competitors.

Positioning Is All About Image

Positioning is all about a brand's image and how the consumer ranks that image relative to competing brands. Well-known authors Al Ries and Jack

Figure 2.2   **Sample Ad: Verizon Wireless**

Source: Created by Natalie Rowan, The University of Tennessee, Knoxville.

Trout in the book *Positioning: The Battle for Your Mind,* define positioning as the process of "owning space in a person's mind." So what is the difference between brand image and positioning? Positioning is developed through advertising and promotional efforts; a brand's image is a result of the target's personal interactions with the brand.

In today's product parity environment, image is often the only feature or benefit a brand has to set it off from the competitors in its category. Unfortunately, not all brands are blessed with a distinct image. Brands without a unique identity require a big idea that identifies an underused or underexposed feature and uses it to develop an exclusive niche or new position for a brand. Ries and Trout also point out in their book that some brands need to look for even more creative ways to stand out in a crowded product category. For example, "If you can't be the first in a category, set up a new category you can be first in." In the 1960s, Volkswagen gained success after positioning the Beetle as a small, ugly lemon. This was a position no one else wanted to belong to and was certainly a unique departure from the big and luxurious positions claimed by other cars at the time.

To stand out when competition in a product category is fierce, brands must take a strong look at their current position within that category. New product categories make securing a position in the mind of the target easier without competing noise. Products that must compete against a stronger, well-known competitor will have a more difficult time securing an individualized and unique position in the consumer's mind.

When a brand has entered its maintenance phase and no longer has to rely on its specific features and benefits to make a sale, it can focus more on its image or reputation to secure a loyal following. Mature products with an established position allow the creative team a little more latitude to expose a brand's exclusivity or cutting-edge science or technology. When there is more focus on image and less on establishing a foundation, the visual/verbal message and promotional activities can be a lot more creative and inventive.

Regardless of market conditions, a good creative idea that resonates with the target and is repeatedly seen can: (1) increase sales; (2) improve brand equity as compared to the competition; (3) increase brand loyalty; (4) promote or solidify a brand or company's reputation; and (5) build brand awareness and thus brand image.

The Business and Politics of Economics

To understand how advertising helps drive the economy in both good and bad times, one must begin by looking at some of the factors that have affected economic growth in the past.

A quick trip through history shows that mild economic downturns typically lead to hodgepodge reform, while more severe crises often trigger great change in both the economic and political sectors. At its most critical, economic collapse may spark revolution. In a 2008 online article for *McKinsey Quarterly,* Robert E. Wright explains: "Scholars are just now recognizing the important role that the real estate bust of 1764–68—when land prices fell by half to two-thirds in about a year and thousands of Americans ended up in debtors' prison—played in the empirical crisis culminating in the events of July 1776. Similarly, the Panic of 1857 in the U.S. and the subsequent recession helped bring on the Civil War by exacerbating sectional tensions over slavery and states' rights and helping the modern Republican Party to coalesce. During the Great Depression, some historians believe, the federal government averted rebellion thanks only to the extraordinary changes ushered in by the first New Deal."

He goes on to say: "The Panic of 1873 and the subsequent long recession, for example, helped spur labor and agrarian unrest. Similarly, the recession of 1893–97 invigorated Populism and Progressivism and paved the way for the turn-of-century Great Merger Movement, which created giant corporations such as U.S. Steel and International Harvester. The Great Depression gave rise to the Glass-Steagall Act (which separated investment and commercial banking for more than 60 years), the FDIC, the Securities and Exchange Commission, and Social Security."

The Evolution of Advertising

How advertising has evolved and affected the economy is simply but effectively expressed by Rosser Reeves in his book *Reality in Advertising* (1981): "Advertising," he states, "is, actually, a simple phenomenon in terms of economics. It is merely a substitute for a personal sales force—an extension, if you will, of the merchant who cries aloud his wares." Perhaps an even better description might be "what goes around, comes around." Personal selling once replaced by advertising is once again the driving force behind all successful brands. But the move from a one-on-one dialogue between buyer and seller took a few years and a few technical innovations before it caught on again.

Before the advent of advertising, the selling of goods and services took place between two known parties. Local merchants knew each buyer by name, and buyers knew the quality of the merchandise they were purchasing. Although interactive, early trade practices did not necessarily favor the buyer. A blatant lack of competition and a limited selection of available goods minimized purchasing options. Without any competition, or advertising costs, or an intermediary between the producer of goods and the consumer, pricing (although often based on a barter or trade system) was relatively static. When a middleman using mass media was introduced into the equation, the process became known as *marketing*. Mass media replaced one-on-one interaction with anonymity, effectively reducing the relationship to a one-way monologue of information. The upside for the consumer, though, was increased competition and a larger selection of merchandise.

Advertising in the United States has been around since the early 1700s, but it only began taking center stage during the Industrial Revolution. Once goods were no longer produced locally, consumers rarely interacted with manufacturers or producers. Because of this, advertising was needed to promote mass-produced goods to a mass audience of consumers. Small local businesses unable to compete against their larger rivals were driven out of business, and the notion of personalized service seemed doomed.

After selling became a one-way monologue, each contact point in the buying process took place through a retailer. When radio, television, and the telephone arrived on the scene later in the century, it gave a new voice to the advertising of mass-marketed and mass-produced goods. The addition of sight, sound, and motion allowed the consumer to visualize and interact with the product or service. It took the advent of the Internet over a hundred years later to resurrect personalized one-on-one service and initiate a dialogue about individual needs. Thanks to the web's vast reach, consumers once again control what, when, where, why, how, and from whom they make their purchases.

Advertising Is a Sign of the Times

Early advertising was not used to entertain or engage the target audience; rather, its job was to announce the product's availability and educate the target audience. Once the Industrial Revolution changed how goods were manufactured, advertisers did little more than keep the public abreast of the newest products and technological advances.

But nothing easy lasts forever. Consumers grew tired of educational ads and dry sales pitches. They needed something more arresting and creative to hold their attention. By the 1960s, a "creative revolution" had overtaken the look and sound of advertising. Bill Bernbach, David Ogilvy, and other leaders in the advertising field introduced simplicity, humor, and personality into creative ideas. The advertised message was all about the visual "big idea," or "the entertaining sale."

Advertising of the1970s—a period often referred to as the "me" decade—typified the materialistic view of the day. Still creative, ads during this time boasted in-your-face messages that featured minorities more prominently and used women less as window dressing and more as an empowered and valuable source of revenue. The 1970s also saw the introduction of sexy designer ads, the banning of tobacco ads on radio and television, and the targeting of children as a market group.

Beauty, wealth, and success defined 1980s advertising. Apple's now famous "1984" Super Bowl ad put the big game on everybody's advertising map and established the Macintosh as an edgy alternative to the IBM personal computer (the latter being portrayed as the machine used by drones). Remnants of the 1980s such as frequent flyer programs, branded goods, and celebrity endorsements still endure today.

The 1990s focused on American individualism, nostalgia, and shock advertising. Brands like Benetton featured ads in the United States that used startling and unusual images to catch a disinterested audience's attention. This was also the decade that introduced the Internet and the "dot-com" boom that followed. Cell phone use was on the rise; children's advertising was still a hot topic; the "Got Milk" mustache campaign was launched; and product placement in movies and on television gained momentum.

The informative and creative ads of the twenty-first century are meant to attract attention and direct consumers to the Internet for more information. Mass markets have been replaced with niche markets, and mass media has given way to more targeted vehicles such as direct mail, mobile marketing, and alternative media vehicles that can once again reach the target with a personalized message. Social sites like Twitter and Facebook take the discussion on brands viral as consumers talk to friends and family and offer valuable feedback to marketers. The Internet has successfully replaced traditional advertising's old monologue approach and reintroduced one-on-one dialogue.

Today's advertising-avoidant consumers know what they want and are fully aware of their buying options. Like the early days of personalized trading, buyers want products tailor made to their specific needs and wants, by a person or company they consider familiar and trustworthy. But unlike the early days, if need be they will go somewhere else to get it. In short, consumers no longer need mass marketing to make buying decisions; personalized service and a high-quality, reliable brand are the critical components needed to build a long-lasting relationship between buyer and seller.

The Internet offers consumers a chance to compare products by moving between sites. They can access information on their own or ask questions online or via a toll-free number. Transactions can be initiated with a few keystrokes or the punch of a few buttons. Credit cards make purchasing safe and easy. And, perhaps best of all, consumers can shop when they want, where they want, and how they want, with or without human interaction.

The balance of power has definitely shifted to the consumer thanks to old-fashioned competition and the Internet. Marketers are no longer in charge of what we buy and when we buy it: The whole world is now open for business.

The art of selling is now about customized products the seller stands behind; more than mere brand loyalty, it is about a tried and trusted faith in the manufacturer. Consumers can communicate one-on-one with marketers, getting information they care about and actually chose to receive through alternative media outlets such as cell phones, or via the web, or through e-mail alerts. This metamorphosis in business and advertising practices was aptly described by famed science fiction writer Isaac Asimov in an online article, when he observed, "It was only with the coming of the Industrial Revolution that the rate of change became fast enough to be visible in a single lifetime." Today, the introduction of some new advertising approach, media outlet, or creative idea can be missed with the blink of an eye. Change in the twenty-first century is measured in industriousness rather than minutes.

Advertising's Role in the Economy: Steps to Take, Steps to Avoid

An economic recession presents a challenge for advertisers, often sparking creative ways to sidestep limitations and enlarge on the possibilities that come with a cyclical downturn. A recession says an FT.com article as defined by the National Bureau of Economic Research is "a significant decline in economic activity spread across the economy, lasting more than a few months, normally visible in production, employment, real income, and other indicators." Advertising's role, then, is to visually and verbally defy those limitations while exploiting any angles that seem to show promise.

History has shown that brands actually jeopardize their positioning and their hard-earned brand equity if they cut back on marketing expenditures during downturns. In contrast, brands that remain in the public eye during hard times tend to reap financial benefits when the market recovers. The reason? When awareness lags, so does image, name recognition, and perceived reliability in a product or service. Research indicates that brands may save money in the short term, but they typically end up spending more money over the long term to regain what they have lost, rarely returning to their pre-recession status. Staying in the spotlight strengthens a brand as the economy emerges from the downturn.

A company that fails to see advertising cost as an investment is missing out on sales and growth opportunities. "It's an article of faith among people in the agency business," says Mark Dolliver in a 2009 article for *Adweek,* "that ad and marketing budgets should be maintained in tough economic times so a brand can keep up its equity, grab share from less-enlightened competitors, reassure jittery consumers, etc., etc." As long as consumers are still spending, it is important that marketers continue communicating with them.

Not all products and services are affected equally by an unstable economy. Consumers usually make the deepest cuts to emotion-laden or luxury-based spending—eating out, personal care products and services, and upscale clothing purchases. Rational purchases such as groceries and health care, on average, see a higher level of spending. Traditionally, higher education enrollments spike as the unemployed or underemployed head back to class. Unfortunately, the "Great Recession" that began in December 2007 differs from previous downturns: Consumer credit is harder to come by; in addition, high credit card debts, diminished personal savings accounts, and a slumping housing market may signal quicker and deeper cuts in more categories than seen in a long time.

In previous economic slowdowns, marketers concentrated their advertising efforts on the most profitable customers, market segments, and specific geographic locations. However, the global nature of the most recent recession may require a broader look. Today's marketer needs to look not only at who is buying but what they are buying and when, and then focus on any emerging profit-potential pockets.

This is also the time to tweak marketing efforts, focus additional attention on offering exceptional customer service initiatives, and reevaluate media options.

Marketing Efforts

When attempting to boost or maintain consumer confidence, it is important that advertising efforts promote product reliability, innovation, and reputation.

To manipulate economic conditions, marketers try to force consumers to make hard decisions. Brands that find creative ways to ease consumers' burdens by keeping prices low, reducing the size of packaging, or offering coupons or two-for-one offers will attract buyers' attention.

For example, marketers promoting packaged goods have noticed that consumers spend more around pay periods and less as the month progresses. Companies like PepsiCo's Frito-Lay and H.J. Heinz Co. are reacting to these cycles by adjusting their promotions to address this spending trend. Their solution: promote larger-sized packages during the first half of the month and smaller sizes during the last half.

Other marketers, like ConAgra Foods, have taken a different approach. In an effort to offset manufacturing costs and keep the price of their Banquet frozen foods fixed, ConAgra has eliminated some food offers and introduced newer ones. Kellogg's responded to the sluggish economy by redirecting its advertising efforts. Products that were once advertised separately were combined with others, resulting in less advertising waste.

Kraft is pushing value by promoting stay-at-home dining, Kool-Aid touts its low cost compared to soda, and the dairy industry used financial guru Suze Orman to expound on the cost benefits of drinking milk. Restaurants are helping out with two-for-one offers, retailers are slashing prices, and the 2009 government-supported cash for clunkers program gave the new car market a much-needed boost.

Still other companies are finding ways to eliminate buyer remorse and reduce general fears by offering rebates, refunds, or special options. One tactic used by some automotive companies prior to the slow but steady recovery in that industry involved an unprecedented return policy: Car buyers were given the option of returning their new vehicle in the event they suffered a job loss within a year of the date of purchase. Other companies allowed new cars to be returned within 60 days if the buyer was not satisfied with the purchase.

Customer Service Initiatives

To keep longtime customers from cutting back or turning to less expensive store labels, it is important to find ways to reassure them that your brand is the one to help them through difficult times. Focus should be placed on creating interactive opportunities between the product or service and the target—for instance, encouraging consumers to call in, stop by a brick-and-mortar store, or blog about their ideas on product enhancements or use.

Media Options

Recessionary periods traditionally keep marketers using tried and true media vehicles to ensure ROI. But marketers need to be where the target is, and that means being seen when consumers are blogging, texting, tweeting and using various other forms of social media. Although traditional media vehicles are considered safe, they may not be as engaging or far reaching as alternative media options. Almost all economic forecasts project alternative media to account for well over 25 percent of all total U.S. advertising spending by 2012.

Since 2008, consumers have been spending more time at home. This recessionary trend allowed marketers to strategically and cost effectively reach the target by incorporating a mix of old and new vehicles, with the bulk of advertising dollars still going to traditional buys.

Harvard Business School professor and economic analyst Michael Porter, in a 2008 Adweek.com article by Tony Case considers innovation "the central issue in economic prosperity." He goes on to point out that "in the midst of the worst economic morass most of us can recall, [we've seen] some of the best innovations in media and marketing—some that look to have lasting influence, others that could prove to be a real game changer for digital media, in-store marketers, the TV networks, even architects of political campaigns. Barack Obama, whose team harnessed the power of the Web as no "brand" ever had, changed how political races are run, and won. Apple's iPhone 3G juiced up the mobile medium. . . . Even slow-to-change, easy-to-write-off old media like magazines and radio came up with some bright ideas—finally learning how digital media can help, rather than kill their business."

A Recession and the Visual/Verbal Message

Creatively, it is not uncommon for advertising efforts to visually and verbally trumpet what is going on in society, no matter what economic factors are at play. The depths of the recession from 2008 through 2010 changed advertising's usually upbeat message. For example, financial ads talked of changes,

Figure 2.3   **Sample Ad: Southwest Airlines**

Are you in need of some family fun?
We have new destinations
with lots of sun!

With airfare starting as low as $29,
you and your family can fly to five of your
favorite sunny locations.

Go straight from Knoxville to the coast.

Relax. We have it covered.

SOUTHWEST
AIRLINES
Your Destination Is Waiting.

Source: Created by Carly Reed, The University of Tennessee, Knoxville.

and packaged goods took a negative message to the public about competitors in an attempt to retain market share. Almost all campaigns referred to value, reliability, and trust. Many brands resurrected old packaging, jingles, and slogans in the hope that a look back would foster a renewed sense of trust and loyalty in existing brands.

Still others addressed consumer frustrations and fears. Many companies expressed anger over waste, perhaps most notably Eastman Kodak. The Kodak "print and prosper" campaign compared inkjet printer ink to oil from the Middle East and stated that U.S. buyers had overpaid for ink cartridges by a whopping $5 million in 2008 alone. Post Shredded Wheat ads poked fun at progress and innovation, relying instead on an image of wholesomeness and simplicity and a recipe that hasn't changed since 1892. Jet Blue ads picked on executives who had to downgrade their private travel modes to public flights with the slogan, "Welcome Aboard." These messages may seem a bit somber or even cynical, but they won over consumers with sass and creativity.

Advertising creative teams continue to look for ways to squeeze every penny out of a dollar. Many agency executives have looked to advertising tactics of the Great Depression era to define value-driven creative expression. For example, a 1932 *Advertising Age* piece noted that Scott Paper Towels didn't sit back and let the depression run its course; instead, they touted the overall quality of their towels in comparison to competing brands. Promoters pointed to research results that showed Scott's competitors made products that were "chemically impure." This successful approach increased sales substantially while improving market share.

As the depression continued through the 1930s, Scott stepped up advertising efforts once again with a bold proclamation of the necessity of paper towels. Although times were tough for a large number of consumers, Scott was able to push paper-based convenience to cash-strapped consumers.

Kellogg's offers another good example of depression-era success. During the 1920s, both Post and Kellogg's were known for their prepackaged cereals, but neither brand was having much success getting consumers to change from the perennial favorite breakfast food, oatmeal. As the economy began to collapse after 1929, both companies had to decide whether to continue advertising or pull back on expenditures. Post pulled back, while Kellogg's moved forward, doubling its advertising budget. Investing heavily in radio, Kellogg's aggressively promoted its new Rice Krispies cereal. As many products stagnated or collapsed under the weight of a stalled economy, profits at Kellogg's rose nearly 30 percent and helped create the successful brand identity that remains more than eight decades later.

More recently, Apple took an aggressive stance by increasing its advertising efforts during the final months of 2008, when many brands were cutting back on ad costs. Always portraying itself as creative, innovative, and socially aware, Apple drilled the point home in its "Get a Mac" campaign, which put cool guy Justin Long (the Mac) up against the far-from-trendy John Hodgman (the PC). These ads helped Apple gain market share in excess of 2 percent, giving them an almost 10 percent share of the personal computer market. In addition, Apple featured ads that helped coax PC users to switch over to a Mac. These ads improved brand equity by highlighting Apple's consistent level of innovation and design. The message also underscored Mac's reputation of exceptional customer service, incomparable user support, and trouble-free performance.

Microsoft attempted to counter the mismatched Apple spokesperson pairing with an odd couple of its own—comedian Jerry Seinfeld and well-known Microsoft co-founder Bill Gates—but they lacked appeal as an advertising duo. The "Shoe Circus" ads failed to prove technological innovation or trouble free use. However, the "I am a PC" campaign that followed did a much better job of improving the brand's image.

Most brands react like Post and cut back on advertising during difficult economic times. Progressive brands like Kellogg's, Scott Paper Towels, and Apple do just the opposite by gearing up their advertising presence and even increasing acquisitions and investments in research and development. Truly innovative brands may go so far as to introduce a new product or service, knowing that weakened competitors will not launch or manufacture a parity product any time in the near future. Others look for merger opportunities, and still others gobble up the unemployed talent not available at any other time.

Research has repeatedly shown that companies that remain in the public eye come out of recessions with a higher share of the market and more brand-loyal consumers than before the crisis. Studies on the recessions of 1921–1922, 1981–1982, and 1990–1991 confirmed that when businesses increased or maintained their level of spending, they grew significantly over competitors who reduced spending in all categories. Furthermore, research has shown that companies that do not base business decisions on changing economic cycles saw their stock prices increase an average of 1.3 percentage points annually.

Don't sit back and weather the economic storm. Here are five great reasons to be innovative and progressive during an economic downturn: (1) available deals on media buys—many that can be locked in for years to come; (2) the need to keep customers up-to-date on both existing and new product introductions; (3) the ability to stand out when competitors are cutting their budgets; (4) no loss of market share if competitors do not cut their advertising expenditures; and (5) finishing ahead of the game when the economy picks up.

3

The Strategy Behind Using Alternative Media

Figure 3.1 **Sample Ad: K•B Toys**

Source: Created by Jason Cowen, The University of Tennessee, Knoxville.

Reaching the Target in Memorable and Strategic Ways

Influential advertiser John O'Toole notes in his 1985 book *The Trouble with Advertising:* "There is no such thing as a Mass Mind. The Mass Audience is made up of individuals, and good advertising is written always from one person to another. When it is aimed at millions it rarely moves anyone." Never has this statement been truer than it is in the second decade of the twenty-first century.

In today's fragmented, economically challenged landscape, it is important that each advertisement matches the target's lifestyle, presents a fresh and innovative message that stands out from competitors, and creates a meaningful and lasting relationship with the target.

Because the cost to replace a loyal user is much higher than retaining current users, it is vital that communication efforts be personalized and interactive. Every touchpoint between the brand and the target must be a positive one, whether it is with a customer service representative, a sales representative, a promotional offer, or a delivery driver. This one-on-one interaction between the brand and target is known as *relationship marketing,* and it is the best way to build or maintain brand-loyal consumers.

Strategy drives more than just the relationship with the target: It ultimately determines the visual/verbal message; whether the ad will educate, demonstrate, use testimonials, or take a humorous approach; how a brand will be positioned against competitors; and whether to use alternative vehicles, traditional vehicles, or a mix of both.

When dealing with alternative media, it is important to realize that the vehicle or message may or may not be alternative; it's the strategy that must be alternative. Typically, the strategy highlights one of three things: (1) the product and its unique features and benefits; (2) the target audience and how the brand will make the target's life easier; or (3) how the target will be viewed by others when using, interacting, or wearing the brand.

Most advertising strategies seen today employ a mix of both traditional and alternative media vehicles. Traditional vehicles are used to reach an undefined mass audience and build awareness; alternative media is all about creatively streamlining and personalizing the message, building a relationship with the target, and highlighting their individual media habits (reaching those who use the web, play video games, or are avid texters). Many traditional vehicles also incorporate some type of alternative media option, such as including a web address in ad copy, using product placement in programming and movies, or inserting samples between the pages of a magazine.

Verizon used a mix of alternative and traditional media tactics to promote its 99-cent prepaid cellular plans. To do this, they promoted 99-cent cab rides from preselected locations in Manhattan. Cabs promoted the fares on promotional signs appearing on the roof of each taxi. The one-day promotion was followed two weeks later with promotional 99-cent ice cream treats delivered via logo-wrapped trucks placed throughout the city and surrounding locations. Accompanying the sweet treats were napkins bearing more details about the promotion. Additional media included transit shelters, digital signs, and wild postings, as well as traditional media such as newspaper, radio, and out-of-home.

Whether employing alternative media alone or a mix of alternative and traditional vehicles, it is important to understand that advertising is no longer about sending a one-way message to a disinterested audience. Ad creators need to find ways to initiate a compelling conversation with the target, ensuring them that they will receive the best product and customer service assistance available.

The innovativeness associated with alternative media is all about making a creative statement that can break through the target's existing cynicism about advertising and its one-size-fits-all message. Today's savvy consumers want to seek out advertising and compare features, benefits, and prices on their own before deciding on a purchase. They want advertisers to solicit their permission to deliver a message they have "opted in" to receive—one that is tailored to their specific interests. The last thing they are looking for is a sales pitch or a laundry list of generic claims.

Because consumers can tune out the majority of messages that invade their day, many strategies attempt to reach the consumer where they are. Joseph Jaffe notes in his book *Life After the 30-Second Spot: Energize Your Brand with a Bold Mix of Alternatives to Traditional Advertising:* "Time is the new currency."

Because most alternative options are placed or used in high traffic areas (for instance, a busy city street, in or around mass transit, on elevator doors, or at malls or events), they can attract a lot of attention and interact with the target unobtrusively during everyday activities. A single event such as having lunch or dinner away from home can be strategically used to reach the consumer with multiple options: Messages can be placed on pizza boxes, chopsticks, carry-out bags, to-go cups, napkins, table-top tents, even bathroom stalls. On the way to their car or mass transit hub, engage the consumer with video-projected messages or street teams, or display a logo on construction barricades, taxi tops, bus sides, or outdoor boards. If the target audience is likely to work out before going home or back to work, consider using branded towels as a message board, or hand out samples that can be used on the spot.

The growth of alternative media was a direct result of marketers wanting their advertising agencies "to do something different." Different morphed into creative, engaging, and often interactive ways to catch and hold the target's attention. A memorable example is the 3-D Chick-fil-A cows, who urge consumers to eat chicken instead of beef. These ads have gone viral since their introduction in 1995, keeping the "please eat chicken" message alive longer than originally intended.

Strategically, the growing popularity of alternative media stems from its ability to:

1. Replace the high cost of most traditional vehicles;
2. Use more effective targeting methods;
3. Often be more creative and versatile than traditional methods;
4. Be more cost effective;
5. Use the element of surprise and creativity to encourage interaction and memorability;
6. Catch and hold the viewer's attention with eye-catching and unusual visuals;
7. Encourage the viral spread of the message;
8. Attract the attention of the hard-to-reach 18- to 34-year-old target group; and
9. Remain unaffected by dwindling readership or listenership.

Growth in alternative media can also be traced to its in-your-face style and one-of-a-kind messages that stand out from mass-produced ads. Because they are highly targetable, alternative media can deliver interactive, attention-grabbing messages that break the mold of the monotone, often irritating, and repetitive traditional media vehicles.

Creatively, the use of an alternative media strategy focuses on nontraditional forms of media, avoiding traditional options altogether or using them as a secondary vehicle to remind and/or educate. To execute this type of strategy successfully, the target market should be small and clearly defined. Messages should focus on whether the brand fulfills a rational need (for instance, food and clothing) or an emotional need (jewelry or expensive spa treatments).

Whatever type of strategy is employed, each creative campaign must find a way to break through consumer apathy to stand out and hammer home its main selling idea. Let's take a look at a few examples.

UNICEF's "Tap Project" found a way to raise awareness about the lack of clean drinking water around the world. The organization placed vending machines across Manhattan with the tantalizingly simple label "Dirty Water" on a picture of a bottle of polluted water. To further emphasize their point, vending buttons allowed pedestrians to select from one of eight types of dirty water, including cholera, yellow fever, salmonella, malaria, dysentery, hepatitis, typhoid, and dengue.

Figure 3.2   **Sample Ad: Verizon Wireless**

Source: Created by Natalie Rowan, The University of Tennessee, Knoxville.

Although no actual dirty water was available for purchase, the goal was to encourage donations either by depositing money directly into the machine, or by sending a contribution via text message. The $0 budget campaign successfully and imaginatively raised awareness about unsanitary water conditions in underdeveloped countries throughout the world. It also generated a great deal of buzz and additional publicity in blogs and local media.

The Canadian Red Cross's Fallen Woman campaign was another attention-getter. This startling campaign placed a full-size color sticker of a woman lying facedown at the bottom of a flight of stairs, legs and arms askew, purse and keys at her side. She appears the victim of an apparent fall. Nearby is a sticker with the recognizable Red Cross logo and the statement:

KNOW WHAT TO DO.
Canadian Red Cross
Learn first aid. www.redcross.ca

A few additional examples of unconventional advertising follow:

- The Discovery Channel set up lifeguard stands complete with a lifeguard and an umbrella in several locations around Manhattan to strategically promote their upcoming Shark Week programming.
- IKEA used alternative media to push the merits of organization, something IKEA is known for, by placing stickers on a flight of stairs depicting row after row of neatly organized drawers of clothing. On the landing was the IKEA logo, along with the phrase: Create space. Organize.
- To publicize its location, a hair salon replaced the white crosswalk lines outside its entrance with white lines painted in the shape of a comb.
- Folgers came up with the perfect way to visually express its coffee with stickers and existing manhole covers. Perforated stickers featuring an aerial view of a steaming hot cup of coffee were placed over city manhole covers. The perforations allowed the naturally produced steam exiting the cover to represent the steam from a piping hot coffee. In a semicircle around the cover were the words: Hey, City That Never Sleeps. Wake up. Folgers. The only thing missing was the smell of brewing coffee.

Many of these nontraditional campaigns are short-lived, one-shot deals that explode on the scene and then disappear, unlike the recurring formats and surfaces used in traditional media campaigns. The "wow" factor is alive and well because the message never gets old, making these ads strong candidates for continued viral discussions.

Unfortunately, not all forms of alternative media are as carefully crafted as the previous examples. Poorly designed alternative vehicles have been likened to junk mail by some critics; however, successful forays into alternative ads often create the memorable first steps toward trial.

With everything alternative media vehicles have to offer, it seems advertisers would flock to use them. Marketers are leery to adopt forms of alternative media, though, because they are untested, a little "over the top," and somewhat risky: Some advertisers are not exactly sure how to use them or how to ensure they accomplish the necessary communication objectives and project a measurable ROI. To overcome these concerns, many advertisers new to the field of alternative media have used special 1–800 numbers or web addresses to measure consumers' responses.

Employing the Best Media Vehicle to Reach the Target

Once the account, creative, and media teams understand the target that needs reaching, the problem that needs solving, and the brand feature that needs promoting, they can more accurately determine the most appropriate promotional mix to reach their goals. The *promotional mix* or category of vehicles employed in the campaign most commonly includes public relations, traditional advertising, alternative media, and sales promotion. How heavily one vehicle is used over another depends largely on budgetary constraints and on how much the target already knows about the featured product or service. Once the creative team knows the promotional and media mix to be employed, they can begin determining how the varied creative ideas will translate between vehicles.

It All Begins with a Marketing Plan

The American Marketing Association (AMA) defines marketing as "the activity, set of institutions, and processes for creating, communicating, delivering, and exchanging offerings that have value for customers, clients, partners, and society at large." Perhaps the best definition as it applies to the relationship between marketing and advertising comes from marketing strategists Al Ries and Jack Trout. In *Positioning: The Battle for Your Mind* (2000), they write: "Marketing is simply 'war' between competitors." It is advertising's job to be sure the competition keeps its head down.

Marketing and advertising teams need to have a thorough understanding of the product and/or service they are promoting in order to pair it with the most appropriate target market. The best way to do this is to dissect the marketing process into digestible parts.

Businesses Use Marketing Plans to Define Action

Great ideas can only grow after the product or service (i.e., the brand) has been thoroughly researched. The client's business plan of action is laid out in a marketing plan that defines sales initiatives, usually for the coming year.

This lengthy, detail-oriented plan of action is prepared by the client. The document looks at the brand's overall strengths and weaknesses compared to the competition; it also examines any opportunities and threats the brand might want to capitalize upon or avoid in the marketplace. The business plan of action is vital for getting a campaign on track: it introduces the target, determines a set of marketing-related (usually sales-oriented) objectives or goals that need to be met, defines a marketing strategy for accomplishing the

Figure 3.3   **Sample Ad: Band-Aid**

Source: Created by Ryan Freebing, The University of Tennessee, Knoxville.

objectives, analyzes competitors, projects a budget, and finally looks at varied implementation and evaluation techniques.

Because today's advertising efforts are consumer-centric, a strong marketing plan needs to incorporate a customer feedback mechanism. Such a mechanism makes it easier to determine a single selling point or key consumer benefit that research has guaranteed will attract the target's attention. It will also assist in defining the overall visual/verbal tone of voice to be used throughout the campaign so that an integrated communicated message is mimicked in all advertising and promotional vehicles, as well as at any customer contact points.

Once the marketing plan is complete, the creative team will receive a smaller, more concise document known as a creative brief, which focuses on communication initiatives.

The Creative Brief Adapts the Marketing Plan into a Communications Plan of Attack

Creative is an idea buried under a pile of research. Each image used—and every word spoken—lies somewhere in the dry statistics that make up the creative brief, so before the creative team comes up with one idea, draws one image, or places one word on the page, they need to review the creative brief. The account executive or agency representative handling an account uses the marketing plan to develop the creative brief. A much smaller document than the marketing plan at no more than one to three pages, the creative brief defines the communications plan of attack. It offers an abbreviated look at what the client wants to accomplish via creative efforts.

Bill Bernbach, in his book *Bill Bernbach Said . . .* (1989), states that the creative team uses the brief to "bring the dead facts to life." Such an undertaking requires that the team undergo a thorough education on the focus of the communication efforts: the goal is not only to solve the client's business problem, but also to strategically reach and talk to the intended target.

The brief, then, is a document that concerns itself with facts, not creative direction. It does not describe or suggest what the creative efforts should say or show. Instead, it serves as an informational springboard the team will use to generate ideas and solidify the campaign's visual/verbal direction.

Briefs, like marketing plans, vary in length and content, but most will include all or some combination of the following: (1) a target audience profile, (2) communication objectives, (3) brand features and benefits, (4) product positioning, (5) a key consumer benefit, (6) a creative strategy, (7) the tone or execution technique, (8) a support statement, (9) a slogan or tagline, and (10) a logo. Let's take a little more in-depth look at each one.

Target Audience Profile

Successful message construction depends on how well the creative team knows the target. This section will briefly define the primary target audience based on demographic, psychographic, geographic, and behavioristic profiles. Sometimes, advertising efforts will focus on a secondary market, or those most likely to purchase the product *for* the initial or primary target or influence their purchase. For example, a nutritious cereal for children may have a primary target of moms, with ads placed in *Good Housekeeping* or *Parents* magazine. The secondary audience may be children, with a message of good taste and fun appearing in advertising spots on Cartoon Network.

The more the team knows about how the target thinks, what their lifestyle is like, and what they find important, the easier it will be to direct the visual/verbal message directly to them. The target audience or target market is the reason the product or service will ultimately succeed or fail.

John O'Toole (*The Trouble with Advertising,* 1985), the former president of Foote, Cone & Belding, explains the importance of knowing the target intimately: "Advertising is about persons. And how a product or service fits into a person's life to make it easier, richer, better."

Communication Objectives

Communication objectives, as opposed to marketing or sales-related objectives, are the goals advertising and promotional efforts need to accomplish—how the target should think or feel about the brand and what the consumer should do after being exposed to the message, whether it be visiting a brick-and-mortar store, doing further research, or buying on the spot.

Brand Features and Benefits

This section is used to educate the creative team on the brand's main features or attributes and how those features will benefit the target. A consumer-focused approach makes it important to push benefits over features. A feature is a specific attribute—color or size, for instance—or may be based on image or status, anything that reflects the target's individual style.

On the other hand, a benefit tells members of the target audience *why* a product or service is important to them. Benefits, therefore, should offer a solution to a problem, enhance image, or improve the target's quality of life. Features cannot sell a product if targets do not know or understand how it will make their lives easier or better. Benefits sell; features support. It is easy for a competitor to match a feature, but impossible to match a benefit without being repetitious and appearing second best. Benefits are also easier to tie to a creative concept because they have substance and are grounded in what the target finds important.

Product Positioning

Positioning refers to how the brand is thought of or "positioned" in the mind of the consumer in comparison to competing brands. This section should compare and contrast the competition's product or service and current advertising with the client's brand. Knowledge about competing products allows the creative team to set the product apart visually and verbally and exploit areas or features the competition may or may not have overlooked.

Key Consumer Benefit

A key consumer benefit is that one feature/benefit combination that research has shown the target is interested in and will respond to. This benefit, if you're lucky, may be unique to the brand, but it doesn't necessarily have to be. Sometimes competitors ignore the most obvious, mutually inherent qualities common to a certain product and fail to feature them in their advertising efforts. Creative teams can take advantage of such a situation, exploiting these untouted features for their own benefit. The key consumer benefit will become the single visual/verbal voice of the campaign. It will be screamed out in headlines, featured in visuals, and expanded upon in body copy.

The key consumer benefit can be promoted as a unique selling proposition (USP), a "big idea," or a multiple selling proposition (MSP). The choice of which one of the three to use is based on the target and objectives of the campaign. If a brand is new or has a unique feature its competitors do not have, chose a USP. Consider the Apple iPhone: It is unique because it broke new ground, and none of its competitors will ever be able to be "first" with this particular piece of ingenious technology.

Use a "big idea" to creatively promote a commonplace brand or feature as unique or find a creative way to make it important to the brand and thus the target. Competing products may have the same feature or sell the same service without focusing on it as part of their advertising and promotional efforts. Aflac made their common brand big by using a duck to repeatedly quack out the company's name, making it both repetitious and memorable. Super Bowl ads also use a "big idea" approach to stand out creatively.

These two key consumer benefit options—the USP and the "big idea"—typically use one repetitive message in a limited number of media vehicles. An MSP, on the other hand, uses rotating multiple messages in multiple media to sell its consumer benefits. This tactic allows multiple messages to reach the target no matter where they are or what they are doing. GEICO uses this approach when rotating between geckos, cavemen, and a spokesperson.

Creative Strategy

The creative strategy of an ad campaign defines how creative efforts will accomplish the stated objectives, promote the key consumer benefit, and talk to the target. If the strategy reflects the key consumer benefit in a way that will attract the target's attention and encourage action, the strategy is considered on-target. If the choice of visual/verbal direction and media mix reflects the strategy, the campaign is said to be on-strategy.

A quote found in the book *Advertising Strategy: Creative Tactics from the Outside/In* by advertising giant Jay Chiat describes the role of a good strategy this way: "Our best work has always begun with a marketing solution, not a creative solution. The ads flowed from the strategy, not the strategy from the ads."

Tone or Execution Technique

The tone or execution technique gives the key consumer benefit a visual/verbal voice and defines the brand's personality and image. The tone may be overtly humorous, tongue-in-cheek, educational, or scientific in nature, to name a few possibilities, and the ad may feature testimonials or demonstrations to drive a point home.

Support Statement

The support statement is an additional feature/benefit combination that further highlights the key consumer benefit. If the key consumer benefit deals with the virtues of electric-start lawn mowers, the support statement might push cutting range, speed, or ease of starting. Its job is to make the key consumer benefit both irresistible and understandable.

Slogan or Tagline

A slogan should reinforce the brand's image. In addition, it must aid in positioning the brand and visually represent the company's mission statement or overall philosophy. Slogans are usually a statement of no more than three to seven words. A good slogan may last the life of the product or until a company is sold, reorganized, or the brand is changed in some meaningful way. Consider some of these notable examples: Calvin Klein Jeans, "Nothing comes between me and my Calvins," IHOP Restaurants, "Come hungry. Leave happy," and Applebee's memorable "Eatin' Good in the Neighborhood."

The only difference between a tagline and a slogan is longevity. A tagline is tied to a current campaign theme and changes with each new campaign direction. Tags associated with brands having a strong brand identity can last a little longer when tied to life cycle stages. Some of the more memorable taglines include Nike's "Just Do It," Eukanuba's "What healthy dogs and cats are made of," and American Express' "Don't leave home without it." Both slogans and taglines can appear either above or below the logo on the brief, depending on the brand's visual/verbal graphic design.

Logo

The logo will close each and every brief. Its job is to represent the company, brand, or service's name, image, or use. It will realistically or abstractly represent the brand's personality, its reputation, its successes, or its failures. A logo can consist of a graphic symbol with or without type, or it may consist of type alone.

Once the marketing plan and creative brief are completed, it is time to develop a media plan that will help decide which mix of vehicles will best reach the target and deliver the message.

Alternative Media Exercise 3.1

1. Develop a creative brief for one of the two visuals that appear within any chapter in this text. Determine to the best of your ability what you think the key consumer benefit and target might be.
2. Pick three additional vehicles to build a campaign around. You can pick one vehicle and use it three different ways, or choose two or three different vehicles depending on direction.
3. Present what you've developed to the class. Be sure to tie vehicle choice to the creative brief and original layout direction.
4. Pick another layout and repeat steps 1–3.

4

The Choice of Media

Figure 4.1 **Sample Ad: K•B Toys**

Source: Created by Brent Harkins, The University of Tennessee, Knoxville.

Telling the Brand's Story Across Varied Media Vehicles

An integrated advertising campaign can be defined as a family of ads that share a visual/verbal identity and promote a single idea to a defined target audience. Multiple targeted media vehicles are used to reach the intended audience with a specific message about a particular product, service, or company. A multi-media campaign's job is to announce a brand's presence in the market, create an identity, build awareness for a product or service, and promote a sale. The integrated choice of media vehicles used in a campaign should reach the target where they are and gain enough attention to influence consumer behavior and attitude. Consumer attention is no longer guaranteed, so the message must be relevant and placed in a location the target is sure to see it.

While it used to be common to see almost every campaign launch using traditional media, today's inventive and highly targeted campaigns may use very few, if any, traditional vehicles. Media choices that can be customized—such as the web-based choices, direct mail, sales promotions, mobile media, or social media outlets—offer the flexibility needed to reach the target.

Campaigns that use multiple vehicles must ensure that the cohesiveness of the visual/verbal message is not lost between vehicles. *Media convergence* is said to be achieved when alternative media and/or traditional vehicles successfully deliver a cohesive message. The target must be able to recognize one branded campaign from another based on the repetitive visual and/or verbal ties that bind it together—such as layout style, character or spokesperson, color, typeface, headline style, and so on—no matter where it appears.

If the visual/verbal message cannot move seamlessly between diverse vehicles, the mix of media vehicles employed to deliver the message must be reexamined.

The most successful use of media will be placed where the target is, and attempt to capture their attention with unusual and engaging devices, among them billboards that smell like steak, direct mail pieces that talk to the target when opened, green messages mowed into hillsides or power washed onto dirty sidewalks, or large-scale advertisements made out of mud or sand. Although these ideas may sound creative, they cannot do their job without a media vehicle to deliver the message.

Strategically, the media vehicles employed in a campaign represent the target in much the same way the creative message does. Television buys and product placement match the target profile to programming; mobile messages reach the busy professional with a message they have "opted in" to receive; interactive websites offer coupons, blogs, and perhaps a contest or sweepstakes offer; out-of-home directs travelers to entertainment venues or other helpful locations; and street teams or portable storefronts interact with the target wherever they are.

Types of Media Categories

There are dozens of ways to classify and label media vehicles. At its most basic, vehicles can be broken down into traditional, alternative, and promotional. Each one has a very specific job to do: The target must be reached, engaged, educated, and inspired to purchase.

Traditional media options, including print and broadcast, are great for advertising mass-produced products (toilet paper, deodorant, and the like) with a large target audience. This one-way form of message delivery is great for building or maintaining brand image and creating awareness. Outdoor and direct mail often housed under the traditional label have creatively moved so far beyond the stagnant world of traditional advertising that they deserve to be reclassified as "progressive traditional." The ever-increasing functionality of alternative media has eradicated lingering taboos associated with blights on the landscape and junk mail. Alternative media is a great way to reach smaller niche markets and create a one-on-one relationship with the target. Not only are they more consumer focused but often less expensive and typically employ less media waste. To encourage trial, consider sales promotion options such as trial at the point of purchase, coupons and rebates, or sampling to boost sales and create valuable word-of-mouth opportunities.

Knowing who will ultimately see or hear the vehicle and its overall pros and cons will help the media team decide on the vehicle(s) that will (1) best promote the visual/verbal message, (2) reach the target with the least amount of waste, and (3) offer the most value for the money. It is important to note that the overall media mix cannot sell a bad product or fix an inappropriately targeted or poorly executed visual/verbal message; it can, however, enhance the viewing or reading experience and become part of the creative experience.

Understanding the Role of Media in Advertising

Understanding the function and character of each of these diverse media categories makes the process of reaching today's consumer more efficient but no less difficult. In the past, knowing what the target was watching, listening to, and reading was far easier to determine; there were only three main television channels, a handful of radio stations and magazines, and one or two daily newspapers per city. Today, media options have multiplied to the point that they can no longer be tracked with ease; throw in out-of-home, direct mail, and the numerous and assorted selection of alternative vehicles available, and reaching the intended target is more complicated than ever before.

Before you can define the role media plays in advertising, you have to understand advertising's role in the marketing process. Advertising is all about the exchange of information and making sure the right people are exposed to the right message at the right time. To do that effectively in today's media-saturated world, you need a creative selection of media vehicle(s) and a visual/verbal idea that grabs the audience's attention to ensure they look at, and respond to, the client's message.

Determining what that creative selection of vehicles will be is the role assigned to media. A *media vehicle* can be defined as any surface, flat or otherwise, that can be used to deliver a message to the relevant target. The options are virtually limitless, but some of the most commonly seen include traditional vehicles, direct mail, out-of-home, websites and banners, T-shirts, calendars, point of purchase displays, posters, shopping bags, product placement, and contests and sweepstakes. A single media vehicle can be further contained within a specific *media class;* for example, *American Idol* is a vehicle that falls under the media classification of television. Once the proper *media mix*—or group of media vehicles that will be employed to reach the intended audience—has been chosen, the next step is to develop a *media plan* that lays out what goals the media needs to accomplish, how it will go about accomplishing them, and what type of media schedule will be used to deliver the advertised message.

Putting Media in Its Place

Media placement is as important today as the creative message itself. The creative and media teams must work together to ensure the target will be reached where they are with a message they are interested in. A thorough knowledge of each vehicle employed will help determine not only strategy but also what type of creative executions can exploit these attributes. The visual/verbal message must appear in the most advantageous media vehicles, meaning the ones the target is sure to see, hear, or use, but preferably ones that are not currently being used by competitors. Getting it right requires significant planning and carefully executed media buys.

Media planning, executed by the media planner, is about laying out a detailed outline that covers a specific amount of time (usually a year) and defines what media vehicles or mix of vehicles it will take to deliver the creative message to the intended target. Media buying, carried out by a media buyer, involves negotiating costs and determining the best media buy or assortment of buys to promote a given product or service.

It is the media team's job to decipher the research; outline budget allocations; place media in local, regional, national, or international markets; and
know who the message is intended to reach, where the target is when they are
exposed to the message, what they are doing when they see the ad, and how
the message will be seen, broadcast, or displayed. The team is also responsible
for determining how many times the ad will be seen and for projecting how
many members of the target will see the message over a set period of time.

Other factors affecting planning and buying include:

1. Where competitors are advertising;
2. What life cycle stage the brand is in; and
3. What vehicles will successfully mirror the brand's image and the
   target's self-image.

Let's take a quick look at each one.

Competitive Advertising

It is important to identify the brand's closest competitors and where they
are currently advertising. When deciding which vehicle or combination
of vehicles will deliver the brand's message, it is essential to determine
if the brand is: (1) innovative with no direct competitors; (2) a leader in
the brand category; or (3) one of many same or similar brands within the
brand category. Strong or innovative brands can compete directly against
competitors using the same media vehicles without fear of losing market
share. Weaker brands should avoid competing directly against brand leaders, choosing instead vehicles that competitors are not currently using;
this strategy helps to increase brand awareness and avoid head-to-head
comparisons. Mass-produced brands in categories with significant product
parity will often compete within the same media class. To stand out, these
brands typically require bigger budgets and more advertising in order to
increase equity and positioning.

Life Cycle Stages

After the initial launch, a campaign's life cycle evolves, ultimately being
improved upon or put out to pasture to make room for the look and sound
of a new generation of consumers. When to scrap a brand's message often
depends on the stage of its life cycle and the overall purpose for advertising.
Most successful brands will go through three specific stages: a new product
launch, a mainstream or maintenance period, and reinvention. Each stage

requires a different message and employs different media vehicles to reach the target. Let's take a quick look at each one.

A new product launch often employs traditional media vehicles because of their reach and ability to build brand awareness and promote image. As the brand achieves mainstream popularity in the marketplace, it requires less advertising but relies more on alternative media to reach loyal users by name, where they are, with a message they will respond to. The goal during this phase is to remind the consumer about the brand, strengthen the relationship with the target, and build or maintain equity.

The main reasons for reinventing a brand are: (1) to update its image with a face-lift; (2) to promote a new and improved feature; or (3) to overcome a damaged reputation. Reinvented brands may rely on both traditional and alternative media to deliver a detailed message and encourage interaction with the brand.

Knowledge of a brand's life cycle stage helps the media team determine their choice of media type(s), the most appropriate combinations of media vehicles, and the projected frequency of the message necessary to prompt the target to make a purchase or seek additional information. Take simple table salt, for example. Not much new needs to be said about salt, but a few carefully placed reminder ads will help maintain sales. Mass-produced and mass-targeted products such as this one typically use a heavy schedule of television and magazines during the summer months, when grilling out is popular, and then again during the holidays. Point of purchase displays in grocery stores are a natural accompaniment, along with a few featured recipes on the web. The summer months are also be a great time to put up a temporary showroom on a heavily trafficked street corner, where local chefs can prepare some tasty and seasoned grilled items pedestrians can try on the spot.

Brand Versus Target Image

Incorrectly placing a brand in a vehicle that does not reflect its image or the target's self-image can damage a brand's earned equity, and thus brand loyalty. A good example of this would be placing an ad for an iPod in *Reader's Digest:* Not only would it affect the product's youthful, innovative image, it would also miss the intended audience. The same would hold true of placing an ad for baby food in a home improvement magazine. Although both may have the same or similar targets, the home repair guru may not be thinking about turning the spare bedroom into a nursery. A vehicle targeted especially at women, such as *Parenting* magazine, would be better suited to advertise baby food, as the reader's interest when skimming that particular publication is firmly focused on children and family issues.

To ensure proper placement, planners must look at the relationship the vehicle has with the target. Radio, for example, offers many different types of music as well as talk radio options. Advertising spots on radio can be aired on AM and/or FM stations and may run during busy drive times or be used to sponsor weather or traffic reports. Television has many of the same options, with programming that targets the very young to retirees. Some programming is directed primarily at women or men; the primetime and late night audiences differ as well, along with fans of comedies, dramas, and documentaries. Magazines also cater to gender, age, and people with special interests. Advertising can appear on the coveted inside or back cover or anywhere in between. Alternative media choices, on the other hand, are more individualized and can easily be placed where the target is. This strategy talks about a specific topic of known interest to that target.

Ultimately, all this careful planning, targeting, and placement must be executed within a set media budget. A media budget details where and when monies will be allocated. Typically, budgets are determined based on the brand, size, and popularity of the product or service.

Advertising budgets are heavily affected by economic ups and downs, so a little creative targeting—such as advertising consumer products to men differently than to women—creates new benefits for features, new visual/verbal creative options, new media opportunities, and perhaps even new uses. Marketers traditionally cut back on expensive traditional media buys during times of economic difficulty, looking instead to alternative media vehicles to deliver the message more creatively and, quite possibly, for a smaller investment.

Research Helps the Media Team Find and Reach Out to the Target

Media planners cannot do their job without research data on the intended target, the vehicles most likely to reach them, and the overall creative strategy to be employed. Typically, planners will use data supplied by research agencies such as Mediamark Research, Inc. (MRI), Simmons Market Research Bureau (SMRB), and individual media vehicles. MRI data focuses on yearly consumer input, and Simmons data focus on specific product categories. Simmons also keeps track of the best media options to reach the intended target.

Individual media vehicles are also a great source of research data. Most larger targeted vehicles, as well as MRI and Simmons, keep a detailed profile on their target audience using demographics, psychographics, and profile product usage to assist planners in matching the media vehicle's image to the target and the brand.

To ensure the proper media coverage, the media team relies on both primary and secondary vehicles to reach the target. Primary vehicles have the most potential to reach the target on a continual basis. One or more secondary vehicles may be employed when (1) a large percentage of the targeted audience will not be exposed to the primary vehicle(s) on a frequent and regular basis; (2) media efforts need to reach a secondary audience; or (3) media efforts need the target to do something, such as visit a website to download a coupon.

Buyers have to weigh cost against the overall return on their media investment. Tracking measurable responses helps determine whether the cost of the media buy was worth it. Quantitative or measurable data looks at items such as audience or vehicle duplication, geographic coverage, and overall cost. Qualitative research helps the buyer match image to the brand and the target, assess the overall quality of the vehicle, and determine placement and/or editorial or programming content.

It is rare for a buyer to buy a single spot or space for a single ad. To manage costs most effectively, they typically negotiate some type of media bundle known as a *value-added program* that saves money.

Like planners, buyers have to do their research on the varying types of media available to ensure the best buy and overall fit for their client. Every medium has different standards, sizes, printing capabilities, and printing and production deadlines—and buyers must be familiar with all of them. Additionally, they must be able to specify sizes, whether measured in inches or feet or in 10-, 15-, or 30-second intervals.

After completing the research, the next step is for the planner to develop a media plan that will determine the best tactics and media mix to promote the brand, its image, and the visual/verbal message.

Determining the Media Plan

A *media plan* outlines what media will be used in a campaign, how long it will be used, and where it will appear. Usually developed by the media planner, most of these plans begin with an overview of what needs to be accomplished. A more detailed look at five particular sections—target audience profile, media objectives, media strategy, media tactics, and evaluation—follows.

The first section of the plan, the audience profile, defines the target's lifestyle, needs and wants, and how they will use the brand. Objectives define the goals of each media buy. Media strategy outlines how the media objectives will be met. Media tactics lay out the steps that will accomplish the strategy. Evaluation determines the overall effectiveness of the media plan. Let's take a look at each one.

Figure 4.2   **Sample Ad: Sharpie**

Source: Created by Caitlin Bradley, The University of Tennessee, Knoxville.

Defining the Target Audience Profile

The media plan uses the same target profile as the creative brief, but in a slightly different way. Planners use it to determine the target's media habits and overall usage. Media habits include whether the target reads magazines, uses a lot of coupons, plays video games, rides mass transit to work, does a lot of shopping on the web, and so on. Usage can be broken down into three basic categories: product usage, brand usage, and category usage. *Product usage* determines how often the target will use the brand: Is he or she a light, medium, or heavy user? *Brand usage* outlines which brand name products the target uses. *Category usage* takes a more generic look at varied product categories such as batteries or shampoos.

Knowing who watches or listens to what programs or who reads what magazines helps advertisers reach the intended audience and eliminate media waste—waste being those messages appearing where the targeted audience will not see or interact with them.

Determining the Media Objectives

Media objectives define how the choice of media vehicle(s) will reach the target audience and how frequently that message will need to be seen or broadcast before it is remembered by the target. Objectives also look at the goals that communication efforts must accomplish and discuss how the budget will be allocated.

Successful media objectives determine: (1) reach; (2) frequency; and (3) media weight. Let's take a quick look at each one.

Reach

Since all media vehicles deal with some combination of reach and frequency, it is important that media buys match the target's lifestyle and known media usage as closely as possible to avoid media waste. Reach determines the total number of people or households that will see or be exposed, at least once, to the visual/verbal message during a set period of time. Effectiveness is based on how many times the target will be exposed to a specific vehicle rather than an individual ad within that vehicle. Each vehicle measures exposure differently. The desired level of reach can be attained using a single medium or a diverse mix of vehicles.

Reach focuses on (1) the size of the target audience; (2) the continued expansion of the audience; and (3) how many times the viewer or reader has been exposed to the message.

Frequency

For an ad to be memorable, it must be more than just creative and informative; it has to be placed in a vehicle the target is likely to see or hear on a regular basis. Frequency refers to how many times the ad will need to be seen or heard by the intended target audience to be remembered and acted upon.

Frequency is defined as the average number of times a single individual or household within the defined target audience is exposed to a single media vehicle during a set period of time, usually lasting from one week to one month. Vehicles that promote one-on-one communication such as the Internet, direct mail, or mobile, are more likely be acted upon than messages appearing in mass media vehicles that require more exposure before being remembered or encouraging purchase.

Exposure is measured in several different ways, depending on the vehicle employed. For example, television measures exposure by the percentage or number of targeted individuals who saw a specific program based on rating points; print relies on circulation, or the number of copies sold. The goal, of course, is to reach as many people as possible as many times as possible. The combination of both reach and frequency determine whether the communications objectives were effective or not.

Message Weight

Message weight refers to the total number of media vehicles that will make up a campaign media schedule. In a nutshell, message weight is a projection of the number of possible exposures an ad or campaign will have in a particular market. Message weight can be defined in terms of impressions, message impressions, gross impressions, and gross rating points.

An *impression* is defined as the number of audience members exposed to the media schedule. *Message impressions* indicate the total number of exposures to a single ad. A *gross impression* refers to the total number of people watching, reading, hearing, or just generally interacting with an ad or promotion. Gross impressions are determined by multiplying the size of the audience by the number of times an ad will be seen or heard. They tell a buyer the possible number of exposures that a particular medium can deliver.

To manage the often hundreds of millions of gross impressions, each medium is given a rating based on the percentage of households exposed to a single advertising vehicle or campaign schedule. For example, in television, rating points assigned to a television show represent the percentage of households watching that program. Each point is equal to 1 percent, so a show with a rating of 15 means 15 percent of households with a television were tuned in. This number does not take into account whether the ad was actually seen, however. Unlike reach, gross impressions do not recognize duplication of exposure.

A *gross rating point* represents the total amount of ratings delivered by a single vehicle or mix of vehicles. To determine the message weight for a campaign employing a mix of media vehicles, the planner needs to combine the ratings of each vehicle together to determine the maximum number of gross rating points or target audience points available for the least cost.

Outlining the Media Strategy

In order for the creative message to reach the target and reflect both the brand and the target's self-image, it must appear in the correct media vehicle(s). The media strategy determines what media needs to accomplish, whether that is launching a new product, maintaining or building awareness, reintroducing an old product with a new image or use, or challenging a competitor's claims.

To strategically accomplish the objectives, the media team needs to focus on:

1. The specific vehicles that will reach the intended target most effectively;
2. The month, times, and days the advertising will appear;
3. The proper positioning for the ad, such as in the first quarter of the super bowl or the inside front cover of a magazine;
4. The length of time the vehicle should be used;
5. The stage in the campaign when the vehicle(s) should be used;
6. The number of ads needed; and
7. The proper size or length of the ads.

Strategy also helps determine what vehicles will best deliver the visual/verbal message and create an interactive and memorable exchange between the target and the brand.

It is also important for the media team to know whether the brand is an emotional or rational purchase. For the most part, rational purchases like food and cleaning supplies require little copy but often need to demonstrate use and employ trial; samples or coupon options often encourage purchase. Emotional purchases like jewelry can wow with visuals in magazines and in-store point of purchase displays. High-end emotional purchases such as cars, boats, and computers, however, require heavy copy and colorful visuals. Media options might include magazines, point of purchase, brochures, direct mail, Internet, e-mail, and event marketing. As mentioned earlier, vehicle choice also hinges on the brand's life cycle stage. Products in their maintenance stage require less media exposure than new or reinvented product launches.

Planning, placement, and scheduling are more difficult than ever before: The number and overall form and format of the varying media vehicles available are daunting. The goal is to employ a media mix that increases awareness, builds or reinforces brand image, captures attention, enhances the brand's visibility, and creates relevant interactive opportunities.

The Media Mix

The media mix refers to the specific vehicles that will be used to accomplish the stated objectives and strategically deliver an advertising message.

Figure 4.3   **Sample Ad: Tuesday Morning**

Source: Created by Stephanie Gilleran, The University of Tennessee, Knoxville.

Determining the right mix of vehicles is as important as what is said and/ or shown.

When a campaign uses multiple vehicles, it is said to take a *mixed media approach*. This is a great way to create a relationship with the target and ensure the choice of vehicles will reach them where they are and when they are most receptive to the message. Most media plans include a mix of traditional and alternative media vehicles. Once the strategy has been determined, planners can chose from either a concentrated or broad mix of vehicles.

Most complex messages employ a *concentrated mix* that offers more frequency over a longer period of time. This type of mix often uses print vehicles over broadcast so the detailed yet informative messages can be digested over time.

Concentrated mixes are great for products in categories with a high level of product parity, since this type of buy increases an ad's chance to be seen and remembered, greatly influencing its share of voice. *Share of voice* refers to a brand's equity or dominance within its brand category based on the percentage of advertising dollars spent as compared to its competitors.

In addition, concentrated mixes are usually less expensive, since the use of fewer vehicles allows for only a small number of diverse messages. For brands requiring less advertising, such as those in their maintenance stage, a broad mix is typically more successful at increasing reach. On the down side, though, this kind of mix can be risky if the wrong media vehicles are used and the target is missed.

The use of a concentrated media mix greatly improves frequency and decreases reach. Basically, the more types of media used, the greater the reach. Concentrated mixes are great for brands targeting niche markets, where interactions take place on a one-to-one basis, or with vehicles like direct mail, brochures, or magazines that can be viewed repeatedly.

A *broad media mix*—one that uses multiple media vehicles—is great for campaigns that need to say a lot and reach a large population of the target audience. The diversified mix of vehicles ensures that the ad is seen repeatedly in multiple places, thus reinforcing memorability. For example, a guerrilla event may take place at the same time an ad is seen on television; street teams might give away samples or promotional items might be used to encourage trial; newspaper, out-of-home, e-mail, or mobile marketing might be used to announce a sale; the Internet may be employed as a research device or used to dispense coupons or as a quick and easy place to make a purchase or talk to other enthusiasts or customer service representatives. Choice should also consider how many interactive or viral opportunities can be built into the mix.

Geographic Placement and Scheduling

Geographic placement deals with where advertising will be placed: internationally, nationally, regionally, or locally. Most international and national media schedules will include a broad mix of vehicles.

International buys must look at individual cultures to determine the best ways to reach the target.

National efforts need to determine whether advertising efforts will appear in all markets or only in specific regions of the country. It is entirely possible that a mix of both national and regional approaches will be necessary, with national advertising efforts spaced evenly across markets but employed more heavily in regions where sales are weak.

Nationally advertised products are usually mass-consumed products such as shampoo or laundry detergents. Products targeted at smaller niche markets concentrate advertising efforts more heavily in certain regions of the country, making a regional or "spot buy" more targeted with less media waste.

Combined efforts are used for those regional pockets where products do not sell as well and require a beefed-up or heavier dose of advertising. Where the product has a greater amount of equity, a light maintenance schedule will maintain market share.

Local advertising focuses on products and services that are located within a city or town. Often tied in to area events, this type of advertising usually features some type of promotion or sale to encourage purchase. Local businesses like grocery stores will often combine advertising efforts with nationally advertised brands. This type of shared exposure is known as *cooperative* or *co-op* advertising; in exchange for exposure, national brands absorb part or all of the advertising costs.

Scheduling

Once the media vehicles have been determined and budget issues have been addressed, it is time to develop a *media schedule*—typically a chart that shows what media vehicles will be used, when they will be used, and for how long.

The most commonly used scheduling models include continuity, flighting, and pulsing.

- A *continuity schedule* maintains a constant level of advertising during the year, dispersing media buys evenly across months. Requiring a large budget, this type of schedule is a great way to build and/or maintain brand awareness over time.
- A *flighting schedule* alternates media buys across months. Some periods will be heavy and other periods will be light or have no advertising at all. An alternating schedule is great for items that are advertised seasonally such as pools and spas.
- A *pulsing schedule* is a combination of both flighting and continuity schedules. This type of schedule maintains a continuous advertising schedule across all months, with an increase in spending during certain months of the year.

Determining which schedule to employ will depend on: (1) target involvement; (2) seasonal factors; and (3) time allotted between purchases.

Target Involvement

Inexpensive everyday purchases take little or no thought before buying and are said to require a *low level of involvement* from the consumer. These are the brand categories that have little brand differentiation and require a broader mix of media vehicles to catch the target's attention and stand out from competing brands. More expensive items, on the other hand, are separated by longer time periods between purchases and require more thought and research by the consumer. High-end purchases such as jewelry, furniture, or certain types of electronics—known as *high involvement purchases*—are influenced not only by price but by input from friends and family members. Because of this, advertising efforts must be seen *prior* to purchase rather than at the point of purchase. High involvement products that are repurchased less often depend less on mass advertising and more on one-on-one individually targeted announcement and maintenance options. The diverse selection of alternative media vehicles guarantees a media and target match no matter what the level of involvement before purchase.

Seasonal Factors

Specialty products such as lawn mowers, holiday items, and snowblowers are advertised seasonally. Seasonal products using a flighting schedule will reach the consumer when they are ready to buy and remind those on the fence about great deals.

Time Allocated Between Purchases

How much advance advertising is needed for a product will depend on how often that product is repurchased. Continuity or continuous schedules are great for commonly used or mass-produced goods such as soap or toothpaste: These ads remind and reinforce brand loyalty, while introducing new and improved options, sales, and alternative uses.

As a rule, most ad campaigns require a media plan that is consistent with the use of the product or service. For example, packaged goods, fast foods, cleaning supplies, and so on advertise all year long. New or reinvented product launches need a heavy schedule of advertising initially in order to build brand awareness and educate the target on use or changes and updates. Efforts are then reduced to a maintenance level to ensure awareness and positioning. Seasonal products like Cadbury Eggs advertise only once a year for a limited number of weeks. Other products like snowblowers have a heavier schedule during peak use and a light schedule just before and after seasonal highs. Understanding how and when a product is used helps avoid media waste and guarantees that exposure opportunities will not be missed.

Alternative media vehicles do not always need to be purchased; many just need to be planned for. Those that take place during heavy advertising periods are more likely to attract attention and encourage positive word-of-mouth exchanges. Because many alternative media vehicles are personalized, the target can be reached directly by e-mail, mobile announcements, direct mail, social networks, and at events and trade shows.

Media efforts can quickly drain a budget, so it is vital the media team knows when to increase exposure and when to cut back or eliminate efforts.

Setting Media Tactics

Tactics define how the media plan will be implemented. Once the strategy has determined how, when, and where the target will be reached, the tactics section will determine what specific vehicles will be used to accomplish both the strategy and the objectives. For example, if using magazines and promotional vehicles, tactics will define what type of promotions and magazines will be used (giveaways, contests or sweepstakes, coupons, and so on). Magazine choices rely heavily on the target to be reached. Professional men between the ages of 25 and 40, for instance, might read *Time, Sports Illustrated,* and/or *Forbes.*

Executing a Media Evaluation

Evaluation determines whether the media plan strategically accomplished the objectives and whether there was a measurable ROI. Evaluation can be carried out by the advertising agency, the client, or an independent source. Tactics might include looking at target feedback, observation, and/or tracking options. *Feedback* is measured by the number of visits to a website, calls to a toll-free number, coupon redemptions, or total number of consumers attending an event. *Observation tactics* involve watching the target in the place where the product or service is purchased or used to determine such things as ease of use, types of comparisons made, level of difficulty to assemble, and so on. *Tracking* evaluates the effectiveness of online ads, participation in a contest or sweepstakes, coupon distribution, and the like.

Media development is complicated. For it to work as intended, the media team must be aware of what the client wants to achieve and what the visual/ verbal message needs to accomplish. The media and creative teams need to work together closely to ensure the buys will effectively and clearly project the creative strategy to the target. Determining the correct choice of media vehicle(s) is critical not only to ensure they reach the target where they are, but to stay on budget as well.

Alternative Media Exercise 4.1

1. For this exercise, use the creative brief created in Chapter 3 to determine a brief media plan. Be sure to consider the following: When will vehicles run, where will they run, and for how long? Will they run alone or simultaneously with one or more vehicles? Will you use a pulsing, flighting, or continuity schedule? What type of reach and frequency are you going for and why?
2. Present media direction to class. Be sure to refer back to the creative brief, the choice of vehicles, and the original layout in order to present your ideas clearly.
3. Pick another layout and repeat the above steps.

5

Conceptualizing the Idea and Choice of Media

Figure 5.1   **Sample Ad: Knoxville Museum of Art**

Source: Created by Victoria Drew, The University of Tennessee, Knoxville.

Taking a Walk Through the Design Process

Creativity isn't all imagination; it's also about solving a business problem creatively. In the world of advertising campaigns, creative execution is the last phase in a lengthy process that started months earlier with intensive research gathering, analysis, projecting, and planning. It is the creative team's job to mold the creative brief into a unique and memorable idea. It is also their responsibility to make sure the idea can be used across multiple types of media vehicles without losing its identity. Exceptional ideas are often elusive and can take a great deal of time and energy to develop. No idea is disregarded, no source ignored. "I have learned to respect ideas, wherever they come from," said legendary advertising executive Leo Burnett in his 1995 book *100 LEO's.*

A great idea is usually built around something concrete, something the target can relate to. The more memorable and compatible the message, the more targeted and successful a truly great idea can be. The creative direction should be reflected in the key consumer benefit. That benefit, in turn, must be strategically expressed in a visual/verbal tone of voice that the target will understand and react to, and the ads must appear in a concentrated or assorted media mix they are sure to see, hear, or view.

Good Ideas Take Their Place at the Front of the Creative Line

Conceptual development, also know as *brainstorming,* is all about thinking the "unimagined." Advertising executive Alex Osborn in the late 1930s, according to an online article by destech.wordpress.com, was the first to come up with the descriptive term, describing it as a way to "use the *brain* to *storm* a problem, in commando fashion." He believed that "it is easier to tone down a wild idea than to think up a new one."

Brainstorming or conceptual development sessions are conducted by the creative team, which is usually made up of at least one copywriter and one art director. Once the team members know what they need to accomplish, the next step is to find a few wild ideas to define it.

Every memorable campaign begins with a good idea that is painstakingly molded to accomplish the initiatives laid out in the creative brief. Many good ideas are accidents. Some others are developed from a couple of bad ideas that have been thoroughly reworked. Still others rely on overactive imaginations, bad senses of humor, keen observations, or vividly recollected past experiences to give them life. A good idea is the hammer that drives the strategic nail.

Good designers need a kaleidoscope of experiences and interests to draw from. They should be open-minded, adventurous, and receptive to others' ideas. A solid creative direction stems from interesting observations of human nature, a well-honed sense of curiosity, and a wee bit of witty cynicism. Ideally, the creative team will be composed of students of human behavior—people who know a little about psychology, economics, art, music, and history. Designers typically venture beyond the bounds of everyday monotony in their search for inspiration. They must be able to employ historical references and use movies, television, and radio references from today and yesterday to represent a brand's image and set the visual/verbal tone for creative direction. They should never get a dreamless night's sleep, pass up an opportunity to do a little inappropriate eavesdropping, miss a much-deserved cocktail hour, or waste a quiet drive home.

Conceptual development sessions allow the creative team to eliminate worn-out solutions and replace them with unique or cutting-edge ideas. The more distinctive the visual/verbal identity, the more a brand can step out and away from its competitors. Unique ideas are the springboards to developing a memorable brand image that solidifies the brand's superiority in the mind of the target.

Brilliant results often take hours of juggling both good and bad ideas. Some will be reworked, and some will be quietly retired, so it is important to generate as many ideas as possible. Every bad idea spoken aloud tends to make the team work harder to find a better, more expressive, more informative alternative. In the end, a creative solution is rarely found in a single idea: usually, several ideas are intertwined to solve an advertising problem creatively.

This intricate collection of ideas is used to promote the right message, to the right target, in the right media. The message is repeatedly tweaked in small but purposeful ways before it is ever presented to the client. Sweating out the details is as much a part of the creative process as conceptual development, copywriting, or design. The creative team usually works on a tight schedule, which does not leave much time to generate ideas. Depending on the product—and in order to make publication or production dates—the team may have anywhere from a few hours to a couple of weeks to complete the creative execution phase. Any art director or copywriter must be able to come up with a creative solution for both major and minor problems with little or no advanced notice.

A successful creative team must:

1. Imagine the possibilities. How can the product be used in new and inspired ways? How will it alter or enlighten the target's lifestyle? What do its size, color, and/or color combinations say or symbolize? Think beyond the obvious.
2. Keep ideas from becoming stale. Obsessive tweaking ensures the

creative solution is in a constant state of organized disorder. Ongoing dialogue with the target will help keep ideas fresh and cutting-edge.

3. Know the brand and the target's image. It is important to ensure the brand's image reflects the target's self-image throughout each media vehicle employed in order to attract attention and engage the target through events, trials, promotion, or purchase.

4. Be well rounded. Good advertising draws on a diverse knowledge of the old, the new, and the futuristic. Good creative teams use research and their diverse arsenal of visual/verbal antidotes to beef up product categories, introduce new uses, looks, or styles, or launch the newest trend or fad.

5. People watch. Go to the mall or the airport or take a seat along a crowded street and observe. Use the array of passing characters as inspiration, taking special note of how their form of dress, their mannerisms, and their sense of style display their individual personalities. Whether they are fat, skinny, bald, hairy, old, young, slow, fast, overdressed, underdressed, spaced out, talking too loudly on cell phones, or dropping a big bite of lunch in their laps, people are unique. Use what you see to give the target a view of life with the brand.

6. Know the brand and competition. Understand the brand's place in the product category as compared to its competitors. How is it different from or similar to the competition? What does the target think about the brand versus the competitors' brands? To find out, consider using both the client's product and the competitors' products yourself to gain insights into their pros and cons.

7. Solve a business problem. Before the campaign can take on a visual/ verbal identity, the creative team must come up with a great idea that stands out from the competition, talks directly to the intended target audience about the key consumer benefit, accomplishes the overall objectives, and stays strategically on-target.

8. Make quick creative decisions. The creative process often consists of one rejection after another, and revisions are an accepted part of the game. The team must be able to make changes quickly and be creative on demand—often for hours at a time. Stress is a big part of the job, and if channeled creatively, it can be a good source of expressive energy and inspiration.

Without an Identity, All Brands Are the Same

Not only is there a lot of product parity out there, there is also a lot of creative repetition. In order to position a brand as unique in its category, it cannot mimic

Figure 5.2   **Sample Ad: Tuesday Morning**

Source: Created by Kelly Bukovsky, The University of Tennessee, Knoxville.

the advertised messages of the competition. The first time the target sees an idea, it is considered an anomaly; once they see it repeated by a competitor, it is dismissed as "me too" advertising or visual/verbal noise and relegated to second place in consumers' minds. Because today's consumers can successfully ignore the thousands of advertisements they are exposed to each day, a product will only stand out if its message is distinctive and directly parallels the target's needs and wants.

A creative team's seemingly endless banter and doodles are the first step toward developing a memorable idea, concept, or theme. The goal of a conceptual development session is to illuminate the obvious and search for a new and innovative direction. At the root of innovation lie clichés and stale ideas. Innovation grows from the unfettered discussion of hundreds of ideas—many of which could be called weird, slightly off-strategy, or downright ridiculous. But successful design is not really about great ideas; it's about selling or promoting a product or service in a memorable way that sets the brand apart from competitors' messages.

Not All Ideas Are Created Equal

The creative phase is the final step in the execution of the client's business plan, so at this point in the process, time is always in short supply. Team members must be able to navigate professionally between what they want and what is best to establish the brand's visual/verbal tone of voice.

Every visual/verbal aspect of a campaign must be developed with the target audience in mind. Creatively, solutions must relate to the target's lifestyle and self-image, as well as solve a relevant problem or fulfill a need. Media choices must be researched scrupulously to assure they reach the target where they are.

A cohesive visual/verbal message is the tie that binds a multiple media campaign together, driving home the key consumer benefit in a way that will attract the target's attention. To be cohesive, all messages must deliver one visual/verbal tone of voice that is recognizable and repetitive in one or more memorable ways. Messages that lack cohesiveness deliver an inconsistent message that directly erodes both memorability and the brand's identity. Every contact point should reinforce and repeat the campaign's message.

Storming the Idea Bastion

Originality can be attained only if the creative team pushes past the mundane to the exotic. Creative problem solving cannot be done on a computer; it still requires a visual/verbal solution that takes shape in the imagination of each team member. Once shared with the group, it becomes a collection of multiple ideas that work together to solve the problem initiated in the creative brief. There are no rules, no boundaries, and no limits to the number of ideas a conceptual development session should generate. The only absolute is to come up with an idea that promotes the key consumer benefit in a creative and imaginative way.

Most brands do ordinary things with expected results. The creative team attempts to find a way of visually and verbally showing the ordinary in an extraordinary, unique, and memorable way. Isolating a brand's creative direction requires an atmosphere of informality where thoughts can be shared openly. Most development sessions never look or sound the same way twice or last for a set amount of time. The only constant is the goal of generating as many ideas as possible. Reliably, dozens and dozens of these ideas will crash and burn on impact; others will linger awhile. Only a small few will live to see further development. These ideas will define the brand's image, talk directly to the targeted audience in a language they will understand, and appear in situations they will relate to. Still fewer ideas will successfully weave the target's self-image with that of the brand, because they are on-target and on-strategy. That is the ultimate definition of a great creative and memorable idea.

What Does a Good Idea Look and Sound Like?

Many young designers and small businesspeople alike often ask themselves, How do I know a good idea when I think of it? The answer is simple! If it hasn't been done before, talks directly to the target audience, strategically addresses the objectives, pushes the key consumer benefit, and has a different visual/verbal tone of voice than the competition, chances are it is a great idea.

The key to solving any problem is not to dwell on it for long. Leave it alone and let it marinate for a few hours, or if time permits a few days, before deciding on a visual/verbal direction. When possible, take the time to search for the best solution. For example, if you normally drive to work, take the bus or train. Look out the window, daydream, go to lunch by yourself and talk to a stranger or two. Ask people to describe your product, to feel it, wear it, or taste it; record their thoughts and reactions. What happens if the product is placed in an unusual setting? How do people react? Manipulate its use or look, compare it to the competition, question its shape or color, find unique answers to questions once thought irrelevant to the brand's image or key consumer benefit. Give the brand a personality. It is more than a toaster, a sneaker, a boat, or a can of peas. Through discussions, experimentation, and basic trial and error, it is only a matter of time before the "I've got it" moment arrives.

Even after the creative team "has it," the idea still faces many hurdles. Tight budget restrictions, time constraints, a client's own creative ideas, and media limitations that often require downsizing or pulverizing the visual/verbal message can have an impact on the overall creative direction of a campaign.

Squeezing Out Both Good and Bad Ideas

If you asked a hundred creative teams how they came up with their great ideas, you would get a hundred different answers. Each team has to determine what works best for them and use it to find a creative solution to the current marketing assignment. Let's take a look at some possible techniques that can help the creative team envision the idea during the conceptual development stage.

Figure 5.3 **Sample Ad: PetSmart**

Source: Created by Maggie Yeager, The University of Tennessee, Knoxville.

Giving Words a Visual Meaning

Visual/Verbal Word Association

When looking for that perfect idea in a dry business document like a creative brief, you often have to look at how a product and its benefits are described for inspiration. Isolating descriptive words is one of the easiest ways to visualize how a product or service works or is used. It is also the first step in interpreting how the target will react to what is said and shown, and how the idea will stand up to different types of media.

Creating a visual/verbal word list is a great way to simplify what a product or service is all about. A typical list is comprised of three separate columns or parts. The first column is used to list as many words as possible to describe what the product looks like, how it is used, tastes, feels and so on, and any preconceived ideas the target may have about the product, whether positive or negative. This is the time to throw anything you can think of into the conceptual development pot. This first list of words is more fact-based than imaginative. Let's take a look at what a small list for a brand of dill pickles might look like:

Column One:
   Green
   Cylindrical
   Sour
   Spear

Using a thesaurus if necessary, the team populates column two with more visual or colorful words to replace the often-uninspiring fact-based words from column one. See the examples below.

Column Two:
   Chartreuse, Ripe, Seasoned
   Elongated, Bullet
   Tangy, Tart
   Slice, Segment, Jab

The third column is where the members of the creative team write one or two sentences on how these words could be visually and verbally used in an ad. Even though some words may not lend themselves to a visual solution, they may make a great headline, tagline, or slogan later.

Column Three:
   The taste of nature.
   Shape defines taste.
   Show people's facial reaction to the tart taste.
   Variety in how used.

Column three is the one that will help define creative direction, so the descriptions should be as interactive as possible. For the pickle example, showcase taste, texture, or experience. A good alternative media option for our pickle list is to get the target to send in pictures of their facial reactions to the first tart bite and use the images throughout the advertising campaign. Street venders can give away food samples that highlight how pickles can be used to complement other ingredients, and so on. Each word in column three should have at least one visual/verbal sentence associated with it. See complete table on the following page.

Column One:	Column Two:	Column Three:
Green	Chartreuse, Ripe, Seasoned	The taste of nature.
Cylindrical	Elongated, Bullet	Shape defines taste.
Sour	Tangy, Tart	Show people's facial reaction the to tart taste.
Spear	Slice, Segment, Jab	Variety in how used.

The next step is to toss out the silly ideas (there will be many) and further develop the ones that have promise.

Techniques such as this one teach you how a good idea is not useable unless it has both a visual and verbal application and adaptability to multiple media vehicles. Many alternative media vehicles allow only a small amount of copy to get the visual idea across, so both solutions must be strong. A typical word association list should be anywhere from 15 to 25 words long to maximize creative options.

Using words to solve a creative problem helps boil down complicated ideas. The team will find it easier to focus on the problem to be solved and the key consumer benefit if they have just a few good ideas to play with.

Laddering

Another good word-based idea-generating technique involves the use of Post-it Notes (or, for that matter, any type of paper that can be attached to a wall and hold an idea). Every member of the creative team comes into the session with a few ideas to toss in the ring for discussion. These ideas can be written down by a moderator and posted around the room, or team members can post their own. Like all idea-generation techniques, this exercise involves building on the original posts to create as many additional ideas as possible, as quickly as possible. Once the initial session has slowed down, each posted idea is reviewed. Ideas that are off-strategy are eliminated, similar ideas are combined together, and so on, creating an extended ladder of varying solutions to the advertising problem. The remaining ladders face a second elimination round until three to five solid ideas are left on the table (or, more accurately, on the wall).

180-Degree Thinking

One of my favorite conceptual development techniques is known as "180-degree thinking." The idea comes from Nancy Vonk and Janet Kestin in their 2005 book *Pick Me: Breaking into Advertising and Staying There.* This very creative technique is great to use when the team is stuck with a day's worth of dull ideas. Go back to the drawing board and have each team member come up with the worst possible way to use or sell the product—something like, "This fajita mix looks like something the cat coughed up" or "This hair spray is guaranteed to give you a helmet-head look and stand up, literally, to the strongest hurricane winds." The goal of the session is to kick a dull and sagging imagination into high gear by seeing the product or service in a new and unique way.

Make It Up, Get Some Help, and Let It Fail

In their book *Bang! Getting Your Message Heard in a Noisy World* (2003) Linda Kaplan Thaler and Robin Koval maintain that exaggerations, interruptions, and failures help foster good ideas. If you're having trouble positioning the brand away from the competition, try coming up with exaggerated comparisons to help identify differences. Sometimes asking the executive in charge of the account, creative teams from other accounts, or even members of the public relations staff to step in with a few fresh ideas can help the team see the brand in a new light. Typically, there will be failures and many starts and stops along the way: Think of them as a rejected line of thinking, not a bad or rejected idea. All bad ideas provide the backdrop for the first step toward the ultimate visual/verbal solution. No idea should be criticized or rejected before it is thoroughly dissected; some small piece might be worth saving.

Cluster Writing

I like to call this technique "the wheel of ideas." It begins with a single posted word that defines the key consumer benefit. That word becomes the hub or center of the idea wheel from which all other words or ideas will be expanded and developed. Once complete, each spoke of the wheel will represent one idea that will inspire a new, and hopefully better, idea.

Starbursting

Like cluster writing, starbursting uses a graphic to organize both the session and the ideas. This technique uses a series of questions to reach a final conclusion or direction. Using a six-pointed star as the original outline, place the words "who," "what," "when," "where," "why," and "how" at the tip of each point. The resulting questions will jut out from each point. Hold off answering any of the questions until round two, when you repeat the exercise.

On the Flip Side

This idea-generation technique is another great way to jumpstart a fried imagination. Looking at a problem from the flip side can be rejuvenating for the entire team. For example, instead of asking the team to come up with an inventive way to sell radishes, ask them instead to brainstorm on why anyone would want to buy radishes?

After having a little fun exhausting all the negative possibilities, flip back to find a positive solution for each.

Charades

This is another great way to loosen up a stiff creative session. Take the best ideas and assign one to each team member. Give them five minutes to think of a way to act out the idea as the rest of the team or outside members attempt to guess what it is. A moderator should write down responses to the actors' interpretive actions.

Each of these techniques centers on reworking and revamping various ideas. Ultimately, the visual/verbal idea is a carefully crafted statement that solves the advertising problem presented in the creative brief.

The more times you go through the conceptual development process, the closer you will get to a visual/verbal solution that will innovatively and uniquely represent the brand in any media vehicle.

Finally, it is important to remember before using any of these techniques that many ideas end up with a visual/verbal identity that has nothing to do with what the brand does, looks like, or is used. The creative team gives it an identity through imaginative positioning; for example, how many of you would have used a caveman to sell insurance (GEICO), or a baby to sell investment services (eTrade)? Most of you would have taken the safe way out and used a pitchman to sell the features and outline the need. Testing the creative waters will help you get rid of the tepid ideas, rework the cool ideas, and settle on the hot "first to think of it" idea.

Ideas are only the first rung on the creative ladder. Execution is the second and most time-consuming element of an advertising campaign. A great idea poorly designed and/or produced will fail as quickly as an idea that is off-target or off-strategy. Good design requires a keen eye for organization, visual/verbal relationships, and a thorough knowledge of technical or production techniques.

Part II

Media Use: How Media Speaks to and Reaches the Target Differently

6

Traditional Advertising

Figure 6.1 **Sample Ad: Morton's Sea Salt**

Source: Created by Ally Callahan, The University of Tennessee, Knoxville.

Traditional Advertising in a Modern Campaign

Advertising is a nonpersonal, paid form of one-way communication that uses persuasion to sell, entice, educate, remind, and/or entertain the target audience about one specific brand. Traditional mass media uses print (newspaper and magazine) and broadcast media (radio and television) to reach an undefined mass audience. While traditional advertising is not the best choice for building a relationship with the target, it is great for creating brand awareness and building or maintaining brand image. Because of its immense reach, it is often used to launch a new or reinvented product or as a reminder for commonly used products such as condiments, milk, soda, toilet tissue, aspirin, cold medicines, and the like. The fact that the message can be repeated helps position the brand in the mind of the consumer, build brand loyalty, and over time gain brand equity.

One of the main drawbacks of any traditional advertising vehicle is that it is not consumer-centric. It relies instead on a passive yet informative one-way flow of information that delivers an impersonal message. Its main job is to inform and build or retain a brand's image, not build a relationship or initiate dialogue between buyer and seller. However, when traditional vehicles offer interactive opportunities, they can become a temporary substitute for one-on-one interaction. For example, newspapers can include coupons, list web addresses, or announce a "limited time only" sale. Magazines can hold the target's interest longer when they feature scratch-and-sniff cards, pop-ups, or multiple folds. Including a website address allows the target to seek out additional information, sign up for contests or sweepstakes, and chat with other users. Covers have also gone interactive by using unusual folds, pockets, movable parts, and even three-dimensional designs to attract and hold the reader's interest. Radio is interactive when participating in remote broadcasts or when promoting a locally sponsored contest such as a call-in trivia game. Interactive television allows viewers to vote for a contestant or order products seen on television commercials or in their favorite shows via their computer, remote, or telephone.

Although it may not have the power it once did, traditional media is adapting, making it unlikely we will see its demise any time soon. Research has shown that consumers are more receptive to advertising in traditional media because they view it when relaxing and engaging in entertainment opportunities. Research also indicates that ads seen in traditional media vehicles are more likely to generate buzz based on a memorable visual/verbal message than advertising seen elsewhere.

Advertisers must pick and choose media vehicles that match the brand's image and the target's needs. Because advertising is only a one-way monologue that delivers an impersonal message, it needs to work with relation-ship-building vehicles to create interactive opportunities. For example, when any traditional vehicle is paired with public relations, it is a great way to promote an event or launch a promotion. When paired with social media, traditional media can lay the foundation for the message consumers share online, increasing the buzz and the frequency with which the message is viewed or heard. Add a website into the mix and consumers can locate additional information, talk directly to a customer service representative, or place an order.

The role of traditional media in a campaign is to ensure advertising efforts:

1. Capture attention.
2. Increase sales.
3. Make a product or service stand out from the competition in a creative and informative way.
4. Develop and maintain both brand identity and image.
5. Announce updates or improvements to existing products.
6. Launch new products or services.
7. Address the target's needs and wants.
8. Encourage buzz.

When you understand the strengths and weaknesses of advertising, it is easier to launch a campaign that has an integrated media mix—one that maximizes exposure and eliminates the costly guesswork involved in finding the target.

Understanding Advertising's Strengths and Weaknesses

Let's take a look at what the varying types of traditional advertising vehicles can or cannot bring to the media mix.

Strengths

1. Buzzing and Branding. A great ad gets noticed and creates positive word of mouth and viral sharing.
2. Guaranteed Exposure. An ad is paid for, so it is guaranteed to run or be seen.
3. Guaranteed Placement. If the space is bought, the ad is guaranteed to run.
4. Image and Awareness. Ads are great for building awareness and launching or maintaining brand image.

Weaknesses

1. Reliability. It takes a long time and frequent exposure before the consuming public will act on the advertised message.
2. Visual/Verbal Control. Standards and regulations keep certain types of advertising (such as cigarette and alcohol advertising) out of certain publications or off broadcast networks.
3. Expense. Buys in major media outlets are often expensive to produce and run.
4. Reach. It is often difficult to target and personalize advertisements.

In the course of this chapter, we will look at newspaper, magazine, radio, and television advertising. Each of these embattled vehicles is fighting to keep up with new media and define its place among them. The art and science of reaching the correct target with the correct message—at the right time and place—is getting more and more difficult. Let's take a look at what each one has to offer. First up, print: newspaper and magazine.

Print Advertising

Defining Newspaper Advertising

Currently, newspapers are fighting for their publishing lives. Many have closed their doors due to a decline in readership, circulation, and advertising revenue. Others have increased subscription rates, downsized their staffs, and reduced the size of the paper in order to survive in a tough economy and compete against the newest technology-driven news vehicles. As newspapers struggle to define their place among twenty-first century technology, their role in retail advertising remains the same: to make a sale and encourage action on the part of the consumer.

One of the oldest and least targetable forms of mass media advertising, newspaper ads were once the only way to get local, national, or international exposure. Newspapers now compete not only with 24-hour televised news channels but also with the Internet and social media sites.

Newspaper advertising is typically divided into two main types: local and national. Local advertising promotes local businesses and events and includes both classified and display advertising. National advertisers like Apple, Target, or McDonald's, for example, feature products that can be purchased locally, online, or by making a toll-free call. It is difficult for both local and national advertisers to reach any one particular target audience. Specialized products that range from lawn mowers to fine jewelry to investment ads are more likely to reach the intended target when placed in a feature section they are sure to read. Therefore, the target audience is often tied to the sports, lifestyle, or business section of the paper. Knowing whom you are trying to reach and what media vehicles they frequently use will help determine whether newspaper is the best media vehicle to reach the intended target. For example, newspaper is a great choice if advertising to baby boomers, who are regular readers, but a poor choice if advertising to millenniums, who favor new technology sources over traditional ones.

As a rule, newspaper advertising is credible, informative, and relatively inexpensive to use. It must have a sense of urgency, must boldly inform the reader about the key consumer benefit, and provide them with an incentive to buy now. What it lacks in beauty and targetability it more than makes up for in loyal readers looking for a sale or a coupon. The ability to localize a national brand, increase store traffic, build awareness, generate excitement for a new product launch, and build or retain brand-loyal customers makes newspaper advertising an effective vehicle in any ad campaign.

Retail Sales Announcements Move Products

Because newspaper advertising usually advertises current sales, it's easy for many advertising efforts to look and sound alike. To ensure compatibility between vehicles within the campaign, the creative team must decide what visual/verbal devices they will use to grab the reader and how to make the key consumer benefit unique and action oriented. Sales should not reflect the current holiday, overstock, or special events. The visual/verbal tone of voice used should take an approach the competition would never use; mirror the personality of the target; and vigorously promote the key consumer benefit, overall strategy, and persona of the product or service.

To attract attention, this timely medium must promote one-time-only sales, limited-time offers, trials, test drives, and the like, or include coupons that encourage action and engage consumer interest. Keeping ads fresh is another way to sustain interest. Newspapers printed on a daily basis make it easy to update or change out current advertising to avoid stale or repetitive offers.

Retail Ads Push Price

Since newspaper advertising is all about making a sale, it is important to high-light price. Pricing sets the product or service apart from competing brands, simplifies comparison-shopping, and makes informative buying decisions easier. There are three main areas where prices can be displayed: the headline, the subhead, and as a callout near a visual(s). Headlines are a great place to feature a specific price prominently. Subheads are better suited for displaying a range of prices. Callouts are a good choice when an array of prices needs to appear near individual images. These small blocks of descriptive copy usually include a bold product-identifying headline, a small amount of descriptive copy, and a slightly larger and bolder price point than the callout headline.

Avoid hiding the price in copy blocks; if it's really a good deal, as all sales are assumed to be, display it boldly. Scream it out, make it big, make it bold, italicize it, let it stand alone, or tie it to a copy point—it doesn't matter where it appears, as long as it's there and easily recognizable.

The only time price is not prominently displayed is when promoting exclusive products that focus primarily on image. These types of ads often eliminate prices and concentrate instead on features and benefits that will enhance the target's lifestyle; special sales and financing packages may also be mentioned.

Determining the Visual/Verbal Voice of Newspaper and Magazines

Each ad, no matter the vehicle, must develop and maintain a visual/verbal identity that (1) features the key consumer benefit, (2) speaks directly to the target audience's needs, wants, and/or lifestyle, and (3) cohesively reflects the visual/verbal tone of voice used throughout the alternative/traditional media mix.

Because print vehicles are informative both visually and verbally, they can define an image, highlight a price, or explain a task, idea, or use. They can use colorful or black-and-white images, project both simplistic and complicated concepts, and encourage action. Print ads use one or more of the essential design elements to tell a story with words—through headlines, subheads, body copy, descriptive copy, and slogans or taglines. Visually, they demonstrate the verbal direction with photography, illustrations, graphics, type and layout styles.

Newspapers incorporate strong black-and-white contrasts in their ads, use a single dominant visual or verbal element, and highlight prices to make the ad stand out on the page. Body copy should flesh out the key consumer benefit and let the target know what the product looks like, highlight any special features, describe how it works, how it will enhance their lives, and where to find it.

Clutter is often a problem when working with newspaper design, so eye flow and placement of each essential visual/verbal design element must be controlled. If using multiple related images, consider grouping them together and using callouts to highlight individual product descriptions and price.

Unrelated images can be organized into a grid, with copy and price discussed independently. If the ad does not have a lot to show, make sure the headline has a lot to say. Consider using graphics, illustrations, line art, or a border to increase the black-and-white contrast on the page.

Framing a Print Ad

Although not a required design element, borders are often used as a decorative element, tying an ad together and setting it off from surrounding copy or other ads.

Borders define the dimensions or edges of a newspaper ad. They can be fat, thin, and double ruled, or defined by graphic images. Most high-end stores peddling expensive merchandise will use a thinner, more elegant-looking border. Advertising for discount establishments are often more cluttered, so a heavier border is required to stand out. A good rule of thumb suggests that the overall weight of a border should reflect the weight of the typeface. Borders need not be consistent in size. Consider making the top and bottom slightly thicker than the sides. This disperses the weight away from the center of the ad, creating the illusion of additional white space and making the ad appear larger. Whatever the look or size employed, be sure the border does not interfere with the visual or the verbal images used in the ad. Borders can also be used inside an ad, particularly around photographs or callout boxes to emphasize an image or any copy points that require special notice.

Frames are not exclusive to newspapers. When borders are used in magazine ads, they are known as *inset graphic borders.* Graphically, they mimic those used in newspaper; instead of defining the edges of the ad, inset graphic borders in magazine ads guard against the accidental loss of some of the ad when the magazine is trimmed to size during printing. These decorative borders can be outlined in any color or tint; background colors may be confined within the border or bleed beyond it. Although borders can grab a viewer's attention, magazine ads typically rely on the white of the page or some type of light-colored background to set off the product or provide additional emphasis.

Cooperative Advertising Divides the Exposure

Commonly used throughout all traditional media vehicles, a cooperative or co-op arrangement takes place when two or more compatible advertisers divide the cost of advertising. Co-op advertising ventures allow advertisers to get more advertising exposure for less money. When products are consistently paired together, the target begins to think of the two as inseparable, or as a two-for-one offer. This type of joint venture is often utilized by national brands in order to get their products exposed in local or regional markets. Wholesalers, manufacturers, distributors, and retailers usually offer cooperative programs. Popular alliances might include airline and cruise ship packages, or the pairing of the Apple iPhone with AT&T or Verizon service.

Defining Magazine Advertising

Magazines chronicle our times with detailed narratives and colorful images. They define a lifestyle built on the target's personal interests, political beliefs, and overall values. Strategically speaking, a magazine can customize the key consumer benefit to directly meet the needs and wants of the target.

Unlike newspaper advertising, which pushes sales and prices, magazine advertising focuses on image—specifically, how a brand will affect or interact with the target's perceived self-image. This type of advertising requires a substantial knowledge of the target and their overall lifestyle. All advertising associated with image must visually and verbally inform the target about the ways in which the product will enrich, change, or improve their lives.

Image-based products such as jewelry and cars are known as high-involvement products, meaning the target's self-image is tied to the brand's self-image; therefore, it is important that the brand's message reflect this image both visually and verbally. Placing sales tags on high-involvement products is discouraged, as it can emasculate both the brand and the target's perceived image. In such cases, the focus should be on the benefits or prestige of ownership.

Magazines are highly targetable and engaging when informative copy, gatefolds, inserts, coupons, order forms, a scratch–and–sniff panel, pop-ups, business reply cards, samples, or three-dimensional enhanced images are included in an ad. Although it cannot evoke a two-way dialog with the target, it can encourage them to take the next step by logging onto a website, calling a toll-free number, or visiting a showroom.

Unlike any of the other traditional media vehicles, magazines have a long life span. The special interest content and exclusive target involvement encourages the target to either retain and/or reread content, or pass it along to others interested in the topic. This increases the advertisement's reach, as new readers give the advertising a second chance to make a first impression.

Magazines connect with the target by focusing on their leisure pursuits, interests, or business concerns. Readers expect and look forward to multiple advertising messages that appeal to their likes. A magazine is read by a target that is interested in its editorial content, so it makes sense for advertising to match the editorial style of the magazine. For example, a do-it-yourself magazine might feature advertising for paint, wallpaper, appliances, or tools.

Fashion magazines typically advertise designer clothing, jewelry, and other accessories. Such ads focus on lengthy fact-based copy that not only educates a receptive audience but also encourages trial or additional research. This targeted medium is an efficient way for advertisers to reach a very specified or niche market. Like all traditional media, magazine advertising needs to be supported by vehicles that are better at building and maintaining a relationship with the target and creating an interactive dialogue with the reader. To make ads more personalized, consider using sales promotions, intercept marketing, or direct or e-mail marketing.

Magazines work well with other members of the media mix by establishing image or by making purchase or research far easier. They can direct the target to additional information or include varied interactive enticements such as coupons, order forms, small samples (of, say, lotions or fragrances), or even CDs.

The choice to use magazine ads is an expensive one; consider it only if the product is geared toward a specific niche market, is a generic or rational purchase, or is an image-enhancing emotional purchase. Magazine advertisements are best suited to educate with lengthy copy or visually show the product in use, either in a particular setting or to portray status or elitism.

The Visual/Verbal Voice of Special Interest Magazines

There are three basic types of magazines: trade, consumer, and farming. Each can be subdivided into special interest categories such as gardening, dog lovers, fashion, and business, to name just a few. These categories can then be further divided into local, regional, or national coverage. Each diverse category presents the advertiser with a very exclusive group of targeted consumers.

Special interest magazines have very loyal readers who repeatedly pick up or have their favorite magazine delivered directly to their home or office. Knowledgeable readers demand a creative idea that is new, different, and relative to their personal experiences.

Magazine advertising should be informative and visually create a mood or define a demeanor or attitude. The choice of visual/verbal imagery will ultimately develop and define the brand's image and overall personality. Copy should reflect the target's interest in, and/or experience with, the product or service being advertised.

When the message is one of exclusivity, sophistication, or education, prices should be minimized or altogether absent. Few image-based ads feature prices or lengthy copy; rather, they let the visual(s) sell the product, the benefit, and the overall visual/verbal experience. Ads that do feature lengthy copy have the ability to hold the reader's interest longer, making it a great vehicle for developing and maintaining a storyline or plot that can be carried across multiple media vehicles. In addition to its educational function, copy that is written creatively will sustain interest and create excitement in the target.

Testimonials are another great way to give copy credibility and build a brand's reputation. How-to ads attract attention by involving the consumer's imagination and skills in the visual/verbal message. If the brand is a food product, consider using a recipe or a coupon for a complimentary item, such as coffee with a coupon for creamer.

Since magazine advertising defines, reflects, and projects image, it is important that the advertised message be striking and visually appealing. This is the time to use bold colors and graphics to make the ad stand out from competing advertising. A creative idea with a unique visual/verbal expression is more engaging and persuasive. If the ad's image reflects both the brand and the target's image, an exclusive relationship is formed between the buyer and the seller.

When the key consumer benefit focuses on image, it is easier to show it than to talk about it, so visuals will take center stage. Copy plays a more dominant role if the product is new or newly reinvented. Use visuals to create an image and copy to define its importance. Each enticing visual and paragraph of informative copy should define the brand's image, ooze elitism, and define the target's personality profile; these goals are best achieved by mirroring the target's self-image, interests, and lifestyle. Magazine advertising can be whimsical, sophisticated, sexy, trendy, informative, and visually/verbally stimulating. It is an excellent vehicle for new products with a truly unique selling proposition, as well as for rebuilding brand image or maintaining an established one. Copy that speaks directly to the target's personal experiences allows the message to focus squarely on situations where the product can be used to solve a problem or enhance an experience.

Advertising in magazines must be planned for months in advance, so any last-minute creative changes resulting from current publicity, scientific findings, or current events should utilize a more frequently published or digital vehicle. Unlike immediate publicity outlets or daily newspapers, magazines may be published as often as once a week or as infrequently as once per quarter.

Consider using magazines to support sales promotions, public relations, event marketing, or direct marketing in publicizing local, regional, national, or global events. The same visual/verbal design influence used in magazine ads to define image or enhance prestige will influence the visual/verbal voice used throughout the event. Once the visual/verbal tone of voice is established, it will be reflected in press releases, packaging, direct mailings, outdoor boards, pledge or thank you cards, posters, flyers, banners, and bumper stickers. Any

Figure 6.2   **Sample Ad: ReNu**

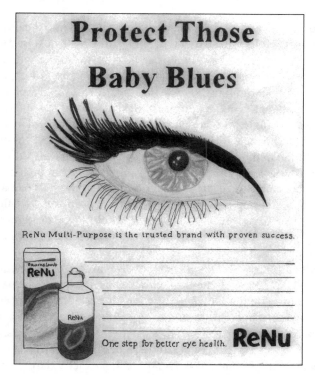

Source: Created by Chelsea Bowen, The University of Tennessee, Knoxville.

sales promotion vehicles such as totes, T-shirts, caps, or water bottles will be easily recognizable as a member of the campaign media mix.

Sizing Up the Ad

A magazine ad can be divided into three important design-influencing parts: trim, live, and bleed. *Trim* is the size of the ad after being printed, trimmed, and bound. The *live area,* located inside the trim, safely confines type so it is not accidentally cut off during printing. A full-size ad measuring 8½ × 11 inches would have a live area around 7 × 10 inches. All images and color blocks can extend beyond both the borders of the live and trim area to the bleed. Bleed is the area beyond the trim. An ad has *bleed* when an image or block of color extends to the edge of the trim on one or more sides. Bleed assures that no white space will show around an ad's edges when the magazine is trimmed to size.

Interactive Folds Give the Reader Something to Do

One way to engage a reader is to incorporate a gatefold into the design. Vary-ing in size, a gatefold refers to one or more folds that face inward toward the magazine's center or spine. Folds can be attached to a single-page ad, to a spread, or to a two-page ad. Most ads employ a single full-page panel. In order to fold without rumpling or creasing, the panel is usually one-quarter to one-half inch smaller than the original page size. Partial page panels are also an option, with a single fold measuring anywhere from two and a half inches to four and a half inches. Although single panels are the most common, there is no limit to the number of gatefolded partial or full-page foldouts used in a magazine ad. Pieces with multiple folds might use a fan or accordion fold that allows the panels to be stacked back and forth on top of one another, or a roll fold, in which multiple panels are repeatedly folded or rolled toward the center. A two-page spread will have a roll fold or gatefold that is placed on both the left and right sides of the spread and folded inward toward the spine or gutter.

Gatefolds can extend the advertised message, invoke curiosity, and engage the reader. When the target interacts with the ad by opening the panels, their interest is focused on the message for a longer period of time. Most panels show accessories or alternative uses for a product; they can also inform the reader about coupons, contests or sweepstakes, upcoming offers, or even a promotional offer such as a product sample. Since gatefolds overlay the bottom photograph, it is important that the images align exactly during printing.

Print Changes with the Times

Today, the traditional media are changing their rules and their look to attract the attention of readers, listeners, and viewers. Until recently, newspapers and magazines never allowed advertising above the fold or on the front cover; now, they are employing both in order to raise revenue.

Magazines in particular are finding ways to change with the times, giving advertisers a louder voice, allowing advertising on their front covers, and using very inventive cover folds, pockets, and interactive options to attract readers. *ESPN The Magazine* took a creative visual approach by adding a foldout flap to half of the front cover that read, "You wouldn't settle for an incomplete cover." Beneath the flap, readers found an ad for Powerade. Others, like *En-tertainment Weekly,* have also added a pocket to the front cover, in this case featuring a pullout ad for the short-lived ABC show *The Unusuals.*

Esquire used its front cover creatively by featuring a picture of President Barack Obama that included a pullback window for the Discovery Channel.

Another ad for the same magazine made use of an old-fashioned substitution cover that allowed readers to mix and match President Obama's chin with George Clooney's nose and Justin Timberlake's eyes. Under each panel, engaged readers saw an ad for the History Channel.

Going one step further, magazine ads are going interactive with a new type of advertising known as *snappables*. Here's how it works: Consumers can take a picture of an advertised product in a magazine, send the shot to the product's manufacturer, and in return they will receive a short code through their cell phone that can be used to shop directly from the magazine.

Newspaper is still finding its way in the ever-changing world of alternative media, but according to the Toronto-based research company Telemetrics, traditional print is responsible for initiating online searches, and those searches keep the advertised message vital.

The next section looks at radio and television's role in the traditional media mix. Broadcast vehicles rely on the listener or viewer's imagination to capture attention. Radio must attract attention with sound only, while television can creatively use sight, sound, and motion to drive home the message.

Radio and Television Advertising

Defining Radio Advertising

Radio reaches a broad and often captive audience through our phones, in our cars, in restaurants, grocery stores, even waiting rooms. Often relegated to background noise, it is a medium that rarely holds our complete attention. Because of this, advertising has to work harder to snap targets out their self-imposed comas with interesting and attention-getting devices—a task made harder when competing against personalized music options such as iPods, MP3 players, and satellite radio.

An imaginative media, radio has the burden of creating a visual/verbal message out of copy alone. Its "sound only" format must draw the listener in by creating a visually stimulating product narrative. The more colorful, informative, and personalized the message, the easier it will be for the target to imagine the product or service in their lives or solving their particular problem. Catchy jingles are a great way to keep the product or service alive for hours or even days after exposure, as the target audience repeatedly replays the lyrics in their heads or shares the bouncy tunes with others.

Like newspaper, radio is timely and adaptable to the latest political, social, or seasonal trends. It is a great vehicle for creating action by announcing sales, publicizing events, or promoting remote broadcasts from local area retailers. Because it is action oriented, it is great for building awareness and creating excitement. Local merchants will find it a relatively inexpensive primary vehicle; larger brands will find it a great cooperative opportunity. In a campaign, radio is often used as a support or secondary vehicle to reinforce the advertised message used elsewhere in the media mix.

Several decisions must be made when using radio, among them whether the radio spot will be 15, 30, or 60 seconds in length and what time of day the spot will air. The two most listened to time slots are the morning and afternoon drive times from 6:00 to 10:00 A.M. and 3:00 to 7:00 P.M. These prime-time slots guarantee listeners; once people leave their cars, however, listenership drops off dramatically, as do advertising rates.

The production of radio ads is relatively inexpensive. Typical costs include hiring talent and incorporating sound effects (SFX) or a musical score or jingle. Total media costs depend on how often the ad will air and the number of stations on which the ad will be placed. Other considerations include the choice of using AM or FM, or a music or talk format. Programming can be broken down further into music types such as rock, hip-hop, country, and so on. Each specialized category allows the message to be personalized to match the target's interests.

Radio challenges the creative team to engage the listeners' minds with information and their imaginations with verbal stimuli. This is made somewhat easier because of its highly targetable format. The ability to produce numerous spots for a relatively low cost can keep the message fresh or allow for an ongoing storyline.

As a viable member of any campaign mix, radio is a great medium for reinforcing the verbal message used elsewhere in the campaign. A good example is to start with the spokesperson or character representative, sound effects, and/or jingle from television, and then mix it with the slogan, tagline, and/or headline style from print. Radio can also inspire immediate action, localize a national brand's message, and increase brand awareness. Like other traditional advertising vehicles, radio talks *at* the target. Promotional events such as remote or on-site broadcasts are a great way for radio advertisers to interact with the target.

Most commonly used in local markets, radio is a cost-effective way for local merchants to reach their target with a relevant message that reflects what is going on in the community. If used nationally, radio has enormous reach. Most national ads will use the same generic message in all markets, but typically, advertisers prefer to exploit radio advertising's hometown, highly targetable, uniquely personalized, special interest format.

For a radio ad to move from background noise to the conscious mind, it

Figure 6.3 **Sample Ad: U-Haul**

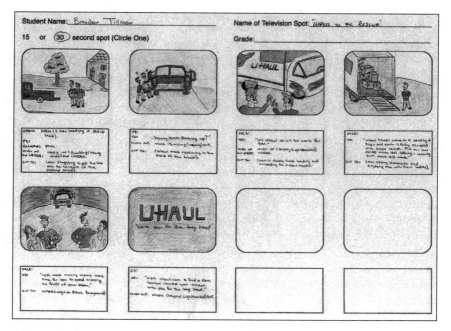

Source: Created by Brandon Tillman, The University of Tennessee, Knoxville.

must engage the listener through startling sound effects or catchy jingles. Promotional opportunities abound when tied to call-in trivia games or remote broadcasts that allow for on-site trials and unsolicited testimonials. Slice-of-life vignettes and ongoing storylines can be used to promote the brand while involving it in dramatic or comedic scenarios that feature local area establishments. This is not only a great way to build curiosity but also to tell an ongoing story listeners can tune into regularly. Consider tying it to a sponsored broadcast such as news, weather, or traffic updates that are "brought to you" ("you" being the listener) by a specific product. This gains repeated exposure and increases brand awareness.

Radio is not the best image-building medium; if the message needs immediate action, consider pairing it with newspaper, the web, texting, and out-of-home advertising to reach a broader swath of public quickly and inexpensively. Public relations can use radio effectively to deliver public service announcements, solicit volunteers, promote blood or food drives, or announce new product launches. If the goal is to educate with detailed copy or promote multiple price points, radio is not the best vehicle. Radio's fleeting message is rarely memorable unless repeated frequently.

Listening to What Radio Has to Say Visually

There are two basic ways to deliver an advertising spot on the radio: live or prerecorded. Simple spots can be written, produced, and aired in as little as a few hours or days and quickly delivered on the air by popular local DJs. Their involvement in the message can be tantamount to a personal endorsement. Listeners trust their opinion, giving the brand a boost of credibility. Popular radio personalities do not read from a prepared script, but are instead provided with a fact sheet. The dialogue is delivered in their own words, without the benefit of sound effects or music, as might be present on a prerecorded version of a radio spot. Depending on the personality, live presentations can be risky, because they are not controlled. However, a DJ who has actually used the product can often talk about its benefits longer than the purchased airtime allows, inadvertently offering a reliable testimony in the mind of the listener.

Radio ads should use a conversational style and have an upbeat and friendly tone. The voice that is chosen to deliver the commercial (announcer or talent) will depend on the strategy and tone of voice used throughout the campaign. Be sure the voice chosen represents the target's personality and voice. Radio copy should be short and full of urgency to encourage a prompt response to the message. Build a visual picture of the product or service's features and benefits and how they can change the listener's life for the better. A radio ad is particularly engaging if a game or a suggested trip to the website will sign up the listener for a contest or sweepstakes, or if a trip to a brick-and-mortar store will get them a sample or promotional item. Let's take a look at a few of the diverse ways a radio spot can be scripted and delivered.

Music and Jingles. A consistent sound is more than just the spoken word or readable copy. It can also be projected in the music played or jingle sung. Music sets a mood without the need for words or visuals. Depending on the genre or tempo, music defines emotions, creates a feeling of nostalgia, and excites or relaxes the listener. Use music to help the target imagine a visual and emotional scene.

Catchy little jingles stay with us long after a commercial message has ended. Consider tying jingles to the key consumer benefit, slogan, or tagline. Every time the target sings or hums a bar, the brand gets a second, third, or fourth shot at delivering its message. A few bars can say as much as a page of dialogue. Jingles not only set a mood but can place boring dialogue to music, making it more memorable.

Narrative Drama. This type of message uses dialogue to tell the brand's story.

Straight Announcement. This no-nonsense type of message delivers only the brand's features and benefits. An excellent option when delivered by an on-air personality.

Celebrity Delivery. This message format is a great way to feature the campaign's spokesperson or character representative.

Live Donut. A live donut is half prerecorded and half live read. The opening and closing are prerecorded, usually with music that fades when the center portion (the ad) is presented live by an on-air personality.

Dialogue. This delivery format is a great way to use testimonials or discuss a brand's features and benefits.

Multiple-Voice Delivery. A multiple-voice approach features two or more characters who speak directly to the listener, usually asking questions and providing answers.

Sound Effects (SFX). Sound can be a visual stimulant. Visual actions shown in other media vehicles can be recycled and visualized on the radio. Sounds such as a ringing doorbell, a belch, or screeching tires can help make a point or solve a problem.

Vignette/Slice-of-Life. A vignette is like a TV sitcom or drama that has an ongoing storyline. The key to recognizing a vignette is the use of repetition—whether characters, sounds, music, slogans, or taglines—to tie the multiple storylines together.

Interviews. Remote broadcasts are a great way to incorporate man-on-the-street interviews into the advertised message.

It is not uncommon to see one or more of these techniques used to deliver a brand's message, create awareness, build curiosity, or entice immediate action. The only rule is to make sure it will engage the target.

Visualizing the Verbal-Only Message

Radio must be able to successfully deliver the key consumer benefit verbally. Reusing devices such as spokespersons, character representatives, music, jingles, or headline devices helps the listener tune in and "visualize" the verbal-only message. In order to reach the target, the message must attract the listener with the brand name and key consumer benefit within the first three seconds. To be successful, radio advertising must:

1. Tune the Listener In. The message has three seconds to engage listeners before they tune back out.
2. Cleverly Identify the Brand. Each spot should open by clearly identifying the brand and key consumer benefit. If the brand is hard to pronounce or has an unusual use, consider incorporating it into a jingle, a rhyming scheme, or through repetition.
3. Have an Identifiable Tone. Each radio spot must adapt the tone of voice used throughout the campaign.

4. Be Chatty. Dialogue that is written in a conversational style is easier to understand and relate to. Punctuate points through short sentences rather than rambling dialogue.
5. Describe the Product. Give the listener's mind something to do, perhaps by describing the product, its packaging, or the outcome of its use.
6. Remind. When listeners are not totally tuned in, copy must repeat the brand name and key consumer benefit often before it is remembered.
7. Be Timely. Tie the brand to local events.
8. Give the Features Real-Life Uses. Don't bore with endless facts; entice with results.
9. Sound Out Carefully. Sound effects work only if they advance the message and are easily recognizable.

A Quick Look at Radio and Television Scripts

The script is where the copywriter goes to give the product or service a voice. In radio, straight dialogue or conversational copy must describe the brand in visual terms in order to stimulate the listener's imagination.

Television can employ sight, sound, and motion to create image, showcase colors, or show the product in use or in a particular setting. Traditionally, both radio and television scripts follow a standard format to ensure readability. Most are double-spaced documents that are set up in multiple columns.

A simple radio script focuses on three things to punctuate the action: dialogue, SFX, and/or music. All dialogue is set in caps-lower-case (sentence style) and enclosed in quotes. To stand out, all SFX are underlined with a dashed line, and all music is highlighted with a solid line (see Figure 6.4). SFX and music reinforce the tone of voice, attract attention, and set a mood. Do not be afraid to use one or more in both radio and television to reinforce the visual/verbal message. All instructions to the talent or production crew will be set in all caps and enclosed in parentheses.

Beyond dialogue, SFX, and music, the more complex television script will include camera shots (or specifications regarding how much of the visual will be shown); camera instructions (describing where the camera needs to be placed during the shoot); and transitions (or how the camera will move between scenes—see Figure 6.5).

To be remembered, both radio and television ads require a hefty amount of repetition. Do not hesitate to repeat the key consumer benefit and product name frequently throughout the spot. Remember, the target is initially unengaged; for the message to be remembered, it must be repeated in a new and creative way each time it is mentioned. Be sure to close the ad with a call to action or with the

Figure 6.4 **Sample Radio Script**

Advertiser: Run Date: Length:	Target: Strategy: KCB:
SFX:	STRANGE STOMACH GROWLING SOUNDS. ‑‑
ANNOUNCER:	"Hey Thompson you going to lunch?" Dialog is always typed in caps/lowercase and enclosed in quotes to distinguish it as spoken dialog. Any speaker who will not be reused anywhere else in the campaign can be labeled as simply announcer.
THOMPSON:	"Uh (MORE GRUMBLING SOUNDS) no. To much to do, this contract is due by the end of the day." (YAWN) "And besides, it takes to long to go out, and it's just to darn expensive to have it delivered. So it's starvation again for me." (SIGH) Quick sounds can be placed within the dialog. Introduce any reoccurring characters to the target by calling them by name.
ANNOUNCER:	"Go out! Don't go out." (EXCITED) "Floozies, will bring you anything from their list of 125 hot or cold dishes within 30‑minutes for only $7.99."
SFX:	(SMALL LITTLE CLAPS OF EXCITEMENT) Hold the listeners attention with some type of noise to help them envision what the speaker(s) are doing. ‑‑
THOMPSON: ANNOUNCER: THOMPSON: ANNOUNCER: MUSIC:	"125" (GROWLING) "menu items?" "Yep" "In 30 minutes for only $7.99?" "Yep" WHAT A WONDERFUL WORLD PLAYS IN THE BACKGROUND. Music can help set the scene without the need for additional dialogue. ‑‑
THOMPSON: SFX:	"Who do I call?" HAPPIER SOUNDING GROWLS. ‑‑
ANNOUNCER:	"It's easy, just dial 555‑FOOD‑FIX or visit www.foodfix.com to order ahead for dinner tonight or immediate delivery."
SFX:	SOUNDS OF THOMPSON DIALING THE PHONE. ‑‑
ANNOUNCER:	"For those of you with a little more time, stop by and see us at 1234 Chop Shop, next to Barney's Golf Accessories. We're open seven days a week from 11 to 9 Monday through Saturday and 12 to 7 on Sundays. See ya soon, and Eat Up." Be sure to close with the product name. If applicable, the location where the product can be found, including landmarks, a phone number or Web address, if easy to remember.
THOMPSON:	"Yeah." (POLITE BURP) "Oh excuse me, Eat Up."

repetition of the slogan, tagline, or logo. In television, when possible, be sure to also show the product and any packaging if unique. Let the target know how to find the product with more than just an address. For locally produced ads, the address becomes visual when attached to local landmarks. Don't give a phone number in radio unless you're lucky enough to be able to use a mnemonic like 1–800‑FLOWERS, since the target is unlikely to have a pencil handy at the pool, in the park, in their car, or on a couch. Be sure to cross promote by including a

Figure 6.5   **Two Frame Sample Television Script**

Frame 1	OPEN:	Open on a deli with a long line of frustrated looking customers.
	MCS:	
	CAMERA:	STILL.
	SFX IN and UNDER:	IN (A lot of stomachs growling and people mumbling in background) UNDER.
	WOMAN 1:	"There has to be an easier and faster way to order lunch?"
	SFX OUT:	(Of people mumbling and stomachs growling in background).
	CUT TO:	Floozies where a woman is picking up her to go order.
Frame 2	MFS:	
	CAMERA:	PAN (restaurant customers eating to a customer picking up her call in order to the delivery driver picking up his to go orders) LEFT AND RIGHT.
	CAMERA:	STILL.
	MCS:	
	OWNER:	"Here is Mr. Thompson's delivery order Dave. This is his fourth order this week."
	DAVE:	"I'm on my way."
	WOMAN 1:	"Yes! Finally freshly prepared food I don't have to wait in line for."
	MUSIC IN and UNDER:	IN (What a Wonderful World) UNDER
	ANN:	"Dine in, carry out, or delivery. At Floozies, you'll never have to stand in line again. Come by and see us at 1234 Chop Shop or call 555-FOOD-FIX or visit us on the web at www.foodfix.com. We're open seven days a week from 11 to 9 Monday through Saturday and 12 to 7 on Sundays. See ya soon, and Eat Up."
	MUSIC OUT:	(What a Wonderful World)
	SUPER:	(Floozies logo with address, phone number and Web address. Deli in background.)

web address in both radio and television; they are relatively easy to remember since they usually include the product or service's name.

Defining Television Advertising

Television advertising creatively shows and tells us what will clean our clothes, the best ways to entertain, and what to drive or wear. It uses sight, sound, and motion to bring a brand's personality to life in a way and in a language the target will identify with and understand. As a primary media outlet, television is an excellent venue for building or maintaining image, creating brand awareness, launching new products or repositioning or reminding the target about mature ones. Like other traditional vehicles, advertising sales on television are slumping. An ailing economy, a disinterested target, and newer more popular alternative media options on the Internet are keeping marketers from investing heavier in the medium.

Television's ability to show and tell, demonstrate, educate, and entertain allows the creative team many options for solving their client's advertising problem. This mass media vehicle makes isolating a niche market a little more difficult than magazine and radio. However, national and cable stations do offer some targetability based on programming. Today's jaded consumer often sees a commercial but doesn't really hear it or process it unless it's visually stimulating, unusual, and/or solves a problem or fulfills a want. Advertisers using television bombard consumers with approximately 18 minutes of advertising per 60 minutes of broadcast programming, leaving them disillusioned, overwhelmed, and uninterested in most advertised messages.

Because television can reach a mass audience, it is perfect for selling generic products such as shampoos, window cleaners, insurance, or furniture polish. For the advertisement to be unique, it must possess or reflect some type of inherent drama or a feature or characteristic that can be used in a subtle but dramatic way to make a point. Leo Burnett, a mid-twentieth-century advertising giant, defined *inherent drama* this way in his book *100 LEO's:* "You have to be noticed but the art is getting noticed naturally, without screaming and without tricks." Subtle today is a little more about being clever or taking a unique approach to solving or addressing a problem; three brands that have utilized inherent drama to the fullest are Apple, GEICO, and Aflac.

Television, like all the other traditional advertising vehicles, talks *at* the target. Any interactive component added to television turns a monologue into a dialogue by holding the target's attention longer and making the message more memorable. Creating interactive opportunities is a great way to engage the target in the message and create a situation that encourages discussion. Consider having the target visit a website for coupons or enter a contest or sweepstakes, visit a showroom, take a test drive, call a toll-free number to request additional information, contribute to a blog, or come out to an event. Direct response marketers often use price incentives or free gifts to encourage interaction and/or immediate purchase. Not only is this a great way to make a sale, but it also meets the target on a one-to-one basis, encouraging loyalty and repeat purchase.

The Visual/Verbal Voice of Television

Television has a short message life and a distracted audience. To make television advertising work, a message must express the key consumer benefit creatively and educationally. Because television incorporates sight, sound, and motion, products advertised on TV can be seen, demonstrated, shown in use, or used to set a mood or spark an emotion. Television ads make the product real and allow the target to imagine the brand in their lives. It is important to show and tell the target how they will look or appear to others using, wearing, or driving the featured product and how it can make their lives more fulfilling. Seeing is believing.

The visual/verbal messaging used in television should match the tone, color choice, and overall style used throughout the campaign. For example, a jingle like the original one used by FreeCreditReport.com is catchy, tells us everything we need to know, and works well on both radio and television. Additional uses might include using the actor's image in print, direct response, out-of-home, and in sales promotion materials, to name just a few ideas.

The high cost of production, editing, and media makes television a very expensive mass media vehicle. Even the simplest television shoots are stressful and exhausting. A few seconds of footage can take hours to achieve. Because of this, a heavily scripted and detailed storyboard is required.

Creatively, a television commercial is made up of two parts: a script and an accompanying storyboard. The audio portion alone is known as a *script,* and the video portions are known as *scenes.* The combined audio and video segment of a commercial is the *storyboard* (see Figure 6.3). Its job is to relate both the visual and verbal message in a detailed way. This very detailed document can also include information on music, SFX, camera shots, scene transitions, and any special instructions to the talent.

Because there are so many people involved in a television shoot, the script must be detailed enough not only for the client and talent to follow, but for the director, editors, camera operators, and any lighting and sound people to follow, as well. The script explains what is going on when, and it spells out exactly where and how each shot will be carried out. Anything less explicit than that can quickly affect both the budget and shooting schedule. Changes at any step along the way are costly.

A typical brand-based commercial will last anywhere from 15 to 30 seconds. When the brand has a lot to say, advertisers will often purchase a single 30-second spot and break it into two separate but related commercials. This "more bang for your buck" buy is known as *piggybacking.* Direct response ads are longer than the typical commercial, usually running around 90 to 160 seconds. The extra time is used to show features, benefits, and uses of the product in question. The granddaddy of all direct response ads is the infomercial.

Infomercials Are Just Long Commercials

Considered more an alternative vehicle than a traditional one, infomercials are long commercials that last 30 to 60 minutes. Most infomercials are endorsed and delivered by a celebrity or an accepted professional in the field. Like direct response commercials, infomercials often feature demonstrations, testimonials, and studies backed by scientists, physicians, or engineers. It is important for the target to get a thorough rundown of how the product works and, if they choose to make a purchase, what's in it for them. Since the goal is to get the target to act, the toll-free number, web address, and payment options should appear on screen continuously or be referred to often by the presenter.

The same basic sales techniques used in traditional commercials—educate and inform—are equally important to the success of an infomercial. This type of direct response commercial has to make both ordering and purchasing fast and simple. With an accepted credit card, the target can easily order from the comfort of their home or office by clicking a few keys or pushing a few buttons. Advertisers who offer 100 percent satisfaction guarantees and make returns easy will ensure customer satisfaction and repeat business.

A Television Shoot Is Hard Work

Most television commercials are painstakingly planned out before the shoot begins. If not, what is already a very expensive and lengthy process can easily go over budget and disrupt the production or media scheduling. A television shoot can take anywhere from a couple of days to several weeks to complete. Add in any computer-generated work or voice-overs and the process can extend to months. Once the art director and copywriter finish the storyboard, the team must (1) hire a director, (2) hold auditions, (3) work with costume, hair, and make-up professionals, (4) decide on a location, (5) find a crew to shoot, edit, and produce the spot, and (6) commission a musical score or perhaps a jingle for the product. The brand's target is matched with programming: Talent must look, act, and sound like the target; lighting, music, wardrobe, and props all must be chosen to project a mood or mimic the target and brand's image.

Finally, the creative team must find an adequate location to shoot the commercial. Locally shot and produced commercials will most often use a straightforward announcer-delivered spot, making them a relatively inexpensive option for small businesses. Established brands, on the other hand, will often shoot in larger markets or in remote locations. A shoot that takes place outside of the controlled environment of a studio is referred to as an *on-location shoot.* This type of production is great for defining image or creating a realistic environment that allows the target to see the product in use and in a definitive setting.

In order to reach the target with a meaningful message, an effective commercial must:

1. Scream out the key consumer benefit in a way that is relevant to the target.
2. Talk to the target in a language they can understand, about problems and situations they can relate to.
3. Ensure the visual/verbal message matches the tone and overall visual appeal of other pieces used in the campaign.
4. Get to the point quickly. Music, sounds, and repetitive statements can help make that point in the allotted 15 to 30 seconds.
5. Address target issues, problems, or interests both visually and verbally to ensure the viewer's connection with them.
6. Define the product identity and that of the target through dialogue, character selection, music and/or sounds.
7. Solve a need or want through the use of testimonials, product demonstrations, and computer-generated images—anything that will build curiosity, entertain, excite, or have some type of personal or social ramifications.
8. Make the key consumer benefit the obvious focus of the commercial.
9. Engage the target by showing how the product works and how it will make life easier, or more satisfying, by focusing on the benefits the product or service offers.
10. Create some type of interactive opportunity.
11. Ensure all speaking parts are accurately timed to easily fill the time allotted.
12. Make sure the final frame shows one or all of the following: the product, the packaging, or the logo to help with memory and brand recognition.

Broadcast Changes with the Times

Clearly, the economy has wrought havoc on the budgets of many local businesses that rely on radio to advertise, including auto dealers, banks, and retailers. However, according to Arbitron, the leading radio research company in the United States, there are some signs of growth: The audience was actually increasing in the second decade of the twenty-first century, especially in smaller markets.

To maintain listenership and accommodate advertisers, radio is considering using more live reads, in much the same way television and movies currently integrate product placement into programming. On-air personalities can seamlessly incorporate commercial messages into pro-gramming in a way that does not break the flow or intrude on the listener. Additionally, radio is moving to the Internet. CBS and AOL have united to bring in excess of 300 radio stations to the web, attracting well over 2 million listeners.

Television still plays a large part in consumer's lives and is still favored by advertisers in both good and bad economic times. Advertisers are finding better ways to reach the target with single-sponsored programming and limited advertising options. The goal is to increase memorability by featuring fewer products that speak directly to a specific target with a specific message. This type of limited sponsorship is nothing new—many shows in the early years of television gained success using single sponsors. The biggest differences between then and now are the power of the remote control and the cost and amount of programming choices available. The goal is to lower clutter and increase brand recall.

Networks like Fox have experimented with showing fewer ads during certain programs. Although it costs more, this technique reduces advertising time to four to six minutes as opposed to the often 18 or more minutes shown during a typical hour-long program. The jury on "Remote Free TV" (as it is referred to by Fox) is still out on how effectively it keeps viewers from changing channels and improving brand recall.

Advertisers are also looking at commercials that are designed to match the programs the target is currently watching. For example, when OnStar bought a spot that aired during the TNT showing of *The Bourne Supremacy,* it tied its commercial message to the scene just aired in the movie by asking, "Are you counting on your cell phone to be your lifeline in a crash?"

Other ways television is responding to advertisers' needs is with "ad-dressable" advertising. This highly targetable form of advertising allows marketers to air two or more spots during the same 30-second time slot; the ads are aimed at different target segments not only around the country but geographically by zip code.

Advertising on demand (AOD) is the newest form of interactive advertising. During a 30-second commercial, a banner will appear at the bottom of the screen. Interested viewers can use their remote to request more information on a featured product or a coupon from the advertisers.

Looking for ways to shorten advertising's interruption time has led to the increased popularity of the 10-second spot. These short and "to the point" spots—often referred to as "mini-mercials"—seem to be more efficient and more memorable. This may be due to their placement immediately following the five-second billboard announcing the closed-caption sponsor; only one spot is available after the billboard, which keeps the ad that follows from being surrounded by any other advertised messages. Because of their short duration, 10-second ads can also be reused online or as mobile ads. GEICO, IHOP, Denny's, and Campbell's are just some of the well-known companies that have successfully used 10-second spots.

Traditional media vehicles continue to play a large part in consumers' lives and are still favored by advertisers working with new technology options. As each medium adjusts to its new role, advertisers will find new ways to adapt the vehicles of old into their new media mix.

7

Out-of-Home
Outdoor and Transit

Figure 7.1   **Sample Ad: Ripley's Aquarium of the Smokies**

Source: Created by Chelsea Lynn, The University of Tennessee, Knoxville.

Out-of-Home Expands the Campaign Message

Aptly named, out-of-home advertising is any advertising seen outside of the home. Vehicles included under this mass media umbrella include outdoor boards, transit vehicles, shelters, terminals, and stations.

The diversity of shapes, sizes, and designs give these varied vehicles an interesting array of looks. Brief, simplified, colorful messages best describe all forms of out-of-home advertising. Its job is to catch the attention of often tired, distracted, and irritable commuters who are either on the move or watching the message pass by their location.

All types of out-of-home advertising are growing in popularity due to the increasingly creative options available to designers. Placement of out-of-home—whether seen locally, nationally, or internationally—is most often concentrated in larger cities and surrounding areas, in or on public transportation, and along interstate highways. It is not unusual to see out-of-home ads at shopping malls, in downtown areas, in airport terminals and bus shelters, and on or in subways, buses, and taxis. Messages appearing inside public transportation reach a captive audience, as this type of advertising cannot be missed, thrown away, muted, ignored, clicked off, or minimized. This great reminder vehicle is most often used by local businesses selling locally available products and services, and by media companies and entertainment providers.

Considered a mass medium, the typical out-of-home vehicle is not consumer focused and must rely on advertising used elsewhere to build a relationship with the target. Most out-of-home vehicles offer a great way to create interest, build or maintain awareness, direct traffic, and reinforce other messages used throughout the campaign. Without any one-on-one contact, these ads must have some type of viral component to get and keep the target talking about the brand.

Because it is limited in what it can say and show, out-of-home is not a great canvas for image-based products. It is, however, an effective vehicle for advertising mature products or promoting events. Most out-of-home vehicles can be changed out easily, making it a great option for campaigns that have an ongoing theme.

Its supporting role to other more traditional or even alternative media makes it ideally suited for teaser ads, new product launches, to maintain or reinforce existing advertising, or as part of a highly visible cooperative opportunity. Creatively, these vehicles have a lot more to show than say. To maintain campaign consistency, consider repeating a color(s) scheme, headline style, character representative, or spokesperson. Visuals are usually limited to one image, so keep it simple but bold if budget and restrictions permit.

This is not the venue to show and tell a detailed story. Copy will be limited, focusing on the key consumer benefit, the slogan or tagline, a logo, and perhaps an exit number, directions, or address. Each message must be expressed in no more than five to seven words. Do not consider this a handicap: Remember, one carefully crafted visual is worth more than a page of copy. Beyond word length, the best boards will:

1. Be creative, unique, and unavoidable.
2. Use a typeface with a consistent weight or thickness. Serif faces with their thick to thin lines should be avoided. The thinner areas of type cannot be seen from a great distance.
3. Be readable from a distance of up to 500 feet, so letterspacing should be slightly increased.
4. Use large text that complements placement. For boards that will be read from up to 500 feet, text should be 15 to 20 inches tall. The text on boards placed in malls, lobbies, and transit terminals should be at least an inch or two tall.

5. Attempt to avoid using all caps and excessive reverses, as these decrease readability and legibility.
6. Keep images simple yet bold, ensuring they can be understood quickly and easily. No one will pull over or stop to reread a board with a confusing message.
7. Use images to deliver the key consumer benefit to the target. Images should reflect any emotions or attitudes you want the target to feel or understand. The attached copy must back up and/or confirm those feelings.
8. Use less copy on boards that are farther away from the viewer.
9. Have a solid background, with no loud patterns or busy background images.
10. Ensure the logo is either placed in the lower right corner or centered at the bottom of the board. This is important since the typical viewer will read from left to right and from the top down.
11. Be sure all colors and visuals employed are in direct contrast to the landscape around it to keep the board from blending in with its surroundings.
12. Be sure the text appears in a contrasting color compared to the background color used on the board.
13. Use primary colors—red, yellow, blue—with a little black thrown in when possible to increase readability and legibility. Avoid colors too close in value (such as red and green); when used together, they can appear to vibrate.
14. Avoid relying on the available technological bells and whistles to carry a bad idea.
15. Be sure the board is lit so it can be seen at night or even add something to the overall design in daylight.

Understanding Out-of-Home's Strength and Weaknesses

Let's take a look at what the varying types of out-of-home vehicles can or cannot bring to the media mix.

Strengths

1. Unavoidable and Repetitious. Commuters and pedestrians can't turn it off or delete it. As a captive audience, they will repeatedly see the message on a daily basis as they travel back and forth to work and other destinations.

2. Location and Size. Messages that are placed in high-traffic areas are sure to be seen.
3. Creative. The diversity of size and creative options makes out-of-home eye-catching and inherently interesting.
4. Affordable. Regardless of the state of the economy, out-of-home is affordable for even the smallest business owner.

Weaknesses

1. Limited Message. Consumers are on the go, so the message must be limited to no more than five to seven words.
2. Preservation. Ads are vulnerable to weather conditions, vandalism, dirt, and pollution that could damage brand image.
3. Location. High-traffic locations are expensive.
4. Availability. Both outdoor and transit need to be reserved months in advance, and they often require lengthy commitments, making out-of-home a poor choice for short runs and time-sensitive advertisements.

Determining the Visual/Verbal Voice of Outdoor Ads

Outdoor boards, also known as *billboards,* can be found along most streets and highways in the United States and around the world, directing commuters to local establishments and reminding them about (or perhaps even introducing them to) local businesses, retail products, or events. Creatively, outdoor boards have come a long way over the past several decades, making them much more interesting to travelers and commuters. Talented creative teams have elevated outdoor boards from ugly blights upon the landscape to a new art form. Key consumer benefits scream off of boards sporting bright colors, cutouts, three-dimensional additions, and electronic movement. Even more attention can be gained by including an extension. When a design extends beyond the main surface of the board by as much as five and a half feet on top and two feet below and/or on either side, it's know as an *extension.* In pedestrian areas, designs have added or dropped pieces down to the sidewalks below to draw attention upward. Three-dimensional additions like those used by the chicken eatery Chick-fil-A are a creative, eye-catching curiosity device that can be continued in print, on a website, on television, or as part of an event.

Ideas both visual and verbal must be flexible enough so they can be molded to fit any vehicle that may be used in a campaign. Fledgling designers often have trouble taking a traditional television or magazine ad and summing it up for outdoor or other alternative media vehicles.

Even when condensed, complex ideas that include lengthy copy or even demonstrations must retain the visual/verbal look and voice used elsewhere in the campaign. David Bernstein, creative director and owner of The Creative Business and author of *Advertising Outdoors,* sums up the process of *creative reduction:* "Solve the creative brief on a poster and you'll have an idea that will work in virtually any medium." Therefore, it is important to start small and work up to presentations that are more complex.

Creative reduction is all about removing what is redundant, inherently understood, or lacking in value to the message. In "An Anecdote of Dr. Franklin" (1818), Thomas Jefferson recalled a conversation he had with Ben Franklin during the drafting of the Declaration of Independence. The following excerpt from that conversation illustrates how "simple" is sometimes "better."

> An apprentice hatter was about to open shop for himself. His first concern was to have a handsome signboard with a proper inscription. He composed it in these words, "John Thompson, Hatter, makes and sells hats for ready money." The image of a hat was included.
>
> He thought he would submit it to his friends for amendments. The first man thought the word "hatter" was redundant, because the words "makes hats" showed he was a hatter. It was struck out. The next man observed that the word "makes" might as well be omitted, because his customers would not care who made the hats. . . . A third man thought the words "for ready money" were useless, as it was not the custom of the place to sell on credit. Everyone who purchased expected to pay.
>
> The inscription now stood, "John Thompson sells hats." "Sells hats?" exclaimed another man! No one expected that the hats would be given away. It was stricken out, and "hats" followed it. So the inscription was reduced ultimately to "John Thompson" [verbal], with the figure of a hat [visual]. (http://www.history.org/almanack/resources/jeffersonanecdote.cfm)

If members of the target audience want more information, they will come into the store or go on the web for answers to their questions.

Keep It Simple, Creative, and Memorable

Outdoor moves fast: If it is not located in a pedestrian area or by a stoplight, its visual/verbal message has only six to eight seconds to make a noticeable impression. Brief and simple messages must be memorable to be successful. With more size and design options available than ever before, outdoor vehicles should not be considered limiting because of their unusual shapes and verbally stunted nature; rather, these qualities should be viewed as an imaginative and creative challenge.

Visible for quite a distance, billboards are an effective advertising device for an array of products and companies. Typically, large highway signs will measure 20 × 60 feet, while most boards placed within city limits measure 14 × 48 feet. Because advertisers can pick a specific location, outdoor can be a fairly targetable vehicle; however, high-traffic areas have a cluttered visual arena. Designs that are clever, unique, or interactive will grab the viewer's attention and stand out from the surrounding visual/verbal noise. Let's take a look at a few good examples.

Orbit (the chewing gum brand) used a billboard to promote its teeth-cleaning abilities. Three-quarters of the board included a close-up headshot of a man and a woman with big toothy smiles. Hanging off the billboard were two 3-D mannequins of window washers with squeegees, each one busily cleaning the models' very white teeth.

American knife maker Zwilling J.A. Henckels placed a billboard in the shape of a kitchen knife in the clef of a Y-shaped streetlight. On the black handle were the company's red and white graphic logo and their name reversed out of the background. Placement in unusual locations is guaranteed to capture the attention of passersby.

A great vertical billboard for Old Timers, a chain of roadside restaurants located off Austrian highways, was placed at the entrance to a tunnel. The top quarter of the board read: "All you can eat rest stop" on the left with the logo directly across on the right. The bottom three-quarters featured a close-up of a woman's face, her upper lip and teeth fitting right over the tunnel's entrance so entering drivers appear to be her next meal.

Heineken, the Netherlands-based brewer, used an innovative vinyl billboard that stretched across two sides of a building. The background was green and the visual was a single bottle of Heineken. It may sound simple, but the creative part is that it looks like a hand is trying to push through the spongy vinyl to grab the bottle from behind.

Silberman's Fitness Center took simple to another creative level with a billboard featuring an obviously overweight man standing on the far right side of a white board. Like a teeter-totter, his weight has lifted the left side of the board up in the air, exposing the board's structure underneath. The tilted copy reads: "Time for Silberman's Fitness Center 899–9501."

Bic set a white billboard out in the middle of a grassy area. The only copy on the board is a small picture of the logo in the lower right-hand corner. Its uniqueness comes from the big three-dimensional Bic razor leaning against the board and the freshly mowed line in the grass that leads up to the razor.

Bloom supermarkets created an outdoor board with an ongoing storyline. Initially, the board showed an oven-mitted hand holding a three-dimensional pan of muffins seen on its side, offering an aerial view. Copy on the oven mitt read "JUMBO MUFFINS," followed by the logo. Below the board, oddly enough, was a small, red compact car with "FOR SALE" signs in the windows. The following week, the pan on the billboard was missing a muffin; the red car below appeared to have been crushed by the weight of the one missing jumbo muffin. Later, once the muffin was removed, both traveled to various Bloom locations as a part of an ongoing promotional event.

Another great vertical board came from the creative team at Cingular. This orange board with reversed copy read: "HATE DROPPED CALLS? Switch to the network with the fewest dropped calls." What made this ad so creative was the hole in the middle of the board where the word "CALLS" should have been. The missing piece could be found lying on the sidewalk below—a great way to pull pedestrians' eyes skyward.

Nationwide Insurance used a triptych, or three separate panels, on the side of a building to illustrate the need for insurance. On the left panel was a fictional ad for Coops Paints, featuring two open cans of yellow paint and one can of blue paint placed at the top of the panel. The eye-catching disaster takes place on the middle panel, when one of the yellow cans of paint is tipped over. Yellow paint pours down the sign to cover the ground and the four cars parked directly underneath. The right panel is the board for Nationwide, the slightly spattered copy stating: "LIFE COMES AT YOU FAST," followed by the logo and, on the bottom, more copy with the stacked words "Investments, Retirement, Insurance."

Another simple yet creative board was used in a campaign for Eskom, a South African electric company. The gradated board goes from solid black on the left to solid white on the right where the words "Use Electricity Wisely" are lit by a single light at night.

South Africa's Nedbank went green with its "Power to the People" board. Loaded up with 10 solar panels that generate more than 100 watts of power each, the board supplied enough power to run the kitchen in a nearby grade school.

The soft drink giant Coca-Cola also went green by powering its digital Times Square outdoor board with wind power. Coke's "Refresh. Recycle. Repeat." campaign then went one step further with a new green ad that premiered on New Year's Eve, 2009 touting its efforts to recycle and reuse all aluminum and plastic containers used in the United States.

Coke's "Live Positively" philosophy was given additional press in early 2009 when it was the featured topic at a recycling event held at the New York Public Library. Participants were not only schooled on the ins and outs of recycling but could take part in interactive games and view an array of recycled items, all compliments of Coke.

Sometimes, atypical outdoor boards can be extremely effective forms of advertising. A European jewelry store replaced the chains normally appearing between concrete blocks or pillars with boards featuring various types of jewelry. Each piece had a jewelry tag attached, along with the jeweler's logo.

To ring in the 2008 holiday season, IKEA used a three-dimensional board to spell out the word "joy" with an aerial view of varied pieces of furniture and happy customers enjoying them. The letter "J" was made with a tan sectional and accompanying red pillows. A white circular table and four chairs featuring a red centerpiece represented the "O." The "Y" was created with two chairs, complete with occupants whose extended legs stretch out to connect with a vertical red coffee table. The only other words—"Decorate for the holidays"—appeared at the bottom, with the IKEA logo in the bottom right corner.

Other IKEA promotions used out-of-home with a twist of guerrilla marketing to launch their "Embrace Change 09" campaign in honor of then–president-elect Barack Obama. This hands-on campaign recreated the Oval Office at Union Station in Washington, D.C., using IKEA products. The campaign also called for the slogan to be placed on local buses and trains, and even included an IKEA motorcade.

In another ingenious inaugural promotion for its diverse product line, IKEA placed multiple pieces of furniture on the tops of vehicles driving around the streets of D.C. This move around town was meant to represent the Obamas' move into the White House. The campaign also featured a website that allowed consumers to design their own Oval Office and sign up for a chance to win a $1,500 gift card.

Many of the aforementioned three-dimensional enhancements can be made out of almost anything—wood, plaster, metal, even real products attached to the board. But one of the most inexpensive enhancements can be blown up and used for both on-site promotions and outdoor boards. It's the *inflatable ad.*

On-site promotions can be enhanced and easier to see if accompanied by an inflatable advertisement. Inflatables can be reproductions of a character representative with a logo or an inflatable tent that customers can enter or stand under to pick up a sample or complimentary beverage while shopping. When used on outdoor boards, these three-dimensional air-filled images project beyond the board, expanding the viewing area. A simple two-dimensional outdoor board becomes an inexpensive and creative three-dimensional statement. Inflatables are memorable and often very creative, but they are subject to damage by severe weather and vandalism.

The Varied Types of Outdoor Boards

Today, all outdoor boards are easy to change out and are made of tough nonfading material that can withstand daily wear and tear. They cannot stand up to extreme

Figure 7.2   **Sample Ad: Wasabi Steakhouse**

Source: Created by Madhuri Jagadish, The University of Tennessee, Knoxville.

weather conditions, vandalism, or excessive pollution, though, so they should be constantly monitored by the outdoor company for any necessary repairs.

No longer a painted surface, the majority of outdoor boards are digitally printed or silk screened onto vinyl, which can be secured by wrapping the vinyl around the board or gluing it into place. Boards may be opaque or translucent, and they are often illuminated externally by lights. These lights are mounted on the front of the board or lit by a light box located between two translucent panels, allowing the image to be seen from both the front and the back.

Campaigns that use multiple boards placed in strategic locations along a main artery can display several different messages or repeat a single message for emphasis. Out-of-home as a whole is a great teaser vehicle for gradually increasing interest in a new product and keeping a brand or company name in the public eye. There are several types of outdoor boards, but the most popular today include vinyl, mechanical and digital LED, wallscapes, and signage.

Vinyl Boards

Vinyl boards are the simplest and most common type of outdoor board. These no-nonsense boards point the way to local businesses and events. The focus is on who is doing the advertising, what they are promoting, and where they are located.

Mechanical Boards

A mechanical outdoor board uses three multi-message or tri-vision views that rotate continuously. Panels are triangular in shape, and as they turn, three different flat-surfaced ads are revealed. Each rotation lasts around five to ten seconds. Often illuminated, these boards make a memorable impression on the target. One board can deliver multiple messages for a single brand or a single ad for three entirely different brands.

A scrolling board is another type of mechanical board that can display up to 30 messages as it scrolls between images. Usually backlit on vinyl, these boards are easy to view both day and night. Mechanical boards are usually placed in heavily trafficked areas like transportation terminals and malls.

Digital LED Boards

The technological advances incorporated into digital LED boards make them the boards of the future. They can be changed with the click of a mouse and rotate every few seconds. Currently, several companies are working on technology that will allow the board to send a message—a coupon or, perhaps, a sales announcement—directly to motorists' cell phones as they pass by.

Digital LED boards are large and can be seen from long distances. However, for safety reasons, they are most often located in high-traffic areas (where drivers must stop for lights or routinely sit in traffic), or in areas with heavy pedestrian traffic.

Kellogg's Special K cereal in 2008 used a digital outdoor board located in Times Square to help New Yorkers looking to lose a few pounds in the New Year. The promotion encouraged weight-loss enthusiasts to text in their weight-loss goals using the short code "New You." Responses were displayed on the large digital boards. Additionally, Kellogg's used online banner ads that asked consumers to share their weight-loss motivations and visit specialk.com for more information on healthy eating and weight control.

Wall Murals or Wallscapes

Wallscapes are basically large outdoor boards that are hand painted on the sides of buildings or printed on vinyl and hung off the side of a building. These highly artistic and targeted murals usually feature bright colors, a bold image, and an eye-catching logo.

Signage

Outdoor signage is also a type of billboard. Businesses large and small need signage to alert consumers to their location and type of business; the best include not only a verbal aspect but a visual one as well.

Outdoor Delivers Its Message in Simple and Alternative Ways

Moving beyond the traditional to the alternative use of outdoor literally places outdoor messages on the move. Let's take a look at some of the more creative options.

Digital Mobile Outdoor Boards

Digitally activated outdoor boards move along with commuters in traffic. Often placed on the side of panel or semi-trailer trucks, the designs on these mobile boards may be stationary or digitally scroll or rotate several messages in the same way digital outdoor boards do.

A digital mobile ad is an excellent way to deliver a targeted message based on the prescribed route of the truck on which it is mounted, or it may be used as a promotional tool for mass-marketed brands. Moving displays change every eight seconds and can appear on both sides and on the back of the vehicle. The message may be constant or can vary with up to nine different visual/verbal options. Mobile outdoor boards are great for product launches, event promotions, and raising brand awareness.

Kiosks can also go mobile: Extravagant three-dimensional kiosks can be placed on flatbed trucks and driven around town or placed outside movie premieres, local festivals, concerts, sporting events, and other venues likely to draw eager shoppers.

Mobile Billboards

Outdoor mobile advertisements are enclosed in clear glass and placed on the back of a truck. A large board measuring over 60 square feet can travel up and down busy thoroughfares, be placed in areas with a high level of pedestrian traffic, near concert or sporting venues, outside shopping malls, or near areas with a lively nightlife. These often three-dimensional experiences may include live people, props, sound, and video. The unique and encased digital outdoor boards can showcase 15 to 30 full-motion videos, including commercials, video games, or movie previews.

Human Billboards

Another form of mobile billboard is the human body. This walking, buzz-building canvas is a great promotional vehicle. For example, Air New Zealand took the human leap and hired participants who were willing to shave off their hair and display a temporary henna tattoo on the backs of their heads that read, "Need a change? Head Down to New Zealand. www. airnewzealand.com."

The airline hired dozens of living, breathing, brainy "billboards"—many of them expatriates or travelers who had visited New Zealand—to go about their daily lives showing off their tattoos. Anyone who asked about the message would get a spontaneous and unscripted response. Many believe human billboards are a new form of reality advertising and social networking.

FeelUnique.com, an online beauty product distributor, also used human billboards in the United Kingdom. Participants promoted the website with temporary tattoos placed on their eyelids. The goal: Create buzz by walking around winking at strangers. The publicity generated by the campaign was so successful it was featured in several local, national, and international articles. The site saw a considerable increase in traffic and generated a large number of links from other sites.

Not all human billboards are successful, as the online gambling site Golden Palace found out. Golden Palace paid boxer Bernard Hopkins to sport a temporary tattoo featuring its web address during a televised match. Both the gambling commission and ESPN, the station that televised the event, were not amused. Always pushing the creative limit on good taste and appropriateness, Golden Palace has gone as far as asking pregnant women to place temporary tattoos on their stomachs, which they bare at heavily attended events.

Taking the human tattoo idea one step further, one young man placed his bare forehead up for auction on eBay. He agreed to display a temporary tattoo for one month to the winning bidder. The winner, Green Pharmaceuticals' SnoreStop. The ensuing free publicity landed the human advertisement on several national news programs; his story also received coverage in newspapers and on the web.

Finally, Dunlop Tires used various events to permanently tattoo volunteers with their logo or its trademarked tire treads—in front of event goers. Participants were compensated with a set of tires worth $500 to $1,000.

Transit's Visual/Verbal Message Gets Around

Transit advertising is any advertisement that appears in or on buses, taxis, subway cars, commuter trains, ferries, transit stations, platforms, terminals, bus stops, or even on benches.

Transit is a great vehicle for reaching an audience of all ages, backgrounds, and incomes. Reach goes beyond riders to pedestrians, other drivers, and people at work who can see them from their office windows. It is a highly effective direct response vehicle and a great way to encourage immediate or impromptu purchases. The enormous range of shapes, sizes, and technologi-

Figure 7.3   **Sample Ad: Ye Olde Steakhouse**

Source: Created by Alex Crutchfield, The University of Tennessee, Knoxville.

cal enhancements make transit advertising a very creative vehicle. Typical of all out-of-home vehicles, transit ads have limited space; therefore, images must be powerful and meaningful, colors must be bright, and messages must be short and sweet. The small amount of copy often limits the designer to showcasing no more than the key consumer benefit, a slogan or tagline, and the logo. Transit advertising's to-the-point message is an excellent reminder and great support vehicle, especially when teamed up with outdoor boards. Let's take a look at a few options.

Interior Cards

Some of these canvases are big, and some are small; however, all are limited in their capacity to deliver a detailed message. Interior cards found on buses, trains, or subway cars are not the most creative vehicles we will look at, but captive commuters have the time to read the message—repeatedly—on a daily basis. Many interior cards have a double-sided message that can be changed out regularly. Copy space is limited, although it is not unusual to see tear-off order forms or applications known as *car-cards.* Passengers can use these direct response cards to place an order, request additional information, or use them to receive a discount on a product or a service. Interior cards come in a number of different framed sizes and are usually placed above the windows of mass transit vehicles. These interior and bulkhead advertisements can range anywhere from 11 inches high by 24 inches wide to 30 inches high by 144 inches wide.

Advertisers have also made use of existing interior fixtures; for example, IWC watches used the straps that standing commuters hold as a handrail to feature an ad for their watches. When commuters put their hands through the straps, they appeared to be wearing the watches on their wrists. The copy says: "Try it here. The big pilot's watch."

Another great example was used by a gym in Germany that made barbells out of the horizontal poles consumers hang onto when riding the metro. Commuters look like they are holding the heavy weights above their heads with one hand.

Exterior Transit Advertising

Companies that have something big to say use exterior bus, train, or car advertising to attract attention and improve brand awareness. These bold, colorful, weather-resistant designs can be airbrushed directly onto the vehicle, or printed on self-adhesive vinyl, foam board, or corrugated plastic.

There are four basic kinds of bus advertising: king, queen, bus backs, and full bus wraps. King-size ads or posters are the most common. Used by both local and national brands, these designs can be placed on either the driver's side or the curb side of the bus and typically measure around 30 inches high by 144 inches wide. Smaller queen-size posters are usually placed on the curb side only and measure 30 inches high by 108 inches wide or 30 inches high by 96 inches wide.

Bus backs, as the name implies, are placed on the back side of a bus. These very popular, creative, "in your face" designs have become a special way to highlight a brand or cause. For example, the Dutch government launched a promotional awareness campaign for the Keep Holland Clean Foundation by placing a back wrap on city buses that replicated two sanitation workers clinging to either side of a garbage truck. The realistic-looking stickers were used to remind commuters not to leave their trash on the bus. To strengthen the visual, a bus with a raised back side was used to more closely resemble a garbage truck. The message worked: Litterbugs thought twice about leaving their trash on the bus.

Duracell made creative use of bus advertising in India. Using a picture of an open battery compartment complete with two exposed batteries, the sticker gave the impression the bus was fueled by the batteries.

Nicotinell gum used a bus back to encourage smokers to quit. This inventive idea featured a picture of a man's face with his mouth placed symbolically over the exhaust pipe. All day long, the man "blew" exhaust out of his mouth in the same way smokers exhale cigarette smoke. A rectangular white box placed behind him had the words "Ready to quit?" printed on it, with a three-quarter view of an open box of the product.

Another group promoting the need to quit smoking used the same idea.

These ads, resembling a door hanger, were also placed over the tail pipes of city buses. The hole in the poster was situated where the mouth of the young woman shown should be. Each time the bus belched exhaust and it exited the young woman's mouth, the up close visual was simulating a smoker exhaling cigarette smoke. Copy underneath the visual stated: "WHAT WE SEE WHEN YOU SMOKE."

Vehicle wraps are another form of exterior bus advertising. This type of wrap is a relatively new creative opportunity. As the name suggests, a vehicle wrap takes a design and wraps it around a bus, car, or truck. A colorful, self-adhesive vinyl literally molds or wraps itself around the entire vehicle or part of a vehicle. Created digitally, these wraps are weather resistant, fade resistant, and can last up to a year. Memorable and relatively inexpensive, wraps are a great support vehicle for generating brand awareness and promoting local sports or news teams and charitable and cultural events.

Wraps often include a punctured window covering that allows passengers to see out but blocks commuters from seeing in. Bus ads are a very creative, unique, and attention-grabbing way to deliver a memorable message.

Do not forget about the front of the bus. A shocking ad for road safety used stickers to represent a man flattened against a cracked, blood-spattered front window to promote pedestrian awareness when crossing the street.

Transit Shelter Posters and Bench Advertising

A great way to continue the creative message used in or on buses is to extend it to bus shelters and/or benches. Transit shelter posters often consist of two identical ads placed back-to-back with a light box in between. These ads can display the same images used on other transit vehicles to reinforce the message or continue an ongoing theme begun elsewhere in the campaign. The posters are usually four-color and measure around 4 × 6 feet.

In New York City, the Field House at Chelsea Piers used bus shelters very creatively to promote activities at the sports and entertainment venue. On the right-hand side of a clear glass shelter, the design team placed a sticker of a soccer player who had apparently just kicked a ball. The action carried through to the left side of the shelter, where a three-dimensional image of a soccer ball is hitting a net. Another great example from this same venue utilized a baseball theme. A sticker of a player who had just hit a ball was on the right; on the left was an image of a shattered piece of glass. Similarly, the Sports Center at Chelsea Piers placed a sticker of a boxer who just landed a punch next to the twisting body of the guy who received the blow.

Transit shelters have also gone interactive. In Chicago, Kraft's Stove Top Stuffing Mix attracted commuter attention by pumping heat into 10 local bus shelters to simulate the warmth of a home-cooked meal. The goal: to conjure up that warm, fuzzy feeling Stove Top delivers to hungry consumers. This form of guerrilla marketing—known as *experiential marketing*—is a way to encourage consumers to interact with a brand, and deliver a soft sell experience rather than the traditional hard sell commercial pitch. Not devoid of a traditional advertising pitch altogether, each shelter had a poster that read, "Cold provided by winter. Warmth provided by Stove Top." Additional campaign components included placing another 40 posters in unheated shelters and using a street team to hand out samples to passersby.

This multi-sensory type of advertising is difficult to ignore, because consumers experience the message rather than just seeing or hearing it. It is nondisruptive and something tangible that consumers can look forward to on those often long, cold waits for public transportation.

Bench advertising need not be limited to bus stops; it can be used on park benches, on boardwalks, at shopping malls, in restaurants, or in airport terminals. Bench signs are one of the fastest growing types of out-of-home advertising because they appear in pedestrian-heavy locations. These highly targetable, low-cost vehicles offer colorful imaging that is visible 24 hours a day.

Taxi Advertising

Taxi advertising can be bold, understated, or technologically driven no matter where it appears. Exterior taxi advertising can appear on roofs, trunks, windows, and as traditional wraps or the more unusual three-dimensional wraps. Advertising can even appear on the roof of a vehicle in the form of illuminated two-sided panels. These constantly moving canvases have a broad reach. When fitted with a GPS system, taxi advertising can change out (depending on where the taxi stops) to highlight shopping or restaurants in the area, making it a great way for local advertisers to promote their message close to their place of business. Like other forms of out-of-home, taxi advertising is most effective when used as a support vehicle. Branding, reminder, and promotional advertising are the most effective forms of taxi advertising. Let's take a look a few examples.

Creative ideas like the one used by a vitamin manufacturer to make a point about memory loss featured baby seats on the roofs of taxis. The passenger side front and back doors show a picture of the product with the words: "Enhances your memory."

HBO also commandeered several New York taxis to promote the TV show *The Sopranos*. Each taxi had a small bumper sticker placed on the right-hand bumper that read: "*The Sopranos,* only on HBO." Along with the stickers, all of the cabs had a fake leg sticking out of the trunk. If you watch the show, you understand; if you do not watch, your curiosity will surely be piqued.

Another simple yet creative idea was used by a restaurant to promote its Monday night hot wings. A sticker of a screaming man was placed on the third tail light located in the back window of local taxis. Very appropriately, the man's tongue was placed over the tail light, so every time the driver hit the brakes, the tongue lit up red-hot.

Terminal Advertising

These large, usually colorful and illuminated posters are a great way to extend a message to travelers waiting for a ride. Used by both locally and nationally advertised brands, their job is to remind travelers about gifts, food, or travel options located near the station or terminal. Terminal posters are often coordinated to match advertising found inside or outside on local transportation.

One travel site, however, decided on a different approach by taking advantage of the floor and the seats at airport gates to advertise its product. The website hlx.com reached waiting passengers very creatively where they had nothing to do except perhaps think about where they wanted to go on their next trip. The rectangular-shaped ad featured pictures of full-sized skis where seated passengers' feet would be, helping them to think winter vacation. At the top of each ad was the destination and price.

Kiosks are another great way to draw attention to a brand. They are usually four-sided, free-standing glass cases located outside businesses and in various terminals, and they provide the chance to actually show the brand, not just talk about it.

Out-of-home is no longer a static announcement directing drivers, commuters, or pedestrians to the nearest truck stop or retail establishment. Today, out-of-home ads are an interactive and engaging experience innovatively representing the product or service.

8

Direct Marketing

Figure 8.1 **Sample Ad: Ray-Ban**

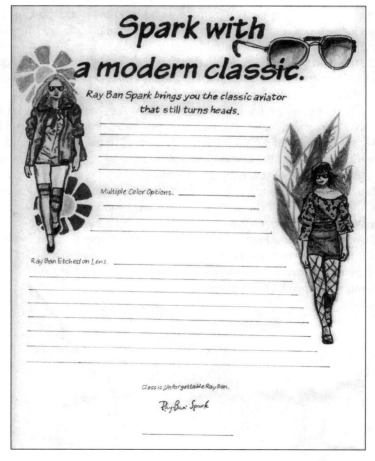

Source: Created by Madhuri Jagadish, The University of Tennessee, Knoxville.

Direct Marketing Personalizes a Campaign

Direct marketing is both a promotional vehicle and a direct response vehicle. A *promotional* device offers an incentive to make a quick sale as opposed to advertising that educates and entertains to make a sale. For direct marketing to work, it must induce a *direct response*—such as encouraging the target to make a call, visit a website for more information, or make a purchase. This very personalized approach initiates one-on-one contact with the intended audience.

Being able to address the target by name and personalize a message that directly addresses their self-interests are direct marketing's strongest benefits. The ability to connect with the target encourages an informative, relationship-building, two-way dialogue between buyer and seller.

Direct marketing has flourished over the last several decades, making it a successful choice for use in a campaign. Product quality, the easy use of credit cards, the Internet, toll-free numbers, top-of-the-line customer and technical service teams, 100 percent guarantees, and easy return policies make buying what cannot be touched before purchase less of a risk.

Today's messages must do more than cleverly entertain (passive); they must get the consumer involved in the message by asking them to do something (active). Direct marketing turns a passive message into an active discussion by finding ways to interact and develop a two-way dialogue between buyer and seller. To further encourage purchase, many direct response offers include an additional promotional incentive to induce the target to "act now." Incentives range from free gifts and upgrades to two-for-one or limited-time offers to the exclusive chance of being the "first to own" a new item. Once a relationship is forged, other contact opportunities might include personal selling, catalogs, direct mail, websites, e-mail, trade shows, seminars, telemarketing, or any other one-on-one interactive communication technique.

Whenever advertising and/or promotional efforts are used alone or together, the goal is to make a sale. But not all sales are meant to be immediate. When used as a member of a campaign, direct marketing's job may be limited to eliciting a response, creating excitement, provoking curiosity, or encouraging additional information gathering, especially if the brand is an expensive one.

Direct marketing is also a great way to launch a campaign, when used as an announcement or teaser device. It is very effective at building or generating interest in, say, a grand opening, a charity function, or a private sale. As a support vehicle, it functions well as a reminder, supplying promotional offers or samples, and making information gathering or purchase quick and easy.

Direct marketing campaigns must be measurable, correctly targeted, and promote a consistently reliable product or service. As a promotional vehicle, direct marketing is successful because it can talk directly to the target, in a language they will understand, about a product or service that will enhance their lives. When combined with the appropriate promotional mix, it can position a product, build both image and brand awareness, and encourage brand loyalty more efficiently and effectively than almost any other campaign approach.

The more that is known about the target's lifestyle, the more personalized the message and the easier it is to talk to them about a brand's specific features and benefits, and how they relate to their interests. This type of intimate approach strengthens the tie between the target and the brand and is the first step to building a lasting brand-loyal consumer.

Customer Relationship Marketing

Direct marketing, also known as *customer relationship marketing* (CRM), is the development and maintenance of the relationship between buyer and seller. Its personalized approach and ability to tie product features and benefits to the target's lifestyle make it a more individualized marketing vehicle. A marketer's job is to initiate contact and deliver a product that meets the consumer's needs and wants. If accomplished, the result is a long-term relationship between buyer and seller. This is particularly important today because consumers decide when, where, and how they buy largely on the quality of a company's customer service.

As consumers work harder to save money, loyalty takes a back seat to the lower-priced brand. To counter this, companies that employ relationship marketing can build loyal long-lasting relationships with the target. A good relationship begins with a quality product that consistently performs at the same level with each purchase. It grows with personalized messages that are tied to the target's lifestyle. It is solidified with quality customer service representatives and a program that allows for customer feedback.

Customer relationship marketing is not a new concept. It began with the small business owners who sold goods and services one-on-one with members of their own communities. Next came direct mail, which was personalized based on a list of addresses from varied sources. Direct marketing took the mailing list one step further, segmenting the target into related groups in order to deliver a specialized message to a small niche of interested target members rather than one mass audience.

It was not until databased marketing came along that the message could be personalized according to an individual target's needs. With the addition of CRM techniques, each individual target member is considered a part of the brand's value that needs to be retained and nurtured, creating a long and mutually beneficial relationship.

This relationship absolutely must be continued after the sale. Consider sending a thank you e-mail or a survey that documents customers' purchasing activities and experiences. Give back to loyal customers in the form of coupons, discounts, and so on. Use this loyal following to gain product feedback.

It is a well-known fact that most sales result from a relatively small number of target users. The *Pareto Principle* or *80/20 Principle* is the best way to define relationship marketing: If 20 percent of the target generates 80 percent of a company's business, then more advertising efforts should be shifted their way. Having a strong relationship with 20 percent of buyers is a great way to build loyalty.

Promotions such as coupons or sales do not create loyalty; ultimately, it is the personalization and overall value of the brand to the target that does. Value is also about reliability and efficiency. It should be easy to reach customer service or technical representatives 24/7. A customer with a question wants answers quickly. When contact is made, representatives should be knowledgeable and courteous. Any problems that do arise need to be handled immediately and resolved on the first try.

A complaining customer should be considered an asset. They are talking to you first before trashing the brand via powerful word-of-mouth or viral efforts. A target whose problem has been addressed and corrected typically remains loyal and satisfied and offers value to the brand with each referral they make.

Relationship marketing is not a science; it is the art of fulfilling a need in a personal way. Consider the following:

1. Know the target, and make all advertising messages personalized.
2. CRM is about give and take, creating a dialogue and solving a problem quickly.
3. CRM helps build a network of powerful brand advocates.
4. Because consumers have a choice, loyalty is declining. They feel they are just a number, and are tired of dealing with automated customer service channels. They also often wonder why all the perks go to new consumers.
5. Technology will never replace human contact.
6. Work at retaining the old reliable loyal consumer, since 20 percent of repeat purchases provide 80 percent of overall business.
7. Make information on a company website easy to find, and make the products even easier to purchase.
8. A relationship begins with brand awareness. Features and benefits tied directly to the target's needs and wants allow the target to differentiate

one brand from the others in its category. Strengthen the relationship with one-on-one dialogue with the target; solidify it with great customer service and an even greater product based on client feedback.

9. Solidify their interest in receiving updated product information by offering the chance to easily "opt in" and "opt out."
10. Give incentives for referrals.
11. CRM works at reinforcing a brand's overall relevance.

Using Databases to Reach and Define the Target

Personalized messages have earned direct marketing the moniker *database marketing,* because its success relies on a detailed list of customer names and contact information to reach the intended target. A simple database stores demographic information such as names, addresses, phone numbers, and e-mail addresses. A more comprehensive database uses psychographic information to hone in on targets' likes, dislikes, interests, hobbies, and so on; identify those most likely to purchase; and determine who has purchased in the past. Geographic information is used to determine location, use, and time of year the target will use the brand. Databases also help in identifying prospects, determining the type of offer needed, and encouraging repeat purchase. Generally, information is gathered from sources such as a company's own past purchase history, magazine subscription lists, the U.S. Census Bureau, warranty and rebate cards, credit card purchases, UPC scanners at the grocery store, any professional organizations the target is affiliated with, and varied corporate interactions such as inquiries for additional information.

How companies use consumers' private information is an ongoing concern. Consumers are reacting to fears about identity theft, spam, and intrusive phone calls by pressuring the federal government to tighten regulations on how companies deal with the selling of database lists. In the meantime, consumers are fighting back by joining "do not call" lists, buying subscriptions to identity theft providers, such as Lifelock, and using software to block nuisance e-mails.

More and more companies feel the need to assure their patrons that consumer information will not be sold to outside businesses. Although more time-consuming, many are building their lists from within rather than buying outside lists; this is best accomplished by encouraging consumers to join reward programs or "opt in" to e-mail promotions. Those who do opt in to receive information are receptive to the message, making direct marketing a great primary or secondary campaign vehicle. Because of this, it is important that Internet databases be accurate and free of misspellings. All recipients should be offered an "opt out" option that is easy to access and guaranteed to work.

Databases that are rented from other companies are expensive and are good for only one mailing. They also forbid names to be added to an in-house database list unless a response has been received. Therefore, it is a good idea to offer some kind of incentive to encourage the recipient to respond.

Traditional Advertising and Direct Response

Traditional advertising is intrusive; the message arrives uninvited to a disinterested, distracted target. Promotional database-driven vehicles like direct marketing deal with one customer at a time, usually addressing them by name, whereas traditional advertising vehicles talk to the masses about a generic problem. Although traditional advertising's reach is greater, its generic message does not always reach the intended target. Jaded, inattentive audiences do not react to a generic message as quickly as they do to a personalized, lifestyle-directed one. Traditional vehicles are employing more and more direct marketing tactics by encouraging consumers to do something, such as visit a website, enter a contest or sweepstakes, receive free samples, or sign up to receive future promotional offers.

In order for a traditionally advertised message to be remembered, it must be seen repeatedly before the target is aware of the message and acts upon it. Direct response actively involves the target with a pointed message that encourages immediate action through limited time offers or attractive incentives that encourage them to "act now" (before the commercial ends) or within a preset time limit.

It is relatively easy to determine return on investment and keep track of direct marketing's success because it is trackable. Unlike advertising, direct marketing asks the target to do something—place an order or fill out a rebate form—which allows marketers to track who responded and pinpoint where the target was exposed to the message. Consumers can inform customer service representatives where they encountered the message by giving them a marketing code (a combination of letters and numbers that appear on coupons, catalogs, and direct mail packages). This type of information helps media buyers track the success of their media buys.

Creating a one-on-one dialogue is more expensive than a singularly delivered monologue. Traditional advertising vehicles often fall victim to wasted exposure whereas direct marketing, a more expensive option, employs less media waste. It concentrates a personalized message on a smaller number of consumers that, through research and past purchase history, have been identified as the most likely people to buy the product or use the service.

Although the response rate is often less than 2 percent, direct marketing

Figure 8.2   **Sample Ad: Knoxville Museum of Art**

Source: Created by Amanda Sherrod, The University of Tennessee, Knoxville.

is more effective at reaching the target with a message they are interested in than any other mass-market vehicle.

Direct marketing has a lot to say, so use it to announce a new product or event, encourage trial, or promote the relaunch of a mature product. Each of these promotional tactics offers great opportunities to attach a sample, build a relationship, and learn more about the targets' needs and wants.

Understanding Direct Marketing's Strengths and Weaknesses

Let's take a look at what the varying types of direct marketing can or cannot bring to the media mix.

Strengths

1. Personalization. Personal information allows marketers to address the target by name and tie the message directly to his or her lifestyle.
2. Immediate Results. Toll-free numbers and websites encourage immediate purchase.
3. One-on-One Assistance. The target can reach a company representative 24/7 to answer questions or assist with a purchase. This relationship–building, one-on-one contact encourages repeat purchases and brand loyalty.
4. Interactive and Engaging. Creative writing, bright colors, testimonials, streaming video, entertaining games, scratch-offs, and samples keep the target interacting with the pieces longer or engaged in the message for an extended period of time.

Weaknesses

1. Expense. Personalized messages are expensive—even more so if a company needs to purchase a list of names rather than generating their own.
2. Junk Messages. If it interrupts programming or arrives unsolicited, it is often looked upon unfavorably.
3. Reach. One-on-one marketing limits the number of consumers the message will reach.
4. Production Time. Depending on the piece and medium used, direct marketing can be very time-consuming to produce.
5. Privacy. The unauthorized selling of consumer information is a major concern.

The Visual/Verbal Voice of Direct Marketing

Some of the more popular types of direct marketing include catalogs; direct mail; brochures; statement stuffers, magalogs, and polypaks; fliers or leaflets; reward programs; interactive television; trade shows; sponsorships; and telemarketing. Let's take a quick look at each one.

Catalogs

Catalogs can be divided into two separate categories: those selling general merchandise such as JCPenney or Sears, and those devoted to specialty goods such as Pottery Barn or Crate&Barrel. So successful are these colorful opt-in sales pieces that can hold the target's attention, they have been referred to as the "art and science of creating desire." If that is so, then it is important to dazzle the target with beautiful visuals that feature the product up close and personal.

Colors, typeface, and image quality should match the target's self-image and the product's projected image. Products should be shown alone and in four-color when possible, surrounded only by a small amount of copy featuring a descriptive head and accompanying body copy and price. Informative body copy can detail copy points and tie the product's benefits to the target's lifestyle. Like print design, featured products should be the largest visual on the page to attract attention and encourage sales. Readers typically look first at the top right of the page then move to the top left, so it is important to place featured products near these areas.

Catalogs, like all media vehicles, should attempt to sell more than just one featured item. Consider placing items that can be used together near the main visual to encourage companion sales. Be sure to use generous amounts of white space around items to keep the page from looking cluttered. Keeping type sizes, leading, and placement around images consistent will also create a sense of organization. Do not let type overwhelm the image; in catalog design, the image is what stops attention—not the headline or copy.

Make purchasing quick and easy by offering several ways to place an order. Options might include an order form, a toll-free phone or fax number, and/or a web address.

Catalogs can be broken down into four basic elements: the front cover, the inside front, the internal or midsection, and the back cover. The front cover should promote two or three featured products along with the logo and volume number. This is the catalog's biggest chance to make a first impression, so be sure to keep this area as simple, focused, and representative of image and content as possible.

The inside front cover typically features a table of contents, primary contact information, and perhaps a letter from the editor. It is also the first view of how products will be featured throughout the catalog. The center sections are organized into themes: for instance, a home décor catalog would have sections on outdoor furniture, kitchenware, living room furniture, dining accessories, and so on. Order forms are usually placed in the center section. The back cover includes the logo and mailing panel as well as any additional featured items.

Direct Mail

Basically, direct mail is defined as the sending of a sales device, an announcement, a promotional device, or a service reminder through the mail to predetermined individuals. Today, direct mail is more than just a letter and an order form; it is an interactive introduction to the product or service. It is not unusual to see direct mail paired with direct response television, Internet events, or e-mail.

Direct mail—also referred to as junk mail because it often arrives without the recipients' consent—does not have to live up to its name. A direct mail package can take on a variety of shapes and sizes and contain an array of visual and verbal pieces. Most pieces are simple promotional devices, but others can include three-dimensional pop-ups and pieces that make noise or have multiple moving parts. Still others might include some type of sample relying on the envelope's lumps and bumps to prompt the target to open it. Each piece should keep the target's curiosity alive by adding and building on what has been previously stated.

There is no set rule as to the number of pieces a direct mail package must contain, but most standard packages will include at least an outer envelope, a personalized sales letter, a colorful informative brochure, a price list or menu, a postcard or business reply card, an order form, and a prepaid return envelope. Each piece must work together to create a cohesive visual/verbal design that complements and reflects the message used on other pieces within the campaign.

If creating a multi-piece packet, consider color-coding each piece, offering the target a kaleidoscope of colorful ideas and offers. Multiple pieces will reflect the same key consumer benefit, headline and typestyle, color(s), character representative and spokesperson, and (when possible) layout style. What is included in the package will depend on what the reader needs to do, such as place an order, make a donation, register for an event, or make an appointment.

To hold the target's interest longer, consider including some type of interactive device—perhaps a scratch-off card, coupons, samples, CDs, game pieces, pop-ups, or some other unusual component. The only requirement is that each piece must fit into an envelope or be self-contained in some kind of self-mailer, and fit within the defined budget.

Direct mail's personalized approach and multiple pieces make it more expensive than most printed pieces in the media mix. However, its very exclusivity makes it a great vehicle for rewarding brand-loyal users, making an announcement, or launching or maintaining a brand's image. For those consumers not currently using the product or service, it is a great way to personally deliver some type of enticement—a coupon or free sample, perhaps—to get the consumer to try the product for the first time or to switch brands.

Do not underestimate the power of direct mail to persuade and make a memorable statement. A quality design, a targeted message, and one or more interactive pieces can turn junk mail into a creatively designed, informative jewel.

When used with public relations, the arrival of direct mail singles out the target for special attention. When paired with traditional advertising, it can build curiosity by announcing its imminent arrival or availability. E-mail is a great reminder vehicle, and a website can offer the target an alternative way to find out additional information, speak to a customer service representative, or participate in a blog discussion. Alternative media or guerrilla marketing events, for example, can make the direct mail piece interactive if used as an invitation to a special event or a ticket for a free gift.

Let's take a look at some of the more common creative devices used in direct mail.

Outside Envelope

Curiosity starts with the outer envelope. Make it as interesting as anything found inside. Give it a bright color, unusual shape, distinctive images, or an attention-grabbing creative piece of teaser copy that reflects the key consumer benefit, the logo, and the slogan or tagline.

Whether the consumer asked for the direct mail package or it arrived unsolicited, it must be attractive, interesting, and intriguing enough to encourage the target to open it immediately. Be sure the visual/verbal design on the envelope mimics what is being said and seen in other pieces used inside the package. Entice on the envelope—do not educate at this point—and fill the package with some type of lumpy sample so even touch induces curiosity.

Interactive Devices

The best promotional devices intrigue and engage the target. The more interactive they are, the more time the target will spend with the piece before possibly tossing it. Big budgets or campaigns whose entire budget is tied up with direct mail should consider using some type of interactive device that is retainable and features the company or product's logo. If it can recite the message when opened, great: It has their attention. If it can be folded like a piece of origami, then it's memorable. If it can be used repeatedly, like a pen or calendar, it's constantly top of mind. If it has movable pieces that can be opened, closed, or pulled to reveal different parts of the message at a time, it's engaging. More inexpensive options include entry forms for a contest or sweepstakes; invitations to open houses, private sales, or events; and/or a scratch-off card. Interactive devices are also a great way to encourage word of mouth as the target displays or uses it at work or home.

It is important to remember that whatever the promotional device used, it can only support a sale, not make it. In the end, a clever interactive promotional piece needs an equally strong visual/verbal message to make the sale.

The Letter

Once the envelope has encouraged the target to open the direct mail package, it is important for it to include a strong, personalized letter. Usually written by the president or CEO, it needs to clearly identify the speaker and inform the target about the promotion.

The purpose of the letter is to whet the target's appetite for additional information in a creative but educational way. The more the letter sounds like it is talking to an old friend by inserting anecdotes, possible uses, and inevitable outcomes, the better. As a rule, lower-priced items can use a more informal tone, whereas more expensive items should be more formal.

The middle paragraphs of the letter have a lot to say. Consider using an intriguing plot or benefit-driven storyline, taken from other campaign pieces, that features the target as the main character and the key consumer benefit as the hero of the story. Interesting copy, even if it is long, will be read if it engages the reader's curiosity, fulfills a need, and entertains.

Asking the target to buy something sight unseen will likely promote a degree of skepticism. If, however, your letter provides information on the who, what, when, where, why, and how of your sales pitch, that skepticism will be cut in half. Boring facts do not sell and do not hold anyone's interest. Facts tied to interests and related to the target's lifestyle will enhance the copy's believability. It is important for direct mail copy to involve the reader in believable scenarios and outcomes that can be backed up with testimonials, endorsements, or some type of reliable study.

Copy should reference each piece found in the mailer, explaining their importance, uses, and so on. Remind the reader how much time they have to purchase, call, or come in before the offer expires. Short deadlines often encourage immediate action. Be sure the storyline includes as many product features as possible, including colors, sizes, manufacturing and design details, price, and ordering options. Including an order form or postcard is a great way to organize orders or to use as a direct response device.

The letter's closing paragraph should be a call to action so the reader knows what to do or how to get to the next step. Give the target as many options as possible such as a toll-free or fax number, a web or e-mail address, and local addresses and phone numbers if the action requires a trip to a brick-and-mortar location. Be sure to include payment options and information on returns, guarantees, or warranties.

Whether the brand is expensive or not, keep the copy organized and clean. Use only three different type sizes—one for the headline, another for any subheads, and the last for the body copy; any more than that can look tacky. Depending on the strategy, price is usually prominently displayed in direct mail, so place it in the headline, the subhead, or in a callout box if more than one price exists. Use the headline to announce the key consumer benefit, multiple subheads to break up long copy, and images to visually show a solution or demonstrate a use. Try to maximize white space to increase readability and legibility. Consider using bullets to highlight important copy points rather than discussing them in long blocks of copy. Be sure tone of voice, color(s), and headline and typestyles consistently match those used in the rest of the campaign's vehicles.

Brochures

A brochure is a colorful, informative, multipage promotional piece that comes in a wide variety of shapes and sizes. They are a great support vehicle for the primary advertisements used in the campaign and a credible way to deliver important information directly into the hands of the target. Brochures are most effective when used to break down individual aspects associated with a particular product or service. If the brand is multidimensional consider using multiple brochures to explain each concept, or develop individualized inserts that can be customized to each target's needs.

The beauty of a brochure is its engaging look, often featuring colorful visuals, unusual folds and cuts, and varying sizes. These usually copy-heavy vehicles should actively engage the reader by slowly unfolding the plot, or important information, as the brochure unfolds. A brochure's job is to educate the consumer with facts that can be backed up with testimonials, the results of solid scientific studies, and useful information such as pricing or a schedule of events, depending on its role in the campaign. Brochures can be broken down into four separate areas: the front cover, the back cover, the inside front left and right panels, and the inside flat.

The appeal of the front cover is important: It should be colorful, pleasing to the eye, and relevant in what it says and shows. A brochure has about three seconds to attract the target's attention. Depending on the key consumer benefit, strategy, and target, the front cover can use an enticing visual, a visual and verbal combination, or nothing more than the company name, logo, and slogan or tagline.

The back cover is the least likely to be read, so it is usually the best location to place any contact information such as phone, fax, address, and website URL. If space is at a premium, place any pricing and/or dates and times on the back, as well.

The inside left and right panels are the most read panels, so make each word count. Focus on highlighting the key consumer benefit, along with need, use, and lifestyle enhancement points.

The inside flat refers to the inside of the brochure when it is opened up and read flat. Continue the storyline here and spice it up with images, bars and/ or boxes, or graphs. Strong photographs, illustrations, or graphics command attention and can say more than a thousand words. Use them to enhance and illustrate the story and don't forget the all-important "call to action." Text should use short sentences and multiple short paragraphs. Multiple subheads should make it easy for the reader to grasp the main points at a glance.

While most brochures used in direct mailers are mass-produced, others can be individualized. These types of designs use a mass-produced shell that features one or more pockets on the inside, where single panel inserts can be individually changed or rotated out to meet the target's specific needs. These inserts are a great idea if the copy can be divided into individualized units that can be mixed and matched as needed. Think of each insert as a separate selling idea or ad. To deliver the message effectively, each insert needs to include at least a headline, subhead, and body copy. More elaborate designs may also include one or more visuals. Be sure to match the layout style, type size and style, placement of the logo, visuals, or any other graphic device between inserts.

If not using individualized inserts, pockets can still be used to hold game pieces, tickets, the direct mail letter, or contact information; as a more expensive alternative, emboss, deboss, or foil stamp the logo onto the inside pocket or front cover.

When used in a direct mail packet, be sure the brochure uses the same tone of voice, colors, and typeface as the letter and/or postcard. A brochure is an excellent way to visually showcase any copy points introduced in the letter in beautiful four-color detail. If the budget is tight, consider adding color by using a colored paper stock. Paper is very diverse, offering an array of colors, textures, and weights. Instead of four-color visuals, a duotone (or two-toned) photograph or a black-and-white shot with a spot color might work well. A well-designed piece doesn't need a lot of bells and whistles, just a solid creative idea.

Creativity in brochure design goes beyond the visual/verbal message. It is also about shape, size, and the number of folds required to deliver the information. Brochures are a great interactive device when cut or folded in interesting ways. The eye is attracted to unusual shapes, so if the budget allows, cut, shape, or trim the brochure in an interesting way. Designs that employ the use of *die cuts,* or a special cutting method that can partially or completely cut out or around a specially designed shape, are an expensive but attention-grabbing option. Simple straight or diagonal cuts used on the front cover, for example, are a great way to expose a visual or headline from the inside panels. The most commonly seen die cuts are the slits placed on a pocket or outside panel to hold a business card or other removable piece.

Reply Cards and Order Forms

A reply card is usually smaller than anything else in the kit, so it must be easy to find. Consider making it a bright or unusual color, or attaching it to the brochure with perforations, making it easy to tear off and drop in the mail. The front needs to have a place for the target's name, complete address, day and evening phone numbers, and an e-mail address. If the consumer needs to make some kind of decision, be sure there is a box to check or a line to write on. Also be sure to repeat payment options and contact information. The back must have a return address and a prepaid postage stamp. Although the likelihood of people actually dropping a reply card in the mail is quite low, it can serve as a great worksheet before calling to make a purchase or ask a question. It is important that all information needed to make a purchase, receive a free sample, or request additional information be available and easy to use and read.

Return Envelope

The return envelope is one of the most expensive pieces to print. Because people are using traditional mail less often to contact a business, many packages are eliminating them all together. If it is included, keep it plain and simple and be sure to include a complete mailing address, the required postage bar codes, and a prepaid postage stamp. It is important that a one-sided reply card or order form fit in the accompanying envelope easily.

Direct mail is only "junk" if it is poorly written and designed. An inventive, engaging package that is cleverly written and unusually designed is likely to entice the reader through the entire package.

Do not scrimp on printing; use bright colors and graphics when possible. Use the envelope to grab the target's attention, or if using a self-mailing piece, be sure it is die cut or cut into an unusual but relevant shape. The more visual the piece, the longer it will hold the target's attention. Always be sure the key consumer benefit is the first thing they see, and push that idea throughout the copy. Use testimonials to validate claims and make the product easy to return. Be sure each piece is relatable to the target and easily leads the reader from piece to piece. If the target does not need a piece to make a choice, leave it out. Every image and color used should help set the tone and sell the product or service.

One way to reduce the cost of direct mail is to team with another marketer in some type of cooperative or shared-cost ad—typically placed in polypaks, bank or credit card statements, or package insert programs (PIP)—to reduce overall costs and extend reach. However, these less personalized approaches can reduce response rates even further.

In the end, direct mail has a lot to say and—unlike most advertising vehicles—a lot of space and time in which to say it. Use each piece to highlight features and benefits, uses, prices and offer solutions to specific problems.

Stuffers, Magalogs, and Polypaks

If your advertising budget is tight, consider using statement stuffers, magalogs, or polypaks to get the message out.

Statement stuffers accompany invoices, statements, or other correspondence regularly mailed by businesses and are a great way to market additional products to the customer. Stuffers usually contain a brief message and either a short-form application, web address, or toll-free number. Statement stuffers typically measure around 3¼ × 6 inches; they need to fit easily into a standard statement envelope without any type of folding or special handling. Stuffers can be used to announce new product information without incurring additional postage costs.

A magalog (magazine/catalog) is basically a multipage mail order catalog that looks like a magazine and includes both editorial material and diversified advertising.

Polypaks are a small bundle of 3 × 5 inch index cards that feature advertising for an array of noncompeting products. Usually arriving by mail, they are used to introduce products or to generate interest in mature products. These simple designs are typically four-color and double sided. The small size keeps information to no more than a short message, a visual, and an order form, phone number, or web address. For ease of use, the back will often include a self-mailer.

Fliers or Leaflets

Fliers and leaflets are inexpensive forms of direct marketing that prove particularly effective for small local businesses. Fliers should be creatively written and designed; just because they are inexpensive doesn't mean they have to look that way. When possible, attach a coupon or some type of discount to encourage the target to try the product or use the service. Coupons are also a quick and easy way to determine ROI. The only form of targeting available when using fliers is geographic, but it is a great way to generate leads for generic or universally used products or services sold locally.

Figure 8.3   **Sample Ad: PetSmart**

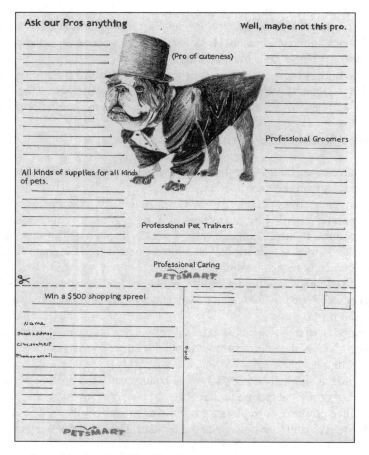

Source: Created by Jessica Kelly, The University of Tennessee, Knoxville.

Another consideration is how consumers receive the flier. Is blanketing local business or residential parking lots or mailboxes the best way to go? What about placing them in other local businesses to be picked up or handed out in trade by other retailers? Or is a one-on-one, hand-to-hand approach more appropriate? The overall product and its image, the degree of cooperation between retailers, and the rules set by local laws will help determine the most appropriate delivery system.

The goal behind employing these types of vehicles is to elicit a response such as calls for further information, purchase, sales leads, or to increase brick-and-mortar retail sales traffic.

Reward Programs

Customer loyalty is fragile in the best of times. Reward programs extend customer service initiatives beyond purchase by rewarding the targets' continued patronage with additional incentives such as:

1. Priority service.
2. Follow-up programs after purchase (for example, thank you cards and e-mails).
3. New product previews, which offer an exclusive peek at a new product. Give loyal customers an opportunity to be the "first to own" before the product is launched to the general public.
4. Incentives to assist with purchase (for example, coupons or a reduced price).

Reward programs such as frequent flyer promotions often begin with one vendor rewarding a customer for using a service or buying a product. Like direct mail, these single vendor offers commonly evolve into multi-vendor programs or cooperatives that offer even greater incentives such as vacation packages with reduced rates at hotels and resorts.

Enrolling in a reward program requires the target to opt in voluntarily, so signing up and accumulating points should be simple and easy. Difficult to use redemption programs or policies that are constantly being reinvented damage both brand loyalty and brand image. Reward programs are an extension of a successful brand maintenance program. Any misunderstandings should be rectified using one or more of the following damage control options:

1. Offer a quick and sincere apology.
2. Offer several solutions to solve the target's problem.
3. Once the solution is identified, fix it immediately.
4. Offer some kind of incentive on the buyer's next purchase.
5. Follow up.
6. Remember: The cost to fix the problem is less expensive than replacing the offended consumer.

Interactive Television

The newest form of televised direct response is known as interactive television. If viewers like the products they see during their favorite programming, they can order what the characters are wearing or using right off their television screens, using their keyboards or remote controls to click on the link provided. With a few keystrokes or punches, they can make a purchase or be taken to a website for more information. This very engaging and interactive advertising vehicle is not intrusive, as the consumer chooses whether to shop or not, and purchasing is easy and less expensive because the sale is made directly to the consumer.

One of the first to embrace interactive television was the cable television channel Bravo. They are developing products that will be tied into and promoted on the series *Real Housewives* and *Top Chef.* All promoted products can be purchased on Bravo's website, making interactive television an innovative way to offset lost advertising revenue.

"This is a fun way to satisfy what we're hearing from our viewers: that they like our shows, they like our taste. It's about giving our viewers a greater immersion in the brand," says Frances Berwick, executive vice president and general manager of Bravo Media in a *New York Times* online article (Clifford 2009). When themes shift, products featured in programming can be changed out easily, thereby accommodating sponsors and holding consumer interest.

Trade Show Advertising

Trade shows allow the target to see, hear, feel, smell, or taste a product before purchase. The one-on-one contact between buyer and seller is a great way to build a lasting relationship. Consumers can ask questions, get immediate feedback, witness a demonstration, or place an order.

This individualized interaction is a great way to develop a rapport and overall sense of trust with consumers who are prepared to buy or place an order. Beyond selling quality products, trade shows allow both buyer and seller to put a face with a name. They provide one of the fastest ways to build not only a relationship but also a loyal client base.

Since most trade show exhibits look pretty much alike, it is important for a brand's booth to stand out in some meaningful way on the crowded showroom floor. Make sure the consumer's visit is memorable and that all interactions reflect the product or service's image. Keep the space open and airy. Be sure to have an ample amount of business cards and offer some type of small sample that includes the brand logo and relevant contact information. Most important, be sure product representatives are knowledgeable, reputable, and well groomed. The goal of a trade show is to make contact and build leads that result in sales. It is important, then, that all leads be followed up before the next show or within 30 days.

Sponsorships

Sponsorships are great exposure vehicles. The target is captive for several hours, so it is a great place to show off a brand and allow the target to interact with it. When trying to reach a particular niche market, it is often a good idea to involve the brand in events, programming, or publications that also target that same niche. For example, the wine and spirits company Pernod Ricard launched a new tropical-flavored vodka, Absolut Mango, which served as a sponsor for RuPaul's web-based series *Drag Race*. They also incorporated TV and event marketing into the media mix. The integrated mix will include televised commercials, stops at major market nightclubs and bars, and an Internet component.

Volkswagen chose to sponsor Major League Soccer (MLS). As a part of their sponsorship, they can display their brand at events, place their logo on jerseys, and be visible at player appearances. Volkswagen will also sponsor a traveling tournament called MLS Futbolito, where a team of four amateur players participate in an ongoing tournament.

It is not unusual for films to have several corporate sponsors. For example, Burger King, Esurance Insurance Services, Nokia, and Kellogg's all featured the latest Star Trek movie in their advertising efforts.

Sony used street teams to promote its small yet sleek VAIO P Series computer during Fashion Week 2009 in New York City. The goal was to promote the P Series as "fashion forward, looking good and ultra portable." Dressed in fashions by some of the top new designers, 10 models or "live mannequins" were set up on New York streets dressed to the nines. Each outfit was accessorized with the colorful and fashionable VAIO P. The models were placed in varied locations for the two weeks prior to opening day. Their job was to showcase the computer's diverse color palette and to entice passing pedestrians to stop and take a look. Designers whose clothes were featured on the live mannequins also designed window displays from their fashions and the Sony VAIO P at the Manhattan SonyStyle store.

Telemarketing

Most consumers find telemarketing calls annoying not only because they arrive at an inopportune time, such as during the dinner hour, but they are also unsolicited. To counter this, many consumers have added their names to "no call" lists in an effort to stop these intrusive calls. However, under "opt in" circumstances, telemarketing does offer several advantages, including (1) determining consumer interest, (2) finding out consumer needs, and (3) providing time to explain technology or complex product features and benefits.

Telemarketers invariably generate negative results when they (1) use inaccurate target lists, (2) push poorly made products, and (3) employ pushy, rude, or inconsiderate salespeople.

The most successful form of telemarketing is in business-to-business marketing, where calls are directed to a more receptive audience. A successful business-to-business telemarketing campaign can:

1. Generate promising leads.
2. Generate appointments.
3. Build an updated database of potential customers.
4. Allow for follow-up calls after purchase or inquiry.
5. Develop long-term relationships.
6. Inform on promotions and reliability of competitive products.

The key to all types of customer contact is simple: If you have nothing important to say, sell, or announce, do not contact the target. All contacts need to be looked upon by the target as important, with outcomes that will benefit them in some significant way. The goal is to build awareness and drive traffic to a website and/or a brick-and-mortar store.

Direct marketing can successfully build consumer relationships, instigate purchase, generate new business, and rejuvenate old business. The greatest assets of direct marketing in a campaign are that it is personalized, convenient, free of hassles, and easy to use. It is also one of the best vehicles for breaking through product parity; product differentiation can be created by developing long-term relationships built around reliable, quality products and courteous and knowledgeable customer and technical service personnel.

9

Sales Promotion

Figure 9.1 **Sample Ad: Knoxville Zoo**

Source: Created by Lindsay Frankenfield, The University of Tennessee, Knoxville.

The Incentive to Use Sales Promotion in a Campaign

The American Marketing Association defines *sales promotion* as "media and nonmedia marketing pressure applied for a predetermined limited period of time in order to stimulate trial, increase consumer demand, or improve product quality."

Sales promotion gives the target an incentive or gift in exchange for loyalty or trial. The goal of sales promotion is to immediately increase sales for the short term; this is achieved by either reducing the price of a product or service or giving the target an added incentive for the same price.

Sales promotion uses an assortment of limited time offers to persuade consumers to make a purchase. The most common types of incentives include coupons, samples, contests and sweepstakes, point of purchase displays, price-off deals, rebates, bonus packs, and premiums. Incentives are most often used to encourage impulse buys or a first time purchase, or to lure consumers away from competing brands.

Promotions are often associated with traditional advertising, direct marketing, the Internet, street teams, and mobile advertising. The major difference between advertising vehicles and sales promotion is that advertising is informative and uses both a visual and verbal approach to show and tell the brand's key consumer benefit. Promotional efforts, on the other hand, engage the target in an activity—for instance, downloading coupons from sites such as couponmom.com, coupons.com, 8coupons.com, couponcabin.com, fatwallet.com, shortcuts.com, and couponcode.com; participating in a taste test; or getting a two-for-one offer to encourage purchase. Used together, one is a great educational device, while the other gives a hands-on view of how the product or service performs.

All of the advertising and promotional vehicles we have looked at so far deliver the message to the target. Sales promotion is less concerned with the message and more concerned with bringing the target to the product through an engaging and interactive device.

Even though sales promotion has little to say on its own, it is important the incentive offered reflects both the product and the target's self-image. Logos, slogans, and taglines should be prominently displayed. Any printed incentives should reflect the color(s), typeface(s), and style used throughout the campaign. If using a spokesperson or character representative, be sure to include them as a part of the promotional look and voice, when possible.

The increasing popularity of sales promotion can be traced directly to the slumping economy and product parity in almost all consumer goods categories. When the economy is doing well, the use of incentives goes down. When the economy is slow or weak, sales promotion efforts pick up. The lack of differentiation between products makes it difficult for consumers to distinguish between brands, causing many purchases to be dictated by price or promotional efforts alone. To attract attention, disrupt competitor sales, and immediately increase revenue, businesses are relying more and more on sales promotion efforts to make their voices stand out from the crowd. Those brands that have a unique and effectively diverse brand image require little or no promotional efforts to increase sales.

Getting the product into the hands of the target is one thing; getting them to repurchase without the use of an incentive is another. Sales promotion cannot improve on a bad product, hide product defects, overcome poorly executed advertising, or reinvent the popularity of an aging brand. It can only enhance a brand's value temporarily, not save it altogether. If the coupon, trial, or premium successfully gets consumers to make a purchase, the product must do the rest in order to make them repeat buyers.

On the down side, the repeated use of promotional efforts can hurt brand loyalty, erode brand equity, and diminish brand image. When consumers get used to repeated incentives, they will often hold off on a purchase until the next promotion comes along. These types of users, known as *brand switchers,* are the most likely to switch from a currently used brand to a new one. Alternatively, those already loyal to a brand will not be swayed by incentives of any kind. However, it is not unusual for even brand-loyal consumers to wait for the next promotion to make a purchase or stock up. Another point to consider is the large amount of incentives that go to waste. Although over 90 percent of all households use coupons, only a small fraction, or less than 1 percent, are ever redeemed.

Making Sales Promotion Work within the Campaign

What does it take to put together a successful promotion? Consider the following:

1. Bring the media to an open house or hand out samples of the product to a heavily attended event.
2. Drop off flyers, business cards, or postcards around the area; or post them on car windshields; or use street teams to deliver them outside a business.
3. Place posters on poles or in windows near the business, but be sure the location and type of product is clearly visible.

4. Place magnetic signs with the company's name, address, and phone number on the side of employee cars or business vehicles.
5. Make sure business cards, signage, packaging, and so on all reflect the brand image.
6. Print up some brochures or promotional car flyers and ask nearby businesses to display them at checkout counters.
7. Create a direct mail package that can be distributed to interested targets.
8. Set up a website and display its URL prominently on all advertising materials.
9. Churn up free publicity by sending out a press release to the local media to solicit a story.

Sales promotion is important in a campaign because it creates dialogue and encourages awareness, trial, repeat purchase, and loyalty. It is great for reigniting interest in a mature brand, temporarily highlighting a new brand, encouraging brand switching or repeat purchase, and reinforcing existing advertising. All types of sales promotion should increase brand interest, be engaging, and require some kind of interaction between the brand and the target.

When used in a campaign, sales promotion draws attention to and/or supports other messages used in the campaign. The choice of promotion depends on the life cycle stage of the product or service, as well as how it can be matched to the brand's image and the key consumer benefit. New product launches for rationally purchased products might use sampling, bonus packs, coupons, games, or contests and sweepstakes to encourage trial. Expensive, emotionally based purchases are not likely to engage in any type of promotion outside of sponsored events. Maintenance stage products might employ the use of games or contests and sweepstakes, if any promotional efforts are used at all. Reinvented or mature brands rely heavily on sales promotion to encourage retrial through coupons, bonus packs, premiums, sampling or demonstrations, point of purchase (POP), specialty packaging, and—if it's a high-end purchase—rebates.

Since most promotions are good for only a short amount of time, many marketers are finding ways to reward longtime consumers by developing ongoing loyalty or rewards programs; examples include frequent flyer rewards or the accumulation of points for a free night's hotel stay.

Understanding Sales Promotion's Strengths and Weaknesses

Let's take a look at what the varying types of sales promotion can or cannot bring to the media mix.

Figure 9.2   **Sample Ad: PetSmart**

Source: Created by Kelly Bukovsky, The University of Tennessee, Knoxville.

Strengths

1. Stimulate Sales. Sales promotion can immediately increase sales and generate income, but only on a short-term basis.
2. Interactive. Incentives ask the consumer to do something more than purchase, such as redeem a coupon, attend a sponsored event, try a companion product, fill out a rebate form, or enter a contest.
3. Trial. Promotions encourage consumers to try the brand at the point of purchase. Loyal users will stock up, and consumers loyal to the competition might consider switching brands.

Weaknesses

1. Sales Drops. The temporary increase in sales will immediately drop or return to prepromotional levels once the sales promotion event has run its course.
2. Depleted Brand Image. Too many promotions may damage a brand's image.
3. Waste. Many incentives go unused.
4. Expense. An expensive undertaking, sales promotions may not reach the target in large numbers. Depending on the promotion, overhead can be costly.

Promotions don't just happen. Before a sales promotion campaign is launched, retail outlets will often receive a preparation kit of display materials to assist with promoting the event. A typical kit includes:

1. Some type of in-store posters and/or mobiles;
2. Out-of-store banners;
3. Shelf promotions;
4. Point of purchase display kits;
5. Buttons and/or badges for sales personnel;
6. Brochures or other incentives or promotional material; and
7. Retailer educational packets.

Let's take a brief look at some of the more popular types of sales promotion.

Types of Sales Promotions

Coupons

Coupons are great interactive devices; they bring the target to the brand and initiate a dialogue about the product or service. One of the most-used forms of sales promotion, coupons offer consumers a savings or other type of incentive on a specified product for a limited time. They are a great way to increase revenue temporarily by offering the target something in return for their purchase, or as an introduction to a new product or service. Since they have to be collected and then presented at the time of purchase, they are a great interactive device.

Coupons can take many forms, including freestanding inserts, bounce-back or on-package offers, grocery receipt backs, direct mail offers, displays, and polypaks, to name just a few. Offers can include cents or percentages off or buy-one-get-one free deals. Most coupons must be redeemed by a certain date, while others, known as *instant redemption coupons,* can be used immediately. Still others have to be used on a subsequent purchase or by varied dates throughout the month.

Some of the best ways to get a coupon into the hands of the target include:

1. Direct mail;
2. Bonus packs;
3. E-mail;
4. Freestanding inserts (FSI);
5. Magazines;
6. Websites; and
7. Mobile phone offers.

Coupons that are not physically attached to an ad are known as a *free-standing inserts* (FSI). Inserted into newspapers after printing, these single-sheet, often double-sided, four-color promotions usually feature coupons or announce a sale. Also known as *supplemental advertising,* FSI are colorful, nationally distributed pieces and may feature folds, perforations, or some type of movable or scratchable part. Sizes vary, but they most often measure no larger than 8½ × 11 inches.

Another customized coupon delivery service is Catalina Marketing. These are coupons that are handed to the shopper with their grocery receipt for use on their next purchase. Usually these coupons are for products that are similar (rather than an exact match) to the current brand purchased.

Yet another popular form of coupon distribution, this one called *cross-product promotion* or *crossruffing,* occurs when a coupon is placed on or within packaging or when brands share a cooperative advertising offer. A good example of a cross-product promotion was developed between Bally Total Fitness and Unilever. When women arrived at the gym to work out, Bally handed each member a sample of Unilever's Dove Body Refresher. This fast and simple alternative to an after-workout shower gave women on the go an immediate chance to try the product and initiate feedback.

This type of targeted sales promotion, known as *venue advertising,* gets the product directly into the hands of those most likely to buy it. Putting the product where it will be used allows participants to see immediate results and marketers to get immediate feedback.

One more example of cross-product promotion teamed buttery popcorn with disposable towelettes: Movie theater concession stands placed Lever 2000 Moisturizing Anti-Bacterial Wipes in popcorn boxes. This "free and handy" type of promotion demonstrates the value of in-venue sampling as a results-driven and measurable device.

The Lucky Brand line of clothing apparel by Liz Claiborne offered a fun and interactive way to pick up a coupon. Customers who visited their website could opt to play a game: The better the player, the bigger the discount awarded. Coupons were good at local retail stores or for online purchases. Discounts starting at 20 percent could be increased to as much as 30 percent depending on the players' ending scores. Interactive components associated with any campaign helps consumers get engaged in a brand. Technology can also help marketers customize and personalize the delivery of coupons. Knowing who is likely to respond to the message because of past interest or purchase ensures they will interact with the coupon and the brand.

Brands using the web to deliver coupons must take special care to ensure that redemption is easy and distribution has both an expiration date and a limited number of available coupons—something KFC overlooked on their promotion for their new grilled chicken. First introduced on the *Oprah Winfrey Show,* the lower-fat chicken recipe was an instant hit. Interested consumers were directed to Winfrey's website to download a coupon for two free pieces of grilled chicken, two side items, and a biscuit. The problem? There were no limits on how many coupons could be downloaded—an oversight that led to a lot of free food being given away before KFC had to halt the promotion and face a barrage of negative publicity. Most coupon offers placed in direct mail packages or in newspapers are limited in number and require the consumer to do something in order to receive the free offer, such as buy one, get the second one for free. In this case, KFC not only gave up control of how many offers could be dispersed but did not require consumers to make an additional purchase.

Why Use Coupons?

Why are some brands placed on sale or featured at a promotional price? (1) To stand out from the competition; (2) to launch a new product; (3) to relaunch a reinvented brand; (4) to feature a brand with sagging sales; (5) to eliminate the competition; and (6) to increase brand equity. Let's take a quick look at each one.

Stand Out from Competing Products. Bargain buys and continual promotions bring attention to a brand. Marketers must be careful, however, that continued promotions do not damage a brand's image.

New Product Launch. Price reductions are a great way to encourage consumers to try a new product. Incentives such as offering a free sample, giving in-store demonstrations, offering taste tests, distributing coupons, or teaming up offers with direct mail can often encourage consumers to switch brands.

Reinvented Brands. Reinvented brands have to break into the product category anew when changes or upgrades have been made to an old formula. The same incentives used to launch a new brand will bring attention to a reinvented brand.

Sagging Sales. Oftentimes when mature products reach the end of their life cycle, promotions can hold off the inevitable, but for only a short while.

Eliminating the Competition. Larger companies and more established brands can keep a price lower for a longer period of time than a smaller independent or highly indebted brand. Price cuts can effectively eliminate lesser competitors.

Increasing Brand Equity. Consumers love a deal, especially if that deal is associated with a beloved brand. Loyal consumers will buy more from less advertised brands that consistently deliver on what they promise. Over time, this consistency helps solidify reputation and thus equity.

Coupons Really Do Need to Be Designed

It is rare for any newspaper ad to have a single coupon. The idea is to get the target to go into a store or purchase a brand more than once. To ensure this, each coupon offer will differ and offer a range of expiration dates usually lasting anywhere from 30 to 90 days.

When coupon offers differ in length, consider alternating line lengths for balance, making sure the baselines align across the coupons. When designing more than one coupon, be sure they are placed together and have a consistent look. Coupons should be both easy to read and understand as well as easy to remove from the ad. The best placement for multiple coupons is to align them at the bottom of the ad because they have a weight to them. Coupons should never pop up in the middle of an ad, interrupting eye flow and corrupting the message.

Consistency balances multiple coupons on the page, so all offers, logos, images, expiration dates, and marketing codes should be the same size, in the same typeface, and appear in the same position on each coupon. Consider drawing additional attention to the coupons by outlining them with a dashed line, visually letting the target know where they need to tear or cut them out. Other important aspects of coupon design include:

1. Coupon Size. Coupon size is not uniform and usually depends on how many coupons will appear on the page. Be sure the coupon is large enough for the offer to be read easily.
2. Make an Offer. Every coupon needs to tell the user what they will get for using the coupon: for instance, "Buy One Large Pizza, Get the Second for a Dollar."

3. Scream It Out. If using a percentage or cents-off deal, be sure to enlarge the offer to make it stand out.
4. Retailer Reimbursement. Grocer coupons will require a small amount of copy that tells the retailer how to redeem or get their money back for honoring the manufacturer's coupon.
5. UPC Codes. Coupons redeemed at the grocery store will need to have a scannable series of vertical thick and thin lines known as a Universal Product Code (UPC). When passed over the computer beam during checkout, the product's price is recorded.
6. Logo. All coupons need to have a logo, since the first thing the consumer will do is tear it out of the newspaper, magazine, or direct mailer.
7. Expiration Date. Coupons do not last forever. Each should display an expiration date for the offer, either enclosed in a box at the center-top of the coupon or in bold type within the coupon copy.
8. Picture It. If the product comes in more than one variety or size, make it easy for the consumer to buy the correct item by including both an offer and a picture of the product.
9. Code It. Marketing codes consist of a set of small letters and numbers and are often placed on a coupon to tell the marketer what media venue the coupon came from. This is a good way to track what media vehicles are working best.

Bonus Packs

Bonus packs give the consumer more of the product for the same price. For example, shampoo may come with a "try me" size bottle of conditioner.

Promotional Pricing

Probably one of the most successful promotions is placing an item on sale. On-sale signage can appear on the product, on its packaging, or on a shelf or poster. The goal is to encourage trial of a new or reinvented product or to get repeat buyers to stock up. Beyond the traditional sale, promotional pricing deals can include refunds and rebates, coupons, varied discounts, bonus pack promotions, and the like.

Specialty Packaging

Creative package designs usually carry holiday or movie themes and are used to attract attention, highlight promotional pricing, or invigorate sales of a mature brand.

Figure 9.3   **Sample Ad: Yankee Candle**

Source: Created by Jared Thigpen, The University of Tennessee, Knoxville.

Package Insert Programs

Ads that are inserted into mail-order deliveries sent from the seller to the buyer are known as package insert programs (PIP). Because the ad hitches a ride with a product the consumer has already ordered, it gets an implied endorsement from a company or brand the target audience trusts. For example, Omaha Steaks offers a PIP to vendors who want to reach their same target base. Most programs consist of no more than four to eight noncompeting pieces. A PIP is very similar to direct mail, only less expensive. This clutter-free, competitor-free vehicle is a great way to reach small, loyal niche markets.

All package inserts should feature a bold headline and a simple key consumer benefit–driven offer. When designing, think direct mail. Make sure to maximize white space, offer several ways to order, and if possible, offer some type of incentive such as a free sample or free shipping. Any PIP that is shipped repeatedly should regularly be changed out to maintain variety and interest.

Samples and Free Trials

Two of the easiest ways to get the consumer to try a product is to offer a sample or free trial at the point of purchase. Consumers are more likely to try a product for the first time if it costs them little or nothing.

There is no better way to create interaction between the target and the brand than handing out a sample, demonstrating how the product works, or allowing the target to try the product on the spot.

Today's marketers are concentrating more on advertising at the point of purchase to help differentiate products and get the brand directly into the target's hands. Reaching the consumer with a relevant message and perhaps a taste test, sample, or coupon provides an incentive to purchase "now." This is a great way to stand out from competing products and assist targets with their purchase, when and where they make a decision to buy. Small or trial-sized samples can generate immediate feedback and lasting impressions.

Another great way to get a sample or coupon into the hands of the consumer is attach it to something usable. Several Japanese businesses came up with an interactive substitute for immediately obtained samples or coupons: pocket packs of tissues that have an advertised message printed on them. It's an inventive way to send a message or attach a coupon that will be kept and reused until emptied.

Some of the other more common sampling platforms include: (1) events, (2) flash mobs, or according to Urban Dictionary, "A group of people who appear from out of nowhere to perform predetermined actions, designed to amuse and confuse surrounding people," (3) point of purchase displays, (4) guerrilla street teams, (5) nightclubs/restaurants, and (6) covert product sampling.

Point of Purchase

Point of purchase (POP) advertising includes inside and outside posters or signage, or the more commonly seen stand-alone displays found along store aisles or at the end of an aisle (the latter being known as *end-caps*).

A creative display featuring unusual or distinctive packaging, bonus packs, special pricing, samples, and shelf talkers placed away from competing brands can make a product step out and away from its competitors.

POP programs should not be considered an afterthought. The visual/verbal message should match what is happening throughout the media mix and not only match the brand's image but that of the store in which it is sold and, thus, the consumer. Products most often employing a POP program include candy, magazines, computers, vitamins, lawn and garden equipment, liquor, and large-ticket items such as workout equipment or cars.

More marketers are looking at using POP for three basic reasons: (1) they often outperform traditional advertising efforts; (2) the dearth of sales personnel available at retail stores makes point of purchase programs interesting to retailers; and (3) along with consumers expecting less help, they are also making more impulse buys.

Refunds and Rebates

Refunds and rebates are two ways to give cash back to the consumer after purchase. Each method rewards the target for their purchase and builds brand loyalty. Many products offer a 100 percent refund of the purchase price if for any reason the buyer is not completely satisfied. Rebates are a form of sales promotion that temporarily lowers a brand's purchase price. Typically, rebates are offered on high-ticket goods; they require the consumer to fill out a lengthy form, answer a series of questions, submit personal information, and/or send along some sort of proof of purchase. Therefore, the savings is not immediate.

Trial Offers

Trial offers allow consumers to try the product in their home or office for a set period of time, usually 90 days, before purchasing.

Promotional Products or Premiums

Sponsored events should mimic both the product and the target. Companion product pairings help achieve both awareness and recall. Event sponsors often pursue these goals further by giving away some type of free gift with their logo and slogan or tagline printed on it. Types of promotional products might include T-shirts, water bottles, calendars, magnets, coffee mugs, key chains, pens, and the like.

Besides sponsored events, premiums can be dispensed via personal selling or attached to a product. Some premiums require consumers to cover shipping and handling or to return a proof of purchase seal.

Contests, Sweepstakes, and Games

Contests require participants to demonstrate a certain type of skill. A panel of judges usually determines winners. Sweepstakes, on the other hand, are based solely on luck, and winners are randomly selected. Purchase is usually not required for participation in a contest or sweepstakes. One good example of a contest is the "create your own donut" contest sponsored by Dunkin Donuts. The company launched a $10 million campaign that employed radio, television, and the web, and the winning culinary pastry was available for purchase at all Dunkin Donuts locations.

The goal of all contests and sweepstakes is to grab the attention of an inattentive audience. Put the sweepstakes offer in a catalog or direct mailer and you have created a way to engage the reader for more than a few minutes. Points to know before executing any sweepstakes or contest include:

1. The Target. Most contestants are older and have low to moderate household incomes.
2. Giveaway Items. Prizes should be of good quality and relative to the price and image of the brand and/or company sponsoring the contest.
3. Brand Switchers. Users will easily switch to an alternative brand once the offer has expired, so maintain the contest or sweepstakes such as McDonald's does with the Monopoly game.
4. Visual/Verbal Message. If the visual/verbal message is not innovative and attention grabbing, the offer will not be opened. Engagement increases the success rate.
5. Multiple Prizes. Offering a number of prizes gives the impression the odds of winning are greatly increased.
6. Legal Disclaimer. It is important to make the rules and any limitations clear and have a lawyer look them over before printing.

Games are another interactive way to engage consumers. Options might include scratch-off cards or the collection of game pieces. Unlike contests and sweepstakes, games usually do require a purchase to participate.

Product Warranties or Guarantees

Full warranties make any type of direct marketing a safe way to shop. If not completely satisfied, the customer can return the product for a refund of the entire purchase price. Guarantees ensure the lowest price. If the consumer does find a lower price, the company will refund the difference.

Trade-In Allowances

A trade-in allowance is a promotion that allows the consumer to lower the price of a new product by trading in an old one.

No matter what the incentive, if the target can taste it, touch it, or smell it, then sales promotion is a great interactive device for demonstrating the key consumer benefit at the point of purchase, especially if a product has no features that distinguish it from its competitors. It can be difficult to tie promotional offers to an existing campaign because the visual/verbal images used in other vehicles are relatively silent in sales promotion. However, these images—along with the strategy, objectives, and target—should guide the design team toward the proper choice of promotion to use.

10

Electronic Media

Figure 10.1 **Sample Ad: Hyland's**

Source: Created by Ally Callahan, The University of Tennessee, Knoxville.

Electronic Media Adds Flash to Traditional and Alternative Media Campaigns

Advertising on the Internet is a personalized way to expand a brand's message. It is a great vehicle for building awareness, developing a relationship, maintaining brand loyalty, and increasing or maintaining equity. Internet advertising uses the same visual/verbal techniques as direct mail and broadcast and print—the only difference is it allows the buyer and seller to personally interact in a two-way dialogue.

The Internet is an extension of traditional advertising methods that serves as an effective way to continue the sales message, engage the target interactively, and educate them about a brand. It is also an excellent repository for information such as current promotions, studies, testimonials, product updates, and advice or tips from relevant experts. Many sites feature blogs where the target can ask questions or exchange information about the brand with other enthusiasts.

How does Internet advertising measure up to traditional advertising? (1) It has news value like newspaper; (2) it focuses product information on brand image and the target's lifestyle like magazine ads; (3) it can give the brand the same sense of immediacy as radio; and (4) it uses sight, sound, and motion to show the product in use or in a setting. What makes it more unique than advertising? It encourages interaction and offers a one-on-one dialogue between buyer and seller via customer or technical assistance.

Web-based advertising makes business transactions easier, faster, and more efficient. It is one of the strongest interactive tools available. The two primary roles of the Internet in a campaign are to educate potential customers and interact with the target by providing access to customer service or technical service providers 24/7. The ease of use allows the target to compare products and make a purchase at any time from almost anywhere. Most consumers begin their shopping experience on the Internet by using it as a primary source of information for a certain type of product, namely, those that do not require a great deal of research or can be confidently purchased without first been seen or touched. Those seeking more data after initial exposure to a message seen elsewhere often use the web as a secondary source to confirm or continue their search for information. The hours spent researching a product and its competitors delivers a target that is better educated about product features, quality, price, guarantees, and customer assistance than ever before.

A website that matches the look of other pieces used in a campaign will make the target's research easier and a product's visual/verbal image and message stronger and more memorable.

Destination and Informational Websites

Once traditional advertising, direct mail, or another type of alternative media has the target's attention, it should direct them to a website for more information. Independently, the target may rely on the web as a neutral source of information when researching or comparing brands before making a purchase.

Internet surfers will find two basic types of websites: destination and informational. A *destination site* should offer activities that will actively engage the viewer and encourage repeat visits. To keep consumers coming back, it is important that this type of site change out content often. It may be nothing more than an updated weather or stock market report, or perhaps the promotion of various contests or sweepstakes, or the inclusion of interesting trivia, coupons, blogs, recipe ideas, audio broadcasts, and the like. Attaching some type of viral component is a great way to spread the word about the site with little or no advertising. Jack in the Box, for example, introduced a site after their popular character representative was hit by a car following the 2009 Super Bowl. Using the accident as a way to introduce their new website and logo, visitors to the site were encouraged to send "get well wishes" during his recovery. As a reward for the targets' continued participation and concern, Jack in the Box planned to follow up the promotion by sending coupons to everyone who wished Jack a swift recovery.

Informational sites are where the target goes to gather product information, find tips or coupons, and get questions answered 24/7. A typical page resembles traditional print media in its look and scope of information. Such sites use broadcast techniques to demonstrate or discuss the key consumer benefit and any supporting features.

All sites should be simple and easy to load and navigate. Carry over any visual/verbal messages from print or broadcast to reinforce both the message and the image of the brand. Websites should also feature any spokesperson or character representative used elsewhere, as well as similar and recognizable layout and headline styles.

Educating and Interacting with the Target

Because consumers choose to use the Internet for research or entertainment purposes, it renders the interaction between buyer, seller, and brand a more positive, less apathetic, one. Consumers determine what they look at and for how long, making web browsing an efficient way to comparison-shop or purchase.

Once the search for product information is complete, the Internet effectively brings the product or service to the consumer. Many products allow the target to not only customize their purchase but also participate in the development of product upgrades and the restructuring of customer or technical service issues. When the target has an active stake in a particular brand, they feel an affinity or loyalty to that brand, and this often results in a lasting relationship. Because the Internet relies on databases, it is easier to target smaller niche markets. Add in e-mail marketing and the target can be reached at any time with a personalized message. Advertisers who match their message to these highly specialized sites will successfully reach the intended target with a message that interests them and they will respond to.

Using cross promotion in traditional mass media vehicles or direct mail encourages a trip to the brand's website. It is important that the creative team knows the role the Internet will play in the promotional mix. Will it use visual/verbal elements to support traditional advertising efforts but be a primary location for obtaining coupons, registering for a free sample, or entering a contest? Or will it be the only location to make a purchase? The answers to these questions will determine how the website will be cross-promoted and visually and verbally designed.

Relationship Development Opportunities

Creating opportunities to develop a relationship with the target is the goal of Internet marketing. Once the relationship is solidified, the need for quality customer service initiatives is crucial to maintaining loyalty. In fact, superior customer service is as important as the visual/verbal message and the product's overall reliability. It must be successful the minute the website launches.

Customer service is more than people, it is policy. Representatives should be knowledgeable and courteous, and policies should ensure immediate feedback, easy ordering and purchasing, quick delivery, a 100 percent money back guarantee, and varied ways to purchase. After delivery, a follow-up e-mail on the quality of the experience and/or a thank you note helps to maintain the relationship with the buyer. Future e-mails can announce sales or specials that match the target's interests.

The more options a consumer is given to make contact with a brand or its representatives, the better. Any attempts to contact customer service must be quick and easy. If contact is made via e-mail or instant messaging, the connection must be immediate. Any responses that require additional time must be articulated and accurate. The goal is to create positive interactions that reflect reliability and encourage trust rather than project negativity and foster distrust.

When developing a site, it is important to take into account whether customer service initiatives will be active or passive. Active customer service includes live discussions via phone or electronic communication via instant messaging, blogs, or Twitter. The goal is to make answering questions and solving problems quick and easy. Passive customer service often features automated phone systems, delayed Internet responses to questions, and a lengthy wait for a sample or confirmation e-mail responses.

Advertising on the Internet

The goal of Internet advertising is to reach the targeted audience wherever they are regionally, nationally, or globally; to create brand awareness; and to pique the target's curiosity enough to click on the ad. Once transferred to the sponsoring website, it should be easy to navigate and gather information or ultimately make a purchase. A well-designed and informative site can simplify the seek, search, and purchase process as well as create an opportunity to develop a database of current or interested customers.

Databases play a large role in maintaining an ongoing relationship with the target. Information is gathered based on their past purchase behavior, search topic history, demographics, permission or opt in e-mail lists, or browser type. Advertisers can also monitor the target's movements by employing several tracking devices—cookies and clickstream tracking among them. These devices leave behind an electronic trail to help advertisers track interests.

Today, Internet advertising is becoming more aggressive. Designers are moving away from the unobtrusive simple banner and skyscraper to "in your face" pop-ups and pop-unders, floating ads and flyovers, and unicast or display ads that showcase both streaming audio and video. Search engine advertising gives advertisers an even broader yet targeted reach, while e-mail and mobile texting can personalize a message based on the target's interest or location.

A website should be every bit as polished as any advertising efforts employed elsewhere. First impressions affect how a brand will be experienced and initially judged in much the same way as an initial visit to a brick-and-mortar store. Because the Internet virtually replaces both a physical location and sales personnel, consumers need to visually and verbally recognize the brand's image in the overall layout, find the site easy to use, and perceive any interaction opportunities as helpful.

With all the work that has gone into designing websites and all the time consumers spend browsing the web, the Internet is still not seeing a feasible return on investment. Since clicking on an ad is voluntary, advertising must be distinctive enough to capture attention: It must be visually attractive, informative, and participatory. If web surfers do not click, they probably will not become customers.

Understanding the Internet's Strengths and Weaknesses

Let's take a look at what the varying types of electronic vehicles can or cannot bring to the media mix.

Strengths

1. Personalized. Sites like Amazon can address a returning customer by name and suggest varied products or services based on past purchase behavior.
2. Targetable. The Internet, like direct marketing, uses databases to reach those who have shown past interest or are most likely to purchase.
3. Expense. Internet sites are relatively inexpensive to maintain. Updates can be done quickly and easily as opposed to print, where any changes require the reprinting of one or more pieces. The greatest expense overall is the initial design of the site.
4. Customer Service. Consumers can make a purchase and ask questions 24/7.
5. Customer-Centric. Because there is no intermediary standing between buyer and seller, a relationship can be nourished starting with the first visit, continuing through the decision-making process and purchase, and ending with follow-up calls or e-mails concerning the target's level of satisfaction with the experience.
6. Cross Promotion. The web address can be easily integrated into other media vehicles used throughout the campaign.
7. Engagement. Consumers visit a site out of interest and to gain information. They choose when they visit, how long they stay, and when and where the contact will be made. The message is accepted and digested on their terms.

Weaknesses

1. Competitive. If the key consumer benefit is not correctly targeted and the site is not interactive or easy to use, the target can easily go elsewhere.
2. Annoyance Advertising. Internet advertising, like traditional advertising, is becoming more intrusive. It is difficult to miss—and often results in an irritated consumer.
3. Niche Sites. Niche sites lower the number of consumers who will be exposed to the message.

4. Privacy. Too many sites are still selling personal data, and hackers continue to put consumer privacy at risk.
5. Technical Limitations. Not all consumers will have the newest and fastest technology. Sites should be accessible to all potential buyers, even those with older computers and slower Internet connections.

Let's begin our discussion of the Internet with a quick look at web page design and technology options. We will then focus on some of the varied ad delivery options available to Internet advertisers such as banner ads, pop-ups and pop-unders, interstitials, permission marketing, floating ads, viral and word-of-mouth marketing, search engine marketing, social media outlets, and pay-per-click.

Website Design

When developing a website, the target must be clearly defined. This important data will draw the target audience to a site, increase the likelihood that they return, and encourage them to make a purchase. Technically, it is also important to keep in mind the varying computer and Internet connections the target may be working with.

Before determining what a product or service's website will look like, designers must understand the site's overall purpose, which might include (1) making brand research easy; (2) developing buyer-to-seller relationships; (3) selling products or services or providing entertainment; and (4) providing outstanding customer service initiatives.

Purpose dictates how a site will be used and what visual/verbal and interactive elements will be needed to meet consumer expectations. The first step requires a preliminary vision of the site's overall look. Most designers will organize a site using what is known as a *wireframe,* which is basically a blueprint of the site that uses labeled boxes to show the tentative placement of visual/verbal elements and ultimately how viewers will navigate from page to page.

Once the visual/verbal direction has been determined, the next step is to incorporate the consumers' needs into the design, thereby ensuring the website will:

1. Be a good place to go for information.
2. Be easy to navigate by providing numerous ways viewers can click their way to relevant information.
3. Not overdo it with technology; it is not a big leap from techno-savvy to creatively tacky.

4. Be clean, interactive, and educational—both visually and verbally—as well as readable and legible.
5. Keep scrolling to a minimum, provide appropriate links, and divide the page using headlines and subheads to highlight important points.
6. Make purchasing easy, be multifaceted, and provide several payment options.
7. Change often to hold viewer interest and encourage them to return to the site.
8. Be carefully proofed for any spelling and grammar errors.
9. Clearly tell the target what you want them to do.
10. Post any relevant articles or press releases on the brand, testimonials collected, any documented research completed, or any pertinent links to other sites.
11. Offer interactive components such as games, music, videos, or photos.
12. Include informative blogs or forums.
13. Offer helpful services such as stock tips, weather forecasts, scores, and calculators.
14. Offer some type of unique feature that competitors' sites do not have to stand out.

Aesthetically, a well-designed site mimics the current campaign, reflects the target's self-image, and directly addresses their needs and wants. Each page should use the same typeface, layout, color(s), and images to express the key consumer benefit and engage the target's interest.

Visual and Verbal Choices on the Web

Typefaces

There are not as many type choices on the web as there are for other vehicles we have looked at. Choosing a standard face will keep viewers' browsers from substituting a typeface for one it does not have, changing the overall look of the page. Since you do not know what type of browser visitors will be using, it is important to understand the attributes of each one. The most commonly used browsers include Safari, Internet Explorer, Google Chrome, and Mozilla Firefox. Knowing how each browser—old and new—displays a page will ensure everyone consistently sees the same thing every time they visit the site.

Once any display issues have been resolved, type use will follow the same rules as those used in traditional print. However, text does require increased leading and kerning to improve readability and legibility online. Copy blocks

Figure 10.2 **Sample Ad: Hills Science Diet**

Source: Created by Emily Huntzinger, The University of Tennessee, Knoxville.

should use short lines of no more than six inches; offer multiple short, descriptive, punchy sentences and multiple paragraphs. Long copy blocks will need multiple subheads and/or visuals to break up lines of text, increase white space, and help lead the reader on an informative journey. Specific points can be highlighted using callout boxes: To give them even more importance, consider making each one a link that will whisk the reader away to a relevant site.

Layout and Color

Each page layout should be consistent throughout the site. Like all campaign elements, it is a member of a family of ads and should match the existing campaign efforts. Place any elements such as navigation devices and logos and any repetitively used graphics in the same place on every page. Any color used on type, graphic images, or as a background should appear consistent from page to page. When using a background color, be sure the contrast between it and the typeface used does not impede readability.

Images

Images on the web can be static, do double duty as a link, be animated, or include sight, sound, and motion. The only nonnegotiable rules include making sure all graphics are representative of the campaign, have an obvious purpose, and work when the target interacts with them.

Body Copy

One way to engage the viewer is to have creative, interesting, and educational copy. Good old-fashioned writing skills are still the best way to hold interest and move the reader toward the desired action. Copy should have the same style and tone of voice as the one used in other print vehicles. Include only what is needed to tell the product or service's story, and then tie it to the target's lifestyle.

Sites with too much copy, however, can be boring and overwhelming. Sprinkle the site with headlines (to divide sections), visuals (to illustrate copy points), and subheads (to help break up long blocks of text). Any links included in the copy should further the target's knowledge about the product or service; if they do not, leave them out. Each visual included should give validity to the copy and help demonstrate copy points; if it does not, get rid of it. When possible, use demonstrations, testimonials, and/or studies to prove a point.

Navigation Devices

Don't make viewers search for information; typically, they will not bother. Make sure navigation devices are both easy to find and use and are placed in the same location on each page. You want the visitor to be able to get around with little or no effort. Navigation schemes that visually guide the viewer through the process of finding answers to questions or making a purchase helps them better manage their time while on the site.

Understanding Technical Limitations

It's important to remember that not everybody has a high-end computer, and not all computer users have a fast Internet connection. Offer the visitor options. The fastest way to lose viewers is to have too many pictures that slow down the loading of a page. If a page does not open fully within 10 seconds, reduce the visual content. Graphics should engage the target's interest, keep them at the site longer, and fulfill their need for instant gratification, information, or assistance. Technology options should not be included in a site for gratuitous reasons. Rather, they should be used for a purpose—to communicate a point or feature, for instance. Consider using such options to demonstrate the key consumer benefit or to highlight testimonials.

Every site should offer interactive options that require the consumer to do something. Media specialists encourage dialogue and help build a relationship between the brand and the target by (1) enabling users to engage a customer service representative or a technical advisor; (2) fostering participation in a blog with current users; and (3) making it easy to sign up to receive a free sample, click on a relevant site, or download a coupon.

The size of a file can also affect the viewer's experience. Remember, simple is better; when possible, be sure to keep each page, file, and image around 40 to 60 kilobytes in size. The same holds true for monitor resolution. It is important to choose a resolution that is common to both old and new equipment. Resolution is defined in pixels: the most commonly used include 640×480, 800×600 and 1024×768. A resolution that is on the higher end may not display all visual or verbal elements in the same way.

Once the site is up, make sure to check for consistency, readability, and legibility, as well as for any spelling and/or grammatical issues. If using simple links or more technically advanced bells and whistles, make sure each one is in proper working order and is easy to use and/or navigate through.

A skillfully designed, thoroughly organized site reflects well on the products sold or services offered by a company. If including a blog or other type of online contact such as e-mail or instant messaging, be sure to monitor the site 24/7. Such measures will pay off with satisfied and involved customers. Other initiatives might include a feature that welcomes visitors back to the site by name or recommends products based on interests and past purchase behavior. These small but important initiatives can help many consumers feel a part of the brand and assist them with future selections and eventual purchases.

Delivery and Visual/Verbal Messaging Options

Podcasts, Webinars, and Webcasts

Podcasts, webinars, and webcasts are more a technological enhancement than an advertising vehicle, but all three can add an interactive component to a web page.

A *podcast* is a free or subscription-based audio or audio/video media file combination that allows web content to be downloaded to a computer or any mobile device such as an iPod or an MP3 player. Information from podcasts is monitored for updates and is available for playback at the user's convenience. Those that include a video format are referred to as *vidcasts.* Certain types of podcasts—known as *enhanced podcasts*—contain both audio and slide presentations.

Webinars, or web-based seminars, allow users to join live meetings, lectures, seminars, or workshops on the Internet either at a predetermined time or on demand. This interactive medium transmits both audio and video to the targeted audience. Multiple viewers can interact with the presenter in a two-way flow of information by submitting questions and receiving immediate feedback. *Webcasts,* on the other hand, deliver only a one-way flow of information to the viewer.

Flash

Flash is a vector-graphic software program, meaning it requires no resolution to be reproduced. It incorporates animation and special effects into web pages. Each movable image also includes sound and various interactive components.

Shockwave

Shockwave is a three-dimensional audio and video authoring tool for presenting multimedia content on the Internet. It is most often associated with games and animation.

RSS

RSS, also known as Rich Site Summary or Really Simple Syndication, is a subscription-based group of web-centered formats that deliver constantly changing audio and video web updates. RSS allows people to stay informed on breaking topics of interest, often on news-related sites and blogs, by sending them to one location rather than to multiple sites. Because these systems are so popular among the coveted 18- to 34-year-old demographic, marketers are wise to employ alternative media such as blogs, podcasts, and RSS advertising in their campaigns.

Rich Media

The advanced bells and whistles seen on websites and banner ads are created using rich media. Examples of rich media banners include streaming video, Flash, Shockwave, search boxes, pull-down menus, and applets for interactivity and other forms of special effects. Rich media is also a great tool for creating games, presentations, and other varied user interfaces and web applications.

For an advertised message to succeed, however, rich media needs to do more than merely entertain and outline facts. It needs to entice the viewer to stay on the site and experience the product or service in some meaningful way. As a business tool, it should define a brand's features and benefits in a way that engages the viewer.

So why add rich media to a website when straight HTML has done a fine job up until now? Because HTML is not as interactive or memorable an experience for the user. Adding rich media spotlights the brand and its image, builds an engaging storyline, and delivers information creatively.

The interactive process is a vital part of the message. This represents a distinctive change from communications theorist Marshall McLuhan's declaration that "the medium is the message" (McLuhan, *Understanding Media: The Extensions of Man,* 1964). McLuhan believed that content is affected by not only the message but by the characteristics of the media vehicle employed to deliver the message.

Types of Internet Advertising

Internet ads have the same job as traditional advertising: to make a sale by encouraging the target to do something, such as place an order online, call a toll-free number, or stop by a brick-and-mortar store.

In order to build awareness, encourage purchase, and create a memorable message, Internet advertising must: (1) be clutter free and to the point—simple ideas are more memorable; (2) showcase the logo in a prominent place and make the logo and other references to the brand large enough to be seen and/ or recognized easily; (3) stand out prominently and tastefully; and (4) feature an interactive component to hold the target's interest longer. Let's take a look at a few of the available options.

Horizontal and Vertical Banner Ads

One of the most common and oldest forms of advertising on the Internet is the banner ad. There are two types of banner ads: horizontal and vertical. Horizontal banner ads are a great way to promote brand awareness, increase website traffic, and, to a lesser extent, generate sales. Banners that are highly targeted will be strategically placed throughout the web and on sites related to the advertised brand. Usually, banners are nothing

Figure 10.3 **Sample Ad: Band-Aid**

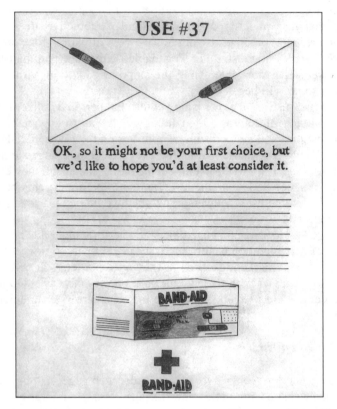

Source: Created by Ryan Freebing, The University of Tennessee, Knoxville.

more than brightly colored bars featuring a logo and slogan or tagline. To capture attention, banners use a variety of visual/verbal images and animation techniques to encourage the viewer to click on the ad. If some type of sales promotion device is attached to the banner, the click-through rate is likely to increase dramatically. Because of its immense reach and specialized targeting, the banner ad remains the Internet's number one mass medium.

Vertical banners, also known as *skyscrapers* or *sidebars,* have a longer time to attract attention because they are larger and cannot be scrolled off screen like traditional horizontal banners. Because of this, their click-through rates are higher. To avoid irritating visitors, though, steer clear of any flashing or otherwise distracting animated images. Technology is fun; too much technology, however, can be annoying.

The most successful banner ads give the viewer a choice of being taken to the sponsoring site immediately; participating in a game, contest, or sweepstakes; or making a quick stopover at some kind of interactive streaming audio and video presentation. Size also attracts viewers' attention; for example, the *New York Times* is now using an expandable ad that takes up half the page when clicked. The more interesting the stopover, the more viral or talked about the banner will become.

Beyond their use as an advertising vehicle, banners can deliver live chats. Intel Corporation in 2009 used technology as a way to engage customers, answer questions, and get consumers' opinions on their new Nehalem Xeon processor. To increase participation, Intel advertised the chat room times online for three days prior to the event. On the day of the event, they employed banner ads that counted down the last 60 minutes before the chat began. The banners also let interested viewers know they would be able to talk directly with Intel experts.

General Electric also exchanged the static ad for banner ads promoting a live webcast discussion on health care issues with their employees.

Conversational marketing is one of the ways marketers are creating opportunities to interact with their target on a one-to-one basis. Options like these banner ads are used specifically to increase consumer interaction and build loyalty.

Pop-Ups and Pop-Unders

A pop-up is an ad that looks a lot like a regular web page. It "pops-up" over the intended website without the viewer's permission, temporarily obscuring the original site from view. Usually smaller than the web page underneath, a typical pop-up features the logo and slogan or tagline and a short message to encourage the viewer to click through to the sponsoring site. When not used as a sales device, pop-ups are a great way for displaying links to information, or as a way for visitors to participate in question-and-answer sessions without blocking content. Unfortunately, most surfers find pop-ups annoying because they have to close the window before they can view the intended site.

A pop-under looks and acts almost the same as a pop-up, the only difference being it opens under the original web page, appearing only when the visitor leaves the site.

Interstitial Ads

A type of pop-up, interstitial ads are more like a TV commercial, often featuring sight, sound, and motion. Interstitial means "in between," indicating that the ad will open up in a separate window, between pages, while a web page is loading. Interstitials usually contain flashy graphics, so make sure the content is relevant and matches the visual/verbal look used in the overall campaign.

Permission Marketing

E-mail marketing or permission marketing is inexpensive and highly targetable. The most successful form requires the targeted consumer to opt in to receive advertising via their e-mail. Consumers who receive e-mails from marketers who did not first solicit their permission are likely to delete them as junk mail, just as traditional direct mail often ends up in the trash.

A form of direct response, e-mail marketing is a great way to build an increasingly in-depth relationship with the targeted audience through personalized messages. The goal is to keep the brand top-of-mind and encourage repeat purchase and brand loyalty.

E-mailed pieces can be simple announcements of upcoming special sales, notification of discounts, or a way to deliver a coupon to the target. Larger pieces such as e-newsletters are used to inform recipients about upcoming events, give details on products, highlight sales personnel, and so on.

Verbal and text-based messages, especially instant messages, should be carefully constructed and proofread before being sent. Likewise, telemarketers have to keep to a script when interacting with the target, following strict rules of phone etiquette. Web-based customer and technical service representatives need to follow "e-netiquette" and create a carefully constructed script before posting. A good e-mail will include: (1) an attention-getting opening or headline; (2) a key consumer benefit and supportive features and benefits; (3) a message that creates want by tying the key consumer benefit to lifestyle; and (4) a call to action.

Be sure each mailing includes a link to the sponsoring website and any other relevant contact information. To keep the message out of the spam folder, avoid the words "free," "order now," "click here," "call now," or "discount offer" in the headline.

E-mail postings are more than a sales pitch. They represent both the company's image and the brand's image. E-mail messages are an interactive way to stand out from the competition. Customer service is often the only difference between products, so it is important to ramp up your brand's service in order to build long-lasting customer relationships.

In a quote from an article for TheMarketingSite.com, Brondmo, founder and chair of Post Communications, sums up the importance of employing e-mail this way: "As interactive marketers seek to keep Web sites 'sticky' e-mail provides elasticity. E-mail reaches out and draws the customer in, and can be individualised for the customer automatically. Production and delivery take hours, not weeks—and measurement is in real time. The database plus the direct communications makes for a powerful combination."

Floating Ads

Floating ads appear when a website is first opened, and they "float" or fly over the page. Lasting anywhere from five to 30 seconds, they will often command center stage while blocking the site beneath them. Many of these ads have the ability to take over a viewer's mouse for the duration of their flight. They are great at gaining the viewer's attention and are usually animated with sound options.

The job of the floating ad is to mimic television commercials by "interrupting programming," making them difficult to ignore or get rid of quickly. Interactive options are engaging and memorable because the target is actively involved in the advertising message, as opposed to the passive nature of traditional advertising. The downside—like most Internet advertising—is their potential to annoy and slow down the search process.

Viral and Word of Mouth

Viral marketing and word of mouth are the terms used to identify user-generated marketing. The difference between the two is subtle. Viral messages are long lasting, whereas word-of-mouth messages are often short-lived. Viral messages are most often delivered via the web, but word-of-mouth messages typically rely on face-to-face discussions. Viral advertising on the Internet is the twenty-first century's version of water cooler gossip; word-of-mouth marketing is gossip around the water cooler.

Viral

Viral marketing is an advertising message passed along between acquaintances. Today, all campaigns should have the potential to generate some type of viral-based message. Most viral messages are passed along via social media sites like Twitter or Facebook; other than face-to-face contact, there is no more personalized place to share information. Because viral advertising is initiated by consumers, it spreads what is known as *user generated content.* The users are doing far more than purchasing a product; they are actively promoting that product to others. Any type of viral advertising originating from a trusted friend or family member makes claims more believable than a message delivered solely through sponsored advertising.

The more creative and engaging the message or event, the more likely the target is to "infect" (in a good way) their contacts' e-mails by forwarding the message. These entertaining e-mails, also known as *viral e-mails,* usually include one or more links that will take the viewer to the sponsoring website. A personal endorsement of this type makes viral e-mails a great way to launch a new product or increase brand awareness.

A good viral message engages the target audience's curiosity, funny bone, or intellect long enough to get them to interact with it. Incorporating a viral aspect into any type of campaign is an important way to get the target talking about the brand. Sometimes, campaign designers create slogans that become a part of everyday conversation, or they come up with characters so recognizable that a logo is no longer needed to identify the brand. These are great ways to create buzz and some of the best ways to incorporate a viral component into the mix.

Word of Mouth

Word-of-mouth advertising can be defined as one satisfied customer telling friends or family members about their experience with a product or service. Word-of-mouth campaigns are inexpensive and low in overhead, but they can bring in a huge amount of consumer loyalty if handled properly. In fact, it is probably the best advertising money *can't* buy. When word of mouth is positive, it will take a brand a long way in building image and awareness among potential customers. However, if the word on the street and on the Internet is negative, nothing can kill a brand's momentum faster.

Any type of positive word of mouth can sustain a brand's message indefinitely, providing the message is constantly upgraded, changed out, unique, interesting, and recognizably tied to other campaign efforts.

Apple, for example, excels in the use of both viral and word-of-mouth advertising to encourage buzz about a product. Always innovative, Apple was the first to create the colored computer, and the company made technological history when it unveiled the iPod and the iPhone. Not only were these cool and one-of-a-kind at the time of launch, but Apple also made them the "must have" products of the day. The products lived up to the hype: They were exciting to own and increased Apple's reach beyond its earlier niche of targeted consumers.

Search Engine Marketing and Search Engine Optimization

Search Engine Marketing (SEM) increases a site's rankings and helps direct interested consumers to a specific website. Sponsors must purchase relevant key words on search engines such as Google and Yahoo to obtain these results.

Search engine optimization (SEO) means making sure a site is linked to other relevant sites to attract traffic. Because the placement of search engine advertising is based on consumers' specific interests, it is very targetable. SEO and SEM are effective ways to promote a business to potential customers on the web.

Social Media

User generated content is the hottest form of online communication: It is found in wikis, on blogs, and on social sites like Twitter and Facebook. These discussion sites allow consumers to voice their concerns, offer quality feedback, start a rumor, or generate buzz about a brand's features and benefits. Social media sites are an excellent forum to promote brand awareness, enhance the brand's image, get answers to questions, and stave off any negative publicity.

Most social media ads have been experimental at best, consisting of sponsorships, ad placements, or brand applications that have not been well received by social media users. Social sites should not be used as an advertising forum, but rather as a viral word-of-mouth forum. Marketers should consider alternative ways to be socially and quietly accepted on social media sites, using methods such as: (1) joining in blogs or forums; (2) openly taking part in a group discussion about the product or competing products and adding to the knowledge of the group; (3) designing a campaign using the target's ideas; and (4) keeping the quality of the brand and customer service initiatives up-to-date.

More and more marketers are using social media sites as a customer service outlet. Twitter in particular has become an important source that lets companies hear from—and respond to—their users. As the Internet's version of "keep it simple stupid," Twitter allows consumers to interact with a brand, a service, a company, or other consumers in little bite-sized discussions. This great viral vehicle can make or break a brand. Twitter is all about immediacy. Information is going back and forth nonstop, allowing marketers to address questions, concerns, and even potential disasters while or before they happen. This form of social media gives marketers a glimpse of public opinion and uses their insights to improve the product or service.

Informative Internet discussions can help marketers adapt their visual/verbal message to reflect public sentiment and overall needs. This type-to-talk social network creates buzz by letting consumers know immediately what is going on with a product or service.

Many corporations like Comcast Cable now have people monitoring Twitter postings full time to address customer comments and stave off any negative discussions before they take hold and flourish. Brands like Bank of America and Apple have gone one step further, providing live customer service representatives on their sites.

Handling and solving problems before they turn negative is what customer service is all about. Helpful, practical advice builds goodwill and good word of mouth. Monitoring social media sites also allows marketers to exploit strengths and opportunities and nip weaknesses and threats in the bud before they become full-blown issues.

Social sites are also a great way to promote a brand, advertise a promotion, or build expectations for an upcoming event. Nestlé's frozen pizza brand DiGiorno, for example, used Twitter along with traditional print and broadcast to launch their new flatbread pizza. DiGiorno tapped into the social outlet's strong following by offering food in exchange for "tweet-ups" (short for "Twitter meetups," or live meetings). For every tweetup hosted by influential tweeters, Nestlé delivered their new flatbread pizza to the event.

The producers of the movie *Sex and the City* used social media sites to build buzz about the movie prior to its opening. They also sponsored a promotional gift-giving campaign that allowed users to send virtual shoes as a gift to fellow Facebook friends. And Esurance, as part of a public relations campaign for their sponsorship of the 2009 summer *Star Trek* movie, created their own homepages on Facebook and Myspace and asked trekky fans to submit videos reflecting their devotion to the ongoing iconic storyline.

Hulu, a groundbreaking member of the Internet entertainment arsenal, was dubbed "one of the great innovations of 2008," by then–NBC-Universal CEO Jeff Zucker. According to a December 2008 Adweek.com online article, Hulu brings television programming to online video. This technological breakthrough delivers consumers' favorite programs to them whenever and wherever they choose. Advertising on the site is done primarily through sponsorships and is relatively unobtrusive.

Pay-Per-Click

A simple text ad, pay-per-click advertising is one of the more successful forms of Internet advertising. Most ads are placed on one or more sites that generate a large amount of traffic. The goal is to capture the surfers' attention and encourage them to click on the link. Fees are based on how long the visitor stays on the sponsoring site. Visits lasting more than five to ten seconds require the advertiser to pay the host a fee.

Technology is evolving so quickly that marketers and creative teams are still trying to figure out how to reach their intended targets through the ever-growing cache of technological breakthroughs available to them. The best combinations will no doubt result in a creative, interactive solution that pushes current technological innovations to the limit.

11

Mobile Media

Figure 11.1 **Sample Ad: K•B Toys**

Source: Created by Heather Burke, The University of Tennessee, Knoxville.

Mobile Communication Moves with the Target

The Mobile Marketing Association (MMA) defines mobile marketing as "a set of practices that enables organizations to communicate and engage with their audience in an interactive and relevant manner through any mobile device or network."

The MMA bases its definition on the following principles:

1. The aforementioned "set of practices" includes activities, institutions, processes, industry players, standards, advertising and media, direct response, promotions, relationship management, CRM, customer services, loyalty, social marketing, and the many faces and facets of marketing.
2. To "engage" means to start relationships, acquire, generate activity, stimulate social interaction with organization and community members, and be present at the time of the consumer's expressed need. Furthermore, engagement can be initiated by the consumer ("Pull" in the form of a click or response) or by the marketer ("Push").

In its simplest form, mobile marketing can reach moving targets with a message delivered near or at the point of purchase through their cell phones, using a Short Message Service (SMS) or text message that may or may not include a link to a sponsoring Internet site. Because wireless communication uses a low bandwidth, messages must contain no more than 160 characters to keep download time to a minimum. This is not considered a deficit, though, since most wireless advertising does little more than remind, reward loyalty with valuable incentives, and encourage purchase. Campaigns that employ SMS technology will find it flexible, measurable, convenient, and affordable.

It is important when planning a campaign strategy that mobile be included in the original media mix. Individualized messages with no foundation are not memorable, will not add to the brand's image, and cannot create brand-loyal consumers.

An independent message is only successful if it can guarantee the target will see that particular media vehicle and need that particular item on that one day or within a week of the advertisement. Repetition, reliability, and quality are what make a brand memorable. One ad in a single vehicle cannot build an image, promote consistency, or guarantee value. To ensure an advertisement is recognizable, understood, and acted upon requires the synchronization of all images and all messages in all media vehicles. If a vehicle is added later in the campaign, for whatever reason, it must be seamlessly integrated into the campaign using the same imaging and messaging devices as the other vehicles.

An integrated message will capitalize on mobile's highly targetable reach, making it more effective and efficient than traditional advertising methods. Research has shown that mobile texts are opened sooner than traditional e-mails and that consumers are more receptive to messages delivered via their mobile phone. A good mobile advertising campaign that reaches the target near hot sale locations makes them anywhere from three to ten times more likely to be engaged by the message, making mobile advertising very attractive.

Targeted consumers who have opted in to receive advertising can be reached wherever they are with a message that interests them. Very flexible, mobile can deliver an array of advertising, promotional, and entertainment options. Beyond text messaging, mobile can employ banners, audio and video, animation, interstitials, coupons, GPS and mapping capabilities, and accelerometers—the latter being a device that allows the phone to detect movement when shaken, making it great for games and controlling the direction of mapping.

The fluctuating economy is helping new and alternative advertising vehicles such as mobile to grow. As marketers slash budgets and pull out of more traditional vehicles, the door opens for smaller, less expensive options such as the web or mobile to see more attention and resources come their way. Areas such as in-game mobile advertising or advergaming, mobile-video, and especially mobile search are some of the areas ripe for growth.

Reaching the Target with More Creative Options

Every day, mobile marketing's reach and capabilities are expanding with options such as (1) premium short message service (PSMS), or the ability to purchase something such as a ring tone; (2) wireless application protocol (WAP), or a wireless web connection; (3) multimedia-messaging service (MMS), an extension of SMS that allows users to send longer text messages and send and receive mobile photographs, as well as audio and video clips; and (4) mobile video (MV), or the ability to watch TV via a cell phone.

This targeted, instantaneous, relatively inexpensive, and measurable vehicle can reach the target with ads or promotions for restaurants, shopping, events, movie theaters, and the like. Mobile marketing can send, receive, inform, and personalize any message. Because the information is sent directly to the consumer, it is timely and often immediately useful, making the advertisement appear more like a service than an intrusion or interruption.

By incorporating mobile advertising into the media mix, a product or service can be cross-promoted and become more competitive. Like most alternative media vehicles, mobile marketing creates a more direct and sustainable relationship with the target and is a great support vehicle for more traditional vehicles. Wireless also delivers:

1. Greater recall and response rates.
2. Increased brand awareness.
3. Increased consumer loyalty.
4. An opportunity to reach high-income professionals.
5. A highly targeted "opt in" consumer market.
6. Increased Internet traffic.
7. Real-time promotions.
8. A way to track where the target originally saw the message through the use of multiple key words.
9. Easy to change out messages.
10. The ability to make a purchase or visit a sponsoring website.

Mobile marketing is different from traditional advertising efforts because it does not interrupt a call like traditional advertising interrupts programming. To receive advertising on their mobile phones, consumers have to "opt in" to receive it. Messages arriving unsolicited create negative word of mouth.

Reaching the Target at the Point of Sale

Mobile's biggest asset is it can now target potential consumers by sending a customized text message about a sale the target is near, as well as offer an immediate link to available coupons. This permission-based service notifies consumers when they approach the sales location and sends an alert that includes the name, address, and link for a coupon or other important promotional information. Basically, it works like a trip wire: Once the target walks or drives by a location—say, a pet shop—it activates a locator device that sends a coupon alerting the target to a sale on their specific brand of dog food.

This makes mobile marketing a great point of sale device, encouraging the target to make an impulse or unplanned purchase. Location-based mobile ads are an effective interactive device and an excellent way to build a lasting, one-on-one, highly targeted relationship with the buyer. To maintain consumer support, it is important that messages be relevant, on-target, and easy to opt in to and out of.

Since mobile carriers have opened up their client lists to advertisers, it is easier for brands to target individual users. Mobile carriers collect a large amount of demographic and psychographic data that can assist advertisers with more precise targeting—where they go, how they use their phones (to make calls to send texts, to surf the web), and even what the target buys. Information gathered is used to build a list or "mob" of consumers who wish to receive promotional materials.

As with e-mail, mobile communications must be carefully targeted. It is

Figure 11.2   **Sample Ad: LensCrafters**

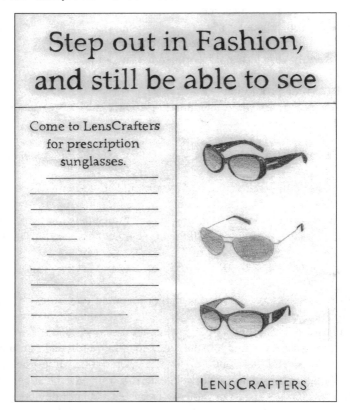

Source: Created by Heather Burke, The University of Tennessee, Knoxville.

important the brand collect enough information to ensure the correct message is sent at the right time and place. Most opt in programs will encourage the target to initially subscribe using their mobile phone and then direct them to an online website where they can complete a more detailed profile. Protecting consumers' privacy is a number one concern for marketers, ensuring they contact only those who have opted in to receive messages; anything else will be considered spam.

Understanding Mobile's Strengths and Weaknesses

Let's take a look at what the varying types of mobile vehicles can or cannot bring to the media mix.

Strengths

1. Quantity. Over 76 percent of the population in the United States owns a mobile phone.
2. Search. Web searches done on a mobile device are expected to exceed those done on a personal computer.
3. International Access. Global users who do not own a computer often do own a mobile phone.
4. Expense. Mobile ads are a more cost-efficient way to reach the target than traditional methods.
5. Location. The target can be reached anywhere with relevant coupons or promotional devices.
6. Response Rate. The target is more likely to respond to mobile messages.
7. Database Development. Consumers who "opt in" to receive information help to build current information on the target as a whole.
8. Generate Buzz. Because messages can reach the target while they are shopping, mobile ads have the potential to generate more buzz or word of mouth as messages are discussed or forwarded to friends or family.

Weaknesses

1. Intrusive. Not everyone wants to receive text messages on their phone.
2. Limited Content. Messages must be short and sweet.
3. Limited Access. Not all brands offer mobile access at this time.
4. Learning Curve. Marketers using mobile are still learning the best way to reach the target with the best message.
5. Opt Out. It is easy for consumers to block advertisers' access to their phones.
6. Technology. Like computers, consumers have both high-end and low-end mobile options to choose from.
7. Reach. Few consumers have yet to catch on to the novelty of mobile access.

Mobile as a Promotional Vehicle

Technology has introduced what is known as "the third screen" into the promotional mix. The three screens include television, computer, and the smaller screen found on mobile phones, iPods, and PSPs.

Researchers have found that small screens are used mostly as a way to kill time. Viewers who use "third screen" devices the most tend to watch sports, real-time news, and music videos. The size and portability of small screens present both opportunities and challenges. They must: (1) offer content that is interesting enough to encourage viewers to opt in; (2) offer multiplatform entertainment and viral opportunities; (3) alleviate boredom and find a way to both educate and entertain; and (4) employ branded entertainment as a way to engage receivers.

Short Codes

Promotions have a lot to accomplish, so it is important to capture the target's attention by getting them to do something, whether it's entering a short code or requesting a coupon. Short codes made up of a series of numbers are frequently cross-promoted in traditional advertising vehicles, direct mail, or as part of an event promotion. Advertising efforts may first employ a radio ad to promote a 25 percent savings on various pieces of sporting equipment if the target texts a specific short code. Once sent, the texter will receive a coupon or promotional code redeemable at sponsoring retail locations. Short code promotions are relatively common, most often used on reality television shows to vote for a favorite participant and as a way to receive promotional items at sporting or entertainment events or download video to mobile devices. These numerical codes can be used at the local, national, and even international level.

One of the most successful uses occurred when short codes played a major role in a political election. Barack Obama was the first American presidential candidate to reach voters by text message. Staffers used texting to encourage voters to cast their ballots and to keep supporters updated on important issues. To reach potential voters, campaign workers set up the short code 62262, which is the tech spelling for Obama on telephone keypads. The short code was used in advertising to encourage supporters to sign up to receive campaign messages. For only a small investment, the Obama camp used texting and social networking to get his message out to those who had opted in to receive the communiqués. Obama's unprecedented use of mobile texting brought renewed attention to the new media vehicle when he used it to announce his running mate to loyal subscribers before anyone else.

Coupons

If the target does not wish to opt in to receive promotions, they can get out their phones, go to the Internet, and simply download a coupon. Unilever is participating in a trial that allows consumers to download select coupons to their cell phone before purchasing the company's products. Like traditional coupons, they are redeemable at the time of checkout; the only hitch is the consumer has to hand their cell phone over to the sales clerk to have the barcodes scanned. After use, each coupon is automatically deleted.

Interactive forms of advertising such as coupons or short codes that are sent via cell phones or made available on the Internet are more memorable and more likely to be acted upon than traditional ads. Campaigns that combine both mobile and Internet options keep information timely and engaging. Messages that include links can say and show more than a simple text message. An interactive mobile ad allows the consumer to click on the link and be taken to a wireless website for more information, and call-through links can hook up the wireless user directly with a customer service representative.

Who's Dabbling in Mobile?

Those who have embraced this new and innovative media vehicle are using it to assist their target to solve problems and differentiate themselves from the competition. Let's take a quick look at how brands in the United States and across the globe are using mobile to interact with and engage their target audiences.

Many mobile promotions use relatively simple but effective ways to build awareness and encourage interaction. PC manufacturer Lenovo, for example, did little more than place banner ads on *USA Today's* mobile web or WAP site (an acronym for Wireless Application Protocol) to receive a click-through rate almost double the industry average.

Instead of running a contest, the men's toiletry brand Axe gave away ringtones to single guys. Participants could choose from a number of songs to separate and announce the identity of their many female callers.

A movie promotion for *Snakes on a Plane* encouraged consumers to go online and use a variety of pull-down menus to submit personal attributes that could be used in a prerecorded phone call from star Samuel L. Jackson.

Many companies use contests to promote a brand and extend a brand's message. Before it was discontinued, Pontiac, to promote and draw attention to its new G6, asked consumers to use their camera phones to take pictures of the car on the streets of their local town. Each photograph that was returned to Pontiac automatically entered the budding photographer into a contest.

To promote their Wimbledon sponsorship and capture the attention of spectators, American Express designed a contest that asked participants to send in their predictions for each day's winners. This very successful promotion garnered American Express a huge increase in brand awareness and a spike in the amount of applications for cards they received.

Wendy's chose to use mobile to distribute coupons to those members of their target audience who opted in to receive them. These instant redemption coupon offers gave consumers immediate access to deals and allowed Wendy's a quick way to track the overall success of their promotions. The only thing participants had to do to redeem their coupons was show their phones to cashiers before use.

Cross-promotion campaigns will often integrate mobile into traditional print and broadcast, out-of-home, and direct mail. This approach increases reach and injects both an interactive element and a high level of engagement into the campaign.

The game show *Deal or No Deal* used television and mobile to extend the competition beyond the confines of the target's living room. The promotion dubbed the "Lucky Case" game asked viewers to text in winning case numbers in exchange for prizes.

Pet food company Pedigree combined direct mail, coupons, and mobile to reach their targeted audience with three different discount offers. The three-month promotion's goal was to increase target engagement with the brand. To ensure memorability, Pedigree applied the "principle of three" to the campaign. This time-tested practice holds that anything seen three times is memorable. The first contact included an initial text message about the coupon offers. The second consisted of a follow-up e-mail reminder about both the coupons and contest. The third reached only those early entrants who received a reminder for each of the three months of the promotion.

Each coupon was good for one month only, so reminders helped encourage recipients to use them before they expired. Along with coupons, the direct mailer promoted a text-to-win program in which entrants could win prizes such as a year's supply of dog food or a digital camera. Single prizes were awarded each month of the promotion if the target texted SMALLDOG to 82222 to enter.

Procter & Gamble successfully paired mobile with the Internet to promote their SitOrSquat.com site. This technology-based campaign allowed the target to rate, locate, and/or recommend clean and fully stocked public restrooms across the country. Verizon also used a combination of mobile and the Internet to launch its "Daily Scoop," a destination site that delivers scores, weather, trivia, coupons, and advertising.

Consumer product giant Johnson & Johnson coupled print with a mobile coupon delivery campaign to reach pregnant women. Print ads were first used to introduce women to the program. In order to be eligible to receive pregnancy-related coupons, the mothers-to-be needed to text their delivery date to the company. Once they had their babies, these new moms could continue to receive coupons for various types of baby products.

Lane Bryant, an established women's clothing store, wanted to reach their consumers while on the go with an opt in mobile program that was initially announced in an e-mail and direct mail promotion. The goal was to build a rich database of information on subscribers and send highly specialized coupons via text to loyal shoppers.

Before initiating any mobile efforts, Lane Bryant needed to determine whether: (1) their target audience was interested in receiving mobile messages; (2) there would be enough interest to successfully sustain an ongoing campaign; and (3) this type of contact would translate into both sales and loyalty.

To ensure compatibility and interest, Lane Bryant's LB MSG ME! mobile push was a double opt in program. To initially opt in, the target could either call, text, or visit the store's website. Once responders received the initial text message, shoppers were required to give their permission a second time before receiving the first coupon offer.

Twice a month, registered consumers were sent a text that contained a coupon code for use on-site or toward online purchases. As a courtesy, every message sent out routinely contained an opt out option. Opting out simply required the target to send the word STOP via SMS.

Putting a spin on the simple and mundane contest, Kidrobot, a small New York firm, chose to use a mobile scavenger hunt they called the "Dunny Hunt" to launch its newest collection of limited edition Dunny action figures, toys, and apparel. The hunt employed a piece of digital technology that is big in Japan but relatively new here in the United States: It uses quick read or QR barcodes. In order for the QR codes to be read, participants had to first download one of two free apps to match their particular type of Smartphone. These readers allowed loyal followers to photograph the codes, which contained collectable virtual images of the new Dunny figure.

To participate in the five-day hunt, the targeted audience could opt in to receive daily mobile clues or choose instead to locate them on Twitter, in Kidrobot newsletters, or in stores where the required promotional codes were located on posters, pedicabs, t-shirts, and/or stickers around the city. Those lucky enough to locate the coded vehicle(s) and photograph or scan the QR barcode were automatically entered into a drawing for Dunny toys. Hunters who uncovered the most or were the first to photograph the code each day were eligible to win additional prizes. To hold participants' interest, a new code was released on each of the five days of the promotion.

Kidrobot chose the scavenger hunt because their target audience is relatively small, consisting of affluent, "first to own" creative types. This personalized niche promotion was simultaneously interactive, engaging, and viral.

Globally, mobile promotions do not differ much from those used in the United States. A slowdown in growth in many international markets has resulted from the routine selling of member information by carriers. However, established brands with an existing loyal following are more likely to find success with mobile marketing.

To get people excited about the 2009 FIFA Confederations Cup and the 2010 FIFA World Cup, the "Fly the Flag for Football" campaign asked fans to SMS FLAG to 41929 to enter a contest for free tickets to matches for themselves and three of their friends. Once entered, entrants immediately received a text message with a link that took them to the "flythesouthafricanflag" mobile website. In order to qualify for the contest, participants then had to find the answers to a couple of easy questions and provide the names and contact information for each friend they planned to take to the matches. Each friend was then sent an SMS message that encouraged them to click on the mobile link and opt in for further information. This successful mobile campaign not only created awareness but also integrated an excellent viral aspect into the campaign.

A slightly more complicated but creative use of mobile advertising was initiated by Swedish clothing company H&M. This campaign used SMS coupons and mobile banner ads that were strategically placed on both mobile and media sites. The mobile site included a click-through slideshow and animated GIF images that showcased H&M's extensive line of clothing. The goal of the campaign was not only to highlight clothing options but also to encourage interested consumers to join the retailer's rewards program.

The job of the banner ads was to get the consumer to the H&M website to sign up to receive coupons and other special promotions. Most offers were good for a limited time, usually no more than a few hours, to encourage immediate purchase. Redemption required the target to show the coupon code at the time of purchase.

The promotion also included a contest for H&M gift cards. Entry into this contest required participants to answer a few questions about their interest in the contest, giving the promotion an interactive aspect. Additionally, H&M hoped to get a little viral mileage from the campaign as loyal adopters sent messages off to friends and family members.

Connection Must Be Easy; Contacts Must Be Relevant

The goal of most mobile campaigns is to increase awareness, build loyalty, encourage immediate purchase, and offer great deals for a much lower cost than traditional methods. It is important that every mobile contact deliver a relevant message, promotion, coupon, update, and so on. Cross-promotional

Figure 11.3 **Sample Ad: Michaels**

Source: Created by Allison Schepman, The University of Tennessee, Knoxville.

use in direct mail, broadcast, print, out-of-home, on the Internet, and through any other alternative media vehicle should help direct the target to additional information and prolong the life of the message. Any time the target pursues more information, they are engaged and interacting with both the brand and the message.

No matter how simple, complicated, or creative a mobile promotion might be, for it to be effective it must:

1. Be relevant to the target.
2. Deliver a specific outcome, such as signing up to receive future messages.

3. Be tied to a campaign message.
4. Be simple and easy to do.

Mobile has been slow to mature as an advertising vehicle, even though cell phones are seemingly everywhere. In reality, less than one-third of Americans were mobile web users in 2010. Also, there is the fact that more than 50 percent of Americans find mobile or m-commerce advertising an annoyance, or even worse, an invasion of privacy. Finally, there are technical issues like mobile platforms and capabilities that make reaching the target difficult.

It is technology, however, that keeps mobile new and exciting as users anticipate each innovative step forward. For example, the introduction of the Apple iPhone took the bland and fledgling industry by storm. The iPhone was the first to make the web mobile and accessible through a handheld device, and the ease of use (with the tap and flick of a finger) is sheer technological brilliance. Smartphones like the iPhone were also quick to introduce mobile apps, which keep the target of many brands invested in the innovative and often time-saving and helpful mobile options.

Kraft was one of the first to jump on the phone app bandwagon with iFood, a mobile destination offering recipes that can be accessed while shopping. The app known as the "iFood Assistant" makes it easier to plan meals and purchase ingredients while on the go. Each recipe comes complete with a convenient shopping list that can be pulled up, along with step-by-step cooking instructions. Good recipes are a great viral component, as cooks send them on to friends and family members.

Kraft's very organized shopping assistant offers more than 700 recipes and even identifies the aisle where the ingredients are found in the grocery store. Once located, each ingredient can be easily deleted from the list to further simplify shopping. This consumer-friendly application also informs the target about any current promotional offers, provides the location of the nearest grocery store, and offers video cooking demonstrations in the various special sections, which include "Recipe of the Day," "Dinner Tonight," and "Budget Dinners." Message boards allow experienced and novice cooks to exchange recipes and ideas.

Kraft also employed mobile display and search ads to drive consumers to their website. The use of multiple media vehicles has helped drive the interactive qualities, holding the target's attention longer.

Applications are now mainstream and considered by many observers an integral part of mobile use, but even more technologically advanced vehicles are emerging. The next phase offers varied types of remote management. Security giant Schlage has already introduced the "Schlage LINK." In a press release, dated September 17, 2009, Schlage describes the innovative new system as a "remote home-management system, which enables homeowners to lock and unlock doors, monitor live camera feeds, and control temperature, lighting and other devices from a computer or Web-enabled mobile phone."

In a very short period of time, mobile has gone from a simple communication device to a personal, business, and home management device. Brands creating and using this exciting, new age telecommunications tool will keep consumers engaged just waiting to see what it will do next.

As brands like Apple and Schlage have shown, advertising does not need to be a visual/verbal sales pitch; innovation and creativity can speak louder than a traditional advertised message and hold the target's attention longer.

12

Guerrilla and Viral Marketing

Figure 12.1 **Sample Ad: Barnes & Noble**

Source: Created by Brady Seymore, The University of Tennessee, Knoxville.

Guerrilla Marketing Is a Campaign Event

Guerrilla marketing uses unconventional means to promote a product, attract attention, and create memorable encounters. The more unique the experience or unusual the locale or surface, the bigger the impact on the target. Because fewer consumers are listening to, reading, or watching traditional advertising, alternative media vehicles like guerrilla marketing must surprise and titillate by giving the target something they do not expect. Brands that create stunts or spectaculars like those used in guerrilla marketing are more likely stand out in the cluttered advertising arena by including the consumer in the experience. The unconventional—and often unexpected—promotional solutions offered by guerrilla marketing help captivate and extend message life through word of mouth.

It was Jay Conrad Levinson (2007) who popularized the phrase "guerrilla marketing" in his book of the same name. Although not new to the advertising creative scene, it has become a bigger part of many business plans in recent years. Levinson's original vision was to find a way for small businesses to complete against their larger, more financially secure, competitors on an inexpensive yet creative level.

Depending on the tactics employed, creative innovation can be broken down into two distinct areas: guerrilla warfare and guerrilla marketing. When the small business owner employs tactics that take the competition by storm, it is known as *guerrilla warfare*. When the small business owner ingeniously creates buzz at little or no cost for days, weeks, or months, it's known as *guerrilla marketing*.

The nontraditional use of space and events is guerrilla marketing's way of creating opportunities to engage the target on a one-to-one basis. Competition, then, is based on the creativity and quality of the relationship and the product, not on the dollar amount spent on the advertising. "The heart and soul of guerrilla marketing," according to Levinson, "is its sparseness of budget and abundance of creativity" (2007).

Today, the term guerrilla marketing is used to describe any form of advertising that does not fit the traditional print or broadcast format. Technically, it can be defined as any alternative, high-impact, niche marketing tactic whose goal is to produce maximum results (sales, awareness) using a minimal investment (time, resources, budget).

Guerrilla marketing is more than a passive newspaper or magazine ad. It works because it penetrates the consciousness of the often apathetic and disinterested modern consumer. It is an active type of promotion that can take on almost any shape or form. Advertisers use guerrilla events to capitalize on consumers' insatiable appetite for creative distractions that are inventive and innovative. The more unique the experience, the bigger the "wow" factor and the more appealing the experience.

Whatever the surface, whatever the brand and message, guerrilla marketing is a great way to get into the consumer's face in an entertaining and memorable way. The more the tactics are talked about on the web, by phone, at work, at home, or in the press, the more powerful and lasting the impact.

As a rule, guerrilla marketing's goal is not to immediately encourage a sale but to encourage word-of-mouth discussions, the strongest and least expensive form of advertising. These unusual and often unconventional tactics are a great way for marketers to interact with consumers, get immediate product feedback, and perhaps encourage them to try the product, use the service, or seek additional information.

The key difference between guerrilla marketing and traditional tactics is its goal: Guerrilla marketing does not preach, educate, or attempt to change the consumer's mind; its immediate goal is simply to entice and create a buzz-worthy event.

It takes imagination and more than a little inspiration to develop a successful guerrilla event. Traditional media is great for announcing, supporting, or launching a guerrilla event, but it cannot sustain one. To do that, the event must be unusual, clever, and downright amazing enough to ensure it stays alive online and in the press long after the promotion has ended. With all that publicity, it is important that the product and any customer service issues are as exceptional as the event. A great idea is only great when the product or service can live up to the initial hype.

By inserting guerrilla marketing events into a traditional campaign, creative teams can reach the target in quirkier, more unforgettable, ways. Add in interactive opportunities, and it becomes a very targeted and consumer-focused member of the media mix. Taking a static print ad and giving it a voice, three-dimensional qualities, a smell, a taste, or a larger-than-life personality gets the consumer talking, and that's good advertising.

To be successful, a guerrilla marketing campaign must:

1. Have impact;
2. Be innovative;
3. Be unexpected;
4. Be able to reach the intended target;
5. Attract maximum attention on a small budget; and
6. Have creative flexibility and ingenuity.

Finding a way to reach apathetic consumers with a message that sticks is getting harder and harder to do. Product parity and the oversaturation of advertising that prevails in the marketplace have propelled guerrilla tactics to the marketing forefront today.

Understanding Guerrilla Marketing's Strengths and Weaknesses

Let's take a look at what the varying types of guerrilla marketing can or cannot bring to the media mix.

Strengths

1. Expense. Guerrilla marketing can be inexpensive to execute when compared with traditional media tactics, making it a great resource for small businesses.
2. High-Impact. Because it is interactive, it attracts the target's attention and makes a more memorable impression.
3. Innovative. Guerrilla marketing events are almost always an imaginative, somewhat unorthodox, and unconventional way to get a message out to the target.
4. Loyalty. Tactics are often one-on-one encounters, making it a great way to build a relationship with the target.
5. Buzz. Many events go beyond viral; if they are picked up by the local and national media, the life of the message is extended even further.

Weaknesses

1. Annoyance Factor. Guerrilla marketing tactics can go too far and annoy the target and/or state and local officials.
2. Measurable. It is not necessarily a great outlet for determining ROI because often the target is not asked to do anything, such as make a purchase.
3. Time-Consuming. It often takes a great deal of time to put a guerrilla marketing campaign together.
4. Not Targetable. It can reach a large audience, but it is difficult to ensure the intended target audience was exposed to the message.

Taking It to the Streets

There are too many guerrilla marketing tactics to list here, but some of the more commonly used and interesting types include stealth and street marketing, pop-ups, video projection, event graffiti, and skywriting.

Stealth Marketing

Stealth marketing—also known as word-of-mouth, buzz, or ambush marketing—often uses actors to talk about or use a product in social situations.

One of the first publicized examples of stealth marketing took place in the 1980s. It involved a beautiful woman asking an unsuspecting man in a bar to buy her a drink. The woman requests a specific brand of vodka. While waiting for it, she talks up the virtues of the brand. Once the drink arrives, she excuses herself and disappears into the crowd. The promotion hinges on the likelihood that the unsuspecting purchaser, left stranded with the woman's drink, will wash down his disappointment with her favorite brand of vodka.

More recently, Sony employed stealth marketing techniques when they hired actors to coerce strangers into taking their pictures. Once engaged, these faux tourists handed over their picture phone while talking up its features.

Detractors label stealth marketing as undercover marketing, since consumers often do not realize they are being targeted. In today's advertising world, however, a sales pitch does not necessarily need to be produced, printed, or announced. The next commercial you hear could be delivered by the elderly couple standing behind you in line at the food court, holding a garment bag from the hippest new clothing store. While you're waiting, the woman may tap you on the shoulder and ask, "Would you wear this outfit?" As the couple pulls it out of the bag, they marvel at how close in age and size you are to their granddaughter. Before you know what hit you, you've gotten far more than your lunch: You now know the price, material, brand name, and directions for where to find the outfit, and you might even walk away with an extra coupon the couple just happens to have on hand.

Street Marketing

Street marketing, like stealth marketing, interacts directly with consumers by using heavily trafficked areas like malls, street corners, parks, or other public places to hand out fliers, samples, or other marketing materials. This more open form of guerrilla marketing brings the product to the target by turning the visual/verbal message found in more traditional vehicles into an interactive, one-on-one experience with the brand.

Pop-Ups

Pop-ups bring a temporary showroom to a public place—like the time a popular brand of shampoo set up sinks and hair stylists to wash and style hair on a busy street corner in New York City. This type of surprise event extends the brand experience to a real-life encounter, creating a highly interactive and memorable event. Another pop-up temporary store, this one set up by Procter & Gamble in Midtown Manhattan, gave consumers coupons, samples, and even beauty makeovers with P&G products. Others such as Unilever and Meow Mix have also interacted with consumers in temporary street locations, offering a one-on-one brand experience.

Video Projection

Video projection advertising takes a recognizable visual image and projects it onto the sides of buildings or reflects it in water, on window frontage, or even on the sides of cruise ships. These larger-than-life displays are another excellent way to generate buzz and connect with consumers during the evening hours in major markets. Usually seen in larger cities, they are often accompanied by street teams handing out samples, free tickets, or coupons. Projected commercials are known as *guerrilla video projection*. These 30-second commercials are most often projected in areas with a high percentage of pedestrian traffic. Other images can include logos and visual/verbal stationary messages. To attract as much attention as possible, the ads are usually projected onto more than one building in more than one location. Outdoor guerrilla video projection can also utilize SMS, video games, and Bluetooth broadcasts.

Event Graffiti

Another form of guerrilla marketing includes event graffiti performances, where highly creative graffiti artists produce an outdoor mural for a product or service. These live six- to eight-hour performances are typically conducted at outdoor concerts, sporting events, or festivals and street fairs. The one-of-a-kind, permission-based outdoor murals (also known as *mural street art*) are hand painted live by the artists, usually on the sides of older urban buildings.

Event graffiti can backfire, however. Sony used it in a 2005 guerrilla event for a PSP handheld game. Street artists were legally commissioned to spray paint images of gamers using the PSP. Local residents objected to the graffiti, and before long all drawings were defaced in some negative and suggestive ways. The campaign ran in several cities with basically the same negative results.

Skywriting

Even the sky is a great place for a guerrilla marketing spectacular. Event advertising can now take to the skies with an environmentally safe machine that spits out specifically designed cloud formations that can be seen for miles. Known as *Flogos,* or flying logos, these clouds have been used by the Los Angeles Angels on baseball's opening day to send up an "A" with a halo from the outfield; they were also used to form McDonald's golden arches and a signature "S" for Sheraton Hotels.

Logo-shaped clouds may be considered a novelty but the sky has been used for decades as a clutter-free venue to reach a large, generally inattentive audience. Blimps, airplanes towing banners, and hot air balloons have all been used to showcase logos and slogans.

The closest promotional vehicle to Flogos is skywriting, a process by which vaporized fluid from a plane's exhaust is used to spell out floating messages that can be seen for miles. These super-sized messages span more than five miles, with each letter reaching heights equivalent to the size of the Empire State Building. Skywriting is out of the ordinary and will catch viewers' attention from up to 15 miles away.

Guerrilla marketing tactics may also employ:

1. Viral, buzz, or word-of-mouth marketing, which is the passing around of advertising between family and friends via e-mail, blogs, and social sites.
2. Presence marketing, or being anywhere the target is, such as on social sites, using product placement in popular shows/movies, and so on.
3. Grassroots marketing, which is more about building a relationship with the target and less about advertising or selling the product.
4. Traditional advertising, since print and broadcast can be used both as a support vehicle to promote the event and as a primary vehicle to build awareness and brand image.
5. Alternative marketing uses any and all surfaces to reach the consumer. The goal is to build a relationship with the consumer that is not considered intrusive.
6. Undercover marketing, or product placement in movies or television programming that does not call attention to itself.
7. Astroturfing, which is a staged viral campaign by the advertiser.
8. Experiential marketing, which promotes an experience that allows the consumer to interact with or use the product.
9. Influence marketing, or the use of public personalities the target trusts to endorse a brand.

Guerrilla Marketing Events Are Creative and Memorable

Small and large brands are using guerrilla marketing not only to promote a brand or set themselves apart from competing products but to bring attention

Figure 12.2 **Sample Ad: PetSmart**

Source: Created by Kate Gustafson, The University of Tennessee, Knoxville.

to community service projects and local and national events in which they are involved. Tactics range from simple one-day events to multi-level promotions. They must be interactive and interesting enough to grab the attention of a lethargic, advertising-avoidant target. Let's take a look at some of the more innovative events that products, services, and charitable organizations have employed to ensnare their target audience's innate sense of curiosity.

A very effective small-budget guerrilla marketing event was initiated by 3M Security Glass. This participatory event placed their entire $500 budget inside a large glass box located on a heavily used sidewalk. To give the illusion there was a great deal more money in the box, promoters filled it entirely with small bills. The event garnered a great deal of curious attention when a security guard was placed at the site. The goal was to encourage pedestrians to try and break the glass with their feet, their hands—anything short of a tire iron or hammer—to prove the glass was unbreakable.

For the 2009 Super Bowl, first-time advertiser Denny's garnered a lot of attention by offering viewers a free breakfast they called an eight-hour Grand Slam giveaway. "This free offer is our way of reacquainting America with Denny's real breakfast and with the Denny's brand," said CEO Nelson Marchioli in a February 2009 online article for *Advertising Age.* The successful event cost Denny's a mere $5 million and gave them an enormous amount of positive exposure.

The simplicity of this one is great: Farmers in a local Canadian farmers' market wanted to publicize their fresh, never frozen, produce. To make their point, they hung fresh apples on a tree that had dropped its leaves for the winter. Each succulent looking fruit wore a sticker that proclaimed its freshness, even in the dead of winter.

Cooperative ventures are an effective way to give a guerrilla marketing campaign unusual flair. For example, Hubba Bubba Bubble Gum teamed up with the German lingerie company Triumph on billboards that featured scantily clad models blowing bubbles—just a little extra unconventional visual for passersby to ponder.

Nissan promoted their new keyless ignitions by losing 20,000 keys in several major markets. Each key had a tag informing the finder the key was useless, since their cars did not require one. Although little fanfare was associated with the event, the buzz it created outlasted the original promotion.

New York City's Times Square has enough traffic to make or break any guerrilla marketing campaign. So, to promote their 2008 interactive game *Goosebumps HorrorLand,* Scholastic Media and its partner, Interface, Inc., arranged for an elementary schoolteacher to display his pumpkin-carving prowess live in Times Square on Halloween. The goal was to break his own Guinness Book pumpkin-carving record of 42 pumpkins completed in just one hour—and capture the attention of the busy and distracted passersby. Sam Ewen, founder of Interface, Inc., was astounded by the event's success in attracting and holding the attention of busy New Yorkers. The goal of a successful marketing event is to not only capture attention but also to interrupt what the target is doing. "Brands" said Ewen, in a December 2008 Brandweek.com article, "[have to] give people something else to think about."

Another example comes from the advertising arsenal of IKEA. For its guerrilla marketing event, the Swedish home furnishing store commandeered an entire monorail train in the Japanese city of Kobe. To showcase its products, IKEA decorated each car using couches, chairs, window treatments, and other home decorating products that riders could find in their new location. Many items sported price tags featuring the name of the item and a web address to help any interested shoppers make a purchase. This interactive display not only announced IKEA's arrival in the area but also let riders actually sit on, try out, and inspect the products as they wound their way through the city to work.

Travel Alberta International used photo wraps and benches in several To-
ronto subway stations to capture attention. Weary travelers who took a seat
while waiting for their train found themselves immersed in a faux winter
scene. The bench was masked to look like a ski lift, the wall immediately
behind wrapped with a wintry scene of the Alberta Rockies; on the floor were
pictures of snow skis that looked like they could be tried on. The beautiful
and restful scene did its job and significantly increased traffic to "skicanadi-
anrockies.com."

Ironman's Organic Coffee used the ocean floor to advertise its brand at the
Ironman World Championship. In order to compete with bigger and better-
financed brands such as Ford and Gatorade, the small coffee brand had to find
a unique way to stand out. The owner decided that building a floating coffee
bar and placing an underwater billboard with an arrow pointing the way to
the "Espresso Bar" would do the trick. The goal was to reach swimmers who
were out practicing for the event. The judicious placement guaranteed the
target would see the sign. It also garnered a great deal of free publicity as
swimmers talked it up in blogs.

Eukanuba aptly used dogs to carry their guerrilla marketing message
through malls in South Africa. The dogs were trained to run between specific
points with a bag of Eukanuba dog food in their mouths. The successful stunt
gained a lot of additional press and increased awareness for the Eukanuba
brand name.

Guerrilla marketing works for social and political issues as well as brands.
For example, in a lead off for the Lights Out for Earth 2008 campaign, the
World Wildlife Fund placed light switch stickers in various locations around
Switzerland. These realistic looking stickers featured copy explaining the
upcoming event. The vehicle was engaging enough to cause passersby to
attempt to flip the light switches off.

KFC has chosen to sponsor potholes in five major cities to promote its
"fresh" message. This buzz-building sponsorship will fill in potholes throughout the sponsored city. Once complete, each patch will sport a temporary
chalk message proclaiming "Refreshed by KFC." Not surprisingly, these
pothole-filling spots have their detractors. Some observers consider them
community exploitation rather than community beautification. Many believe
these goodwill ads, even temporary ones, are detrimental to public spaces.

Attaching an advertising message to nonprofit organizations, events, or
community cleanup projects is usually good public relations. Corporate sponsors such as Kellogg's and Starbucks, to name just a few, have also placed
their brands on community projects.

Meow Mix, found a way to encourage cat adoptions by hosting a reality
show on Animal Planet. Placing webcams in a house they dubbed the "Meow

Mix House," cats could be observed being cats in 10 shelters around the country. At the end of each week, Meow Mix would announce which cat(s) had been voted out or adopted. Adoptive parents received a free year's supply of Meow Mix. The resulting publicity not only increased adoptions but also increased brand awareness for Meow Mix.

To make a point, it is not beneath a guerrilla campaign to scare the target into action. In 2008, Bosch Security Systems focused a guerrilla marketing campaign on several neighborhoods in the city of Johannesburg, South Africa. Advertising agency DDB sent out guerrilla teams to the area to "scare up" interest in security systems. Focusing on over 300 homes in high-crime-rated neighborhoods, the guerrilla teams took Polaroid shots of each home. Once developed, a sticker was placed on the back that read: "With a CCTV Security System, you would have seen me outside your house." The photo-turned-advertisement was then placed in the homeowner's mailbox. Not only did the sale of home security systems go up, but the campaign garnered additional publicity in the local press.

Scaring consumers does not always garner favorable publicity, however. Arguably one of the first and most memorable guerrilla campaigns, considered a disaster at the time, was the "War of the Worlds" radio broadcast launched in 1938 by Mercury Theatre on the Air. This highly imaginative broadcast by Orson Welles led radio listeners to believe that a Martian invasion was taking place on Earth. CBS Radio took a great deal of heat when the broadcast's news-bulletin format was labeled "cruelly deceptive." The ruse was easier to pull off because the program aired without commercial breaks. But it did its job—we are still talking about it nearly 75 years later because it was memorable, creative, unusual, inventive, and engaging.

In a more recent example, the 1999 movie *The Blair Witch Project* heated up both viral and word-of-mouth discussions. This thriller features a group of young college students trekking through the Maryland woods to prove and film the existence of the Blair Witch. The movie was not successful because of multi-million-dollar financing—actually, it was made on a shoestring budget—but because the word on the street was that the Blair Witch really existed: A very successful viral campaign got the rumor going and growing. Movies like this one, and other simulated events, can make it difficult for consumers to tell the difference between great advertising and subterfuge, or what's known as *astroturfing,* a media term that refers to the creation of artificial buzz.

Most *experiential marketing,* or marketing that is both participatory and personally relevant to the target, is successful because it is both unconventional and unexpected. But marketers need to be sure their attempts do not go too far and annoy consumers, as the California Milk Producers' guerrilla marketing campaign did in San Francisco. Chocolate chip scent strips were placed in bus shelters throughout the city. The goal was to encourage commuters to have a tall glass of cold milk with a chocolate chip cookie. This great "scentsational" idea did not go over well with many who encountered it. Almost immediately, commuters complained that the conjured-up smell gave them headaches, made them hungry, or aggravated their allergies.

A small video game company found out just how easy it is to offend when they wanted to place ads on tombstones. Their promise to pay for the privilege was condemned by the public in general and varied religious sects specifically. Protecting their reputation, they assured the community they were only kidding and quickly put an end to their quest for afterlife advertising.

Brands employing guerrilla marketing events need to thoroughly research state and local laws or clear events with city officials to keep promotional events from igniting negative publicity. Campaigns that have malfunctioned include Cartoon Network's *Aqua Teen Hunger Force* bomb scare in Boston (projection boxes set up in public places were thought to be bombs) and Microsoft's failed "fly by" (thousands of stickers printed with butterflies were dropped on unsuspecting New Yorkers, resulting in a fine for Microsoft, along with a forceful request for immediate cleanup).

Guerrilla campaigns that fail affect brand image, so before launching one, creative teams must have a thorough understanding of how large a distraction the target will tolerate, or whether they might find the event annoying or offensive. If you believe in the old saying that any publicity, even negative publicity, is good publicity, then these were successful at keeping the brand's name on consumer's lips, in online discussions, and in the local and national news media long after the events ended.

Campaigns that employ guerrilla marketing tactics are a melting pot of ideas; some are loud and unconventional, while others are clever and less obtrusive. Some are expensive extravaganzas, while others intrigue. The most successful are those memorable enough to be given a second life through viral sharing online.

Getting the Event to Go Viral

A marketing effort that is remarkably creative or that interactively engages viewers, readers, or listeners enough to have them share it with friends and/or family results in advertising that begets advertising. This type of shared promotion is known as *viral* or *word-of-mouth marketing*. The consumer initiates viral campaigns with no assistance from the sponsoring brand. It is often immediate and can be sent through e-mail, spread through face-to-face discussions, or appear as a viral video or within a blog. Unlike guerrilla

Figure 12.3   **Sample Ad: Paper Clips**

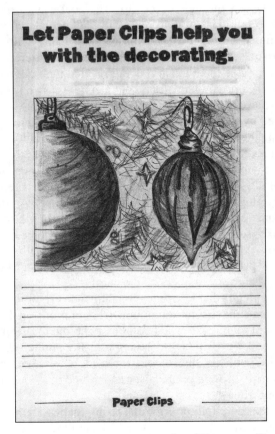

Source: Created by Ally Callahan, The University of Tennessee, Knoxville.

marketing, viral marketing cannot be generated artificially; it is the result of an unsuspected encounter with the product or service.

It is not unusual, however, for guerrilla events to help get the conversation started. *Influence marketing* pairs up a brand with influential members within the target's life—such as hairstylists, DJs, artists, and favorite store owners, to name a few—to openly discuss a given brand's perceived virtues. Since people trust word-of-mouth over traditional advertised messages, reputable individuals are a trusted source for opinions and recommendations on anything from new products to fashion, movies, books, and restaurants. Influence marketing is a great way for a brand to quickly gain credibility in certain targeted circles.

More than anything else, viral marketing is a form of gossip; it's all about sharing information with others. The most influential form of buzz is generated by the product or event itself. In 2008, for example, *Paranormal State,* a ghost series airing on A&E, ran a campaign that questioned the existence of ghosts. The venue? A wallscape near a graveyard in New York City. To promote the idea, A&E placed a sonic transmitter on top of a nearby building that made passing pedestrians hear whispers as they walked by the cemetery. The transmitter was an instant success, garnering a lot of viral and word-of-mouth discussion. However, not all viral campaigns are guaranteed to generate positive publicity. There were numerous complaints that A&E was using people's brains as a transmitter for audio signals, definitely not good public relations. On the flip side, the word-of-mouth campaign that ensued picked up momentum as calls from as far away as Japan managed to beam their versions of the campaign around the world.

HBO bombarded the viral market with information to promote its series *True Blood.* The bloodsucking storyline informs us that vampires are alive and well among us due to a new synthetic blood product. To publicize the series, HBO developed a list of vampire/science fiction enthusiasts from varied blogs and websites catering to the horror genre. This exclusive list of individuals received the initial mailer containing an obscure letter that featured copy written in some type of ancient language—and nothing else.

The second mail drop focused on the synthetic blood product. HBO used print ads that ran simultaneous to the second mailing, explaining that the product could be found in local stores. Additionally, "sold out" signs for the blood products were placed in convenience store windows and on vending machines. The print ads gave the first clue that the product was bogus and really just a promotional event for the HBO series when the disclaimer at the bottom proclaimed "HBO advises vampires to drink responsibly."

Promotional websites that supported each mailing featured fan comments and excitement for *True Blood*'s premiere. They also allowed enthusiasts to create and post their own videos to the sites. The goal of HBO's viral campaign was to give the fictional show a reality base fans could share in.

When viral events take advantage of the surrounding landscape or personalities, the tactics seem less like advertising and more like an everyday occurrence. For example, when struggling Adidas gave up-and-coming rappers in New York City a pair of the company's shoes, it got a big boost from Run-DMC with the release of the song "My Adidas." The resulting publicity and sales put Adidas back on the shoe map.

Brands that offer something new or unusual automatically become a talking point, which will ultimately spread and infect other consumers. The best way to generate viral discussions is to get the brand in the hands of the target for free or at a discount.

Blogs

Blogs (short for weblogs) are a type of electronic conversation between multiple posters. They allow consumers to talk about their experience with a brand and give the brand's CEOs or public relations representatives an opportunity to join in on the conversation.

Blogs can help build and/or sustain target relationships; they can highlight brand flaws and help to improve the brand. They also can echo the marketing message or disclaim it, so it is imperative that all companies have a plan of attack in mind to respond to negative blog postings before they become a major issue. Likewise, a brand should seize on and play up all positive endorsements.

Since blogs are free, they are a great way to get target feedback for little or no cost. Those customers who frequently visit and spend time on a blog are looking for credible and compelling content. Honest, straightforward discussions are the key to success in the blogosphere. If a blog misleads intentionally or otherwise, the blogger will no doubt face negative word of mouth when exposed. For example, Walmart posted a blog about a couple who parked overnight in Walmart parking lots while traveling the United States. It did not take dedicated bloggers long to figure out these postings were untrue and nothing more than an unannounced public relations stunt.

Messages delivered virally or via word of mouth are not only the least expensive form of advertising but also the most credible. This form of real-life testimonial is much more believable and more powerful than any million-dollar ad campaign. Consequently, it is important a brand have a dedicated customer service and/or technical service staff where consumers can easily go to lodge a complaint or get assistance. It is equally vital that users be encouraged to contact brand representatives for reassurance that everything possible will be done to solve their problem or answer their questions. The magnitude of the damage done by dissatisfied customers is backed by solid research: Studies show that the average person probably will not lodge a formal complaint against the company but will likely tell their friends and/or family instead. This can result in irreparable harm to the brand.

Positive word of mouth originates from:

1. A well–made, soundly performing product or service.
2. Actively seeking feedback from current users. It is important that feedback be acted upon rather than ignored.
3. Excellent customer service and/or technical service representatives.
4. Exceeding customers' expectations.
5. Offering a 100 percent money-back guarantee.

Regulations

The Federal Trade Commission (FTC) in 2009 attempted to place stricter guidelines on Internet bloggers and social network users who endorse or give testimonials about a product or service. The commission wants to hold both the company and bloggers liable for any misleading or unsubstantiated statements made by the recipient of a free sample of the product (in advance of the product's general or nationwide availability). Although it is not a new practice to give something in return for free or positive press, it is relatively new to recruit nonmedia mouthpieces to promote products in return for samples or promotional gifts. Leaders in the advertising industry still lobby for self-regulation, because they feel the new rules could inhibit creativity in this emerging field.

It has been difficult for government regulatory agencies to keep up with the changes in technology and the opportunities and threats they present to consumers. The proposed regulations mark the first time the FTC has updated its endorsement guidelines since 1980. Richard Cleland, assistant director for the FTC's advertising practices division, notes in an article on FT.com, "These guides needed to be updated to address not only the changes in technology, but also the consequences of new marketing practices." He goes on to say, "Word of mouth marketing is not exempt from the laws of truthful advertising."

Understanding Viral Marketing's Strengths and Weaknesses

Let's take a look at what viral marketing can or cannot bring to the media mix.

Strengths

1. Publicity. Viral marketing is a free form of advertising.
2. Referrals. It is a great way to get the brand name in front of the target via someone they trust, such as a friend or family member.
3. Interest. Viral marketing can drive traffic to a website.
4. Rewards. To encourage message sharing, loyal customers should be rewarded with some type of incentive.
5. Expense. It does not get any cheaper than free.

Weaknesses

1. Spam. Information sent to acquaintances is not necessarily solicited or appreciated.

2. ROI. It is difficult if not impossible to prove viral marketing increases traffic to a site or sales.
3. Niche Audience. Viral is not feasible for brands with a large target audience.
4. Publicity. Marketers cannot control what is said or passed along about the product or service.

Viral marketing can take a product from obscurity to mainstream popularity with very little effort. Its reach and frequency—although immeasurable—can vastly surpass that of a carefully planned media mix.

13

What If It Doesn't Fit Snugly into Any of the Other Categories?

Figure 13.1 **Sample Ad: Knoxville Museum of Art**

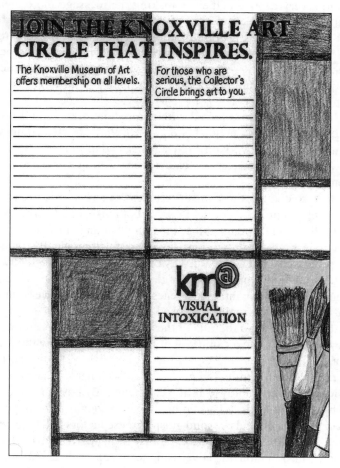

Source: Created by Justin Cooter, The University of Tennessee, Knoxville.

Some Vehicles Are So Unusual, They Defy Classification

The best definition for a vehicle that defies classification is that it does not fit snugly into any of the other niche categories such as out-of-home, direct marketing, electronic media, and so on, making its visual/verbal voice and role in the media mix difficult to define. Like many alternative media vehicles, these specialty vehicles cannot deliver an integrated message alone. To be understood and remembered, the message must be cross-promoted elsewhere.

Many of the misfit vehicles included in this specialty category fulfill nothing more than a functional role—say, coffee cups and sleeves or shopping bags serving as surfaces for an ad. Some, like bathroom advertising, can be highly targeted to a very captive audience, making the message more memorable but failing to build a relationship and certainly not enhancing a product or service's image. Cinema, product placement, and gaming are great reminder vehicles, but they can annoy if they are overt or get in the way of the viewer or player. Others vehicles—augmented reality, for instance—are participatory. They rely on their very uniqueness to capture and hold the target's individual attention like no other vehicles or events previously discussed.

Most often vehicles are paired with compatible brands: Soda ads are a natural on gas pumps, athletic shoes go well with exercise equipment, investment opportunities work on ATM screens, and local restaurants or shops within walking distance can be featured on parking meters or on empty storefronts.

With few exceptions, these misfit vehicles have very little to say; images, not words, play a prominent role. Designs both visual and verbal rely more heavily on the brand's image rather than on what any current or previously advertised messages or promotions say or show. Strategically, the majority of these vehicles cannot deliver the key consumer benefit effectively or build or maintain a relationship with the target. Their strengths lie in their ability to engage, initiate, or maintain awareness. Oftentimes this very uniqueness makes it difficult to determine use, need, and overall ROI.

In order to understand the role of these specialty vehicles and where and how they will be used in a campaign, it is important to know the following: (1) what the advertising efforts need to accomplish, (2) who the target is, (3) where the brand is in its life cycle stage, (4) what primary and secondary vehicles will be employed in the campaign, (5) how the brand works, and (6) how much needs to be said or shown to convince the target to try a product or to switch brands. A solid grasp of these factors will help determine how each of these points can be exploited or supported. Armed with this foundational information, the advertising team can compare each medium's strengths and weaknesses against other vehicles in the mix and predict how the target will interact with the vehicle (picking it up, watching it, driving or walking by it, or opting in to receive it). Additional questions address other concerns: Does the vehicle have enough reach? Is the brand new, old, reinvented, or an age-old favorite? Does the message need to inform with long copy, demonstrate a use, or reflect satisfied customers through testimonials? Is the surface big, small, colorful, smooth, or textured? Will advertising be expensive and time-consuming to produce, or inexpensive with a quick and easy turnaround? This and other considerations will help determine whether or not any of these vehicles will reach the target, with the most appropriate message, at the right time.

Memorable Mass Messages Increase Awareness

The choice of a specialty vehicle, just like traditional or alternative media vehicles, depends largely on the target to be reached, the objectives to be accomplished, the strategic tactics to be employed, and the ways in which a brand will be differentiated from its competitors. Specialty vehicles cannot launch or reinvent a brand or build an image like traditional vehicles; furthermore, they are less targetable than alternative media vehicles. However, they do offer an element of freshness: They are self-promoting, in-your-face, engaging, and interactive pieces that are often unusual and not overly employed.

Designed to reach a mass audience, specialty vehicles rarely speak to the target about their needs and wants and will not enhance their lifestyle in any meaningful way. They cannot build a relationship, but they are functional and because of their innovative approaches can command attention and create strong viral or word-of-mouth discussions. Specialty vehicles do not educate with large blocks of copy, demonstrate use, or directly define how a brand can enhance the target's lifestyle, but they can be used as a vital component in maintaining name recognition. They are meant to awe, entertain, and surprise, and as such they tend to capture and hold the target's attention longer than other messages. Specialty vehicles are generally inexpensive to use and can be placed directly in the consumers' hand or line of sight, making them more memorable than any multi-million-dollar 30-second spot or colorful, page-turning magazine spread featuring the latest fashions or trends.

Specialty vehicles take a "stop, look, and listen" approach; sometimes, they offer participatory messages. Most of them are unique and innovative forms of mass-produced advertising for assorted types of products and services. Creatively, they are often tied to other advertising efforts by nothing more than color, a logo, a spokesperson or character representative, or a slogan or tagline.

Understanding Specialty Vehicles' Strengths and Weaknesses

Let's take a look at what the varying types of specialty vehicles can or cannot bring to the media mix.

Strengths

1. Unique. The unique use of space can stop attention.
2. Creative. No surface is ignored or considered inappropriate.
3. Inexpensive. Small projects can be very cost efficient compared to traditional options.

Weaknesses

1. Mass Targeted. Most are better at reaching a mass audience rather than building a relationship.
2. ROI. No way to determine whether vehicles were seen or acted upon.
3. Expense. Since many of the vehicles are disposable or promotional, they are used for only a short time, which can make them very expensive to produce.
4. Short Message. Surfaces are all relatively small, unable to hold more than the key consumer benefit, logo, slogan, or tagline.

Giving the Misfits a Visual/Verbal Voice

Many of the visual/verbal messages in this misfit category are edgier or more technologically based than other vehicles. They tend to "wow" with what technology can do rather than what the brand can do for the target. Let's take a look at some of the more creative and effective specialty vehicles.

Gaming

In-game advertising can be loosely defined as using the computer, television, and/or mobile marketing vehicles to promote advertising within the storyline of a video game.

The first examples of in-game advertising included static or unchangeable virtual billboards or varied product placements. Many played no role in the games at all, while others could actually become obstacles the players must tackle. Today's in-game advertising is dynamic and can be

Figure 13.2   **Sample Ad: McCay**

Source: Created by Allison Schepman, The University of Tennessee, Knoxville.

easily changed out to accommodate a new product launch or reinvention, to promote an event, or to advertise a political candidate's position on the issues.

Many brands are considering and actively using in-game product placement. But just like their TV cousins, they must be woven into the playing field seamlessly so as not be intrusive. In addition, the product placed in a game must be appropriate for that particular game: Putting an ad for a floral-scented hand lotion in a male-dominated futuristic game is probably not a good idea. Because the gaming audience is actively engaged, however, on-target product placement is a great way to build brand awareness.

Companies such as Dairy Queen have used games as an interactive and fun way to keep their name top of mind year-round. "DQ Tycoon" is a time-management game that has players race against the clock to complete restaurant management tasks such as stocking the refrigerator, taking orders, and preparing Peanut Parfaits and dipped ice cream cones. Games like this one renew the brand and keep DQ in the minds of kids without advertising to them directly.

Gaming's popularity with the 18- to 34-year-old target group has helped to make it a great vehicle to carry political advertising. Barack Obama again rewrote the way a candidate could reach his constituents by using in-game advertising during his run for the White House. The ads were used to remind players to register to vote and to visit the Obama website for more information on his campaign goals.

Another type of gaming ad, known as *advergaming,* is the prominent placement of advertising on mobile devices or free online videogames. Nissan used computer games to build buzz for the launch of its GT-R sport coupe. Food and beverage companies like Cheetos and Burger King have also used videogames as a reminder vehicle and for attracting attention.

Product Placement

Very simply product placement is the placing of a clearly recognizable brand in a movie, television show, or game. A subtle form of advertising, product placement can be accomplished in three major ways: (1) the product is clearly recognizable in a scene; (2) the brand is used by an actor in a scene; or (3) an actor actually refers to the product by name in a scene.

Product placement has gone from a form of free publicity to a vehicle that requires a lot of upfront cash: Studios are asking for upwards of 50 percent of the cost of integration to guarantee prominent placement. Today, it is considered a viable substitute to traditional or more passive forms of advertising. Brands that can be tied to a main character or theme will be the most memorable and successful.

Getting a brand logo a close-up is a good use of product placement; getting it integrated into the plot and mentioned in the dialogue is a great way to build brand image and create brand awareness. Subway, for example, took their product and slogan placement one step further by actually having the slogan worked into a script for NBC's *Chuck:* In the episode, one character delivers the recognizable sandwich to another and—as part of the dialogue—recites the sandwich maker's familiar "$5 footlong" slogan. This type of product placement is actually a mini-commercial appearing inside popular programming.

These types of programs, along with the emergence of other narrowly defined programming channels such as the Food Channel or HGTV, which have a small but loyal following of interested viewers, make it easier to promote the embedded products featured in the programming. It is important that placement not disrupt: The point is to get away from intrusive, in-your-face sales pitches by showing the product in use.

Wild Postings

If you want to encourage members of the target audience to take the ad with them, consider using rip-away wild postings. Wild postings reach the target where they are on the street. These weather–safe, creative posters encourage the target to rip a single poster from a pad and use it as a decoration for home, office, or dorm rooms. Types of wild postings include street posters, window-cling posters, sidewalk chalk drawings, decals, and door hangers, among others. Like many specialty media options, these unconventional advertising tactics are a quick, easy, and inexpensive form of out-of-home advertising. This is a great way to reach a small, concentrated niche market—living in specific neighborhoods or downtown areas, for instance—quickly and easily by placing the posters on nearby walls, telephone and utility poles, outside of local schools, throughout shopping districts, and so on.

Street posters can range in size from a small (standard 8.5 × 11 inches) all the way up to very large (27 × 40 inches). The amount of coverage depends on the amount of posters ordered. A blanket street-postering campaign makes sure there are two or more posters on every available pole so they can be seen from all sides.

This type of vehicle is great for launching new products or announcing a local event. Target engagement can be sustained via a teaser campaign or by showcasing a unique concept, design, or tagline.

Pump Top TV

Gas pump top TVs are another great way to reach a captive audience. These LCD screens, often 19 inches wide, are located on top of gas pumps and can deliver multiple 15-, 30-, or 60-second full-motion video commercials.

Gas pump nozzles are another unavoidable surface ideally suited for logos, slogans, or taglines. A little more unconventional but attention getting are gas station pumps that play an audio commercial when the nozzle is placed in the fuel tank.

ATM Machines

Heavily used ATM machines are ideal for ads because they are repetitively visited by consumers. Like gas pump advertising, ATMs use an LCD screen to deliver a short ad for local businesses or for mass-produced brands that can be found locally. These types of screens can also be found near escalators, moving walkways, on subways and trains, along high-traffic pedestrian walkways, and even in bathrooms.

Street Graphics and Stickers

Street graphics encompass any design that can be found on public thorough-fares, sidewalks, or parking lot surfaces. The following examples show how a sticky ad can be eye-catching and memorable.

The television premiere of *Batman Begins* was creatively promoted by placing bat stickers over footpath lights so the famous bat signature would appear skyward.

China used stickers on city streets to raise awareness of unsafe drinking water; the stickers featured a puddle of water with a skull floating inside.

To raise awareness about skin cancer, the Israel Cancer Association found real stains on sidewalks near beaches and placed framed transparent stickers over them. The point? If you see an unusual spot, go have it checked. The bottom of each sticker featured the logo, a web address, and copy that read: "Unknown stain on your body? Go see a dermatologist!"

UNICEF used round coaster-sized stickers to raise awareness about land-mines. Placed on the floor, the stickers were almost invisible to passersby. Each sticker had a tacky or sticky topside that, when stepped on, stuck to the bottom of the person's foot. When removed, the underside featured a picture of a landmine. Copy informed them that in many areas around the world, stepping on something as inconspicuous as the stickers would have killed or maimed them.

To advertise new barbecues, one imaginative entrepreneur used the sewer grates on local city streets as an advertising surface. The grates represented the grill, and stickers represented cooking implements such as spatulas, skewers, and large two-pronged forks. Stickers were also used to advertise the retailer's phone number so interested pedestrians could call for more information.

IKEA used large stickers that looked like holes in the ground as an adver-tising vehicle. When viewers peered into the flat image, it appeared that they were looking down into a three-dimensional fully furnished room. Topside, street teams handed out store catalogs.

One of the best ways to promote green advertising is to use green graf-fiti. Done using stencils and a power washer that does nothing more to the environment than wash away the dirt and grime from around a template, the clean result leaves a temporary message on the sidewalk, street, or side of a building. Amsterdam, the capital of the Netherlands, used green graffiti to advertise Michael Moore's documentary, *Capitalism: A Love Story.*

Another great interactive green ad was used by SOSrainforests.com to bring attention to energy waste. Light blue stickers were placed over light switches. Each sticker had a cutout for the switch. The copy at the top of the sticker reads: "Would you like to save energy and help decrease the effects of global warming?" Consumers interested in energy conservation efforts could participate by flipping the switch.

How do you show a smooth shave? Wilkinson Quattro Titanium Razors used eggs. When shoppers opened the carton, they not only saw an ad for the razor pasted on the back of the lid, but eggs with stickers of various clean shaven masculine faces looking back at them. Now that signifies a smooth shave in a much more innovative way than the old-fashioned baby's behind.

Malaysia Airlines placed stickers on their pull-down seatback trays showing a pair of seated legs and a picture of a beautiful location meant to encourage the flier to checkout other destinations on the airline's schedule.

One company that sold both men and women's sexy undergarments placed little round stickers of bottoms wearing slinky underwear on the bottom of ketchup bottles. One slap to the bottom of the bottle was very suggestive.

Exercise Equipment

Another great place to find a captive audience is at the gym. Members can use branded touch screens attached to the workout equipment to watch TV, surf the web, or e-mail while working out.

Vacant Storefront Advertising

The unstable economy has left a lot of storefronts empty as more and more businesses close. Retailers who survive the downturn have requisitioned those storefronts for use as additional advertising space. Once considered tacky by many brands, they are now considered an inexpensive way to extend their brand's message. Empty storefronts are an excellent surface because they are often in high traffic areas such as malls or busy downtown walkways.

Intel chose to use storefronts that featured digital billboards showing time-delayed messages about their future plans and a promotion for the fantasy/horror movie *Coraline*. As reported in the *New York Times* (Clifford, May 11, 2009), Intel's ads used the darkened spaces to create holograms where "children would appear out of thin air in an environment that looked to be 20 feet deep, and float up to the window." Others brands like Delta, Nestea, and Snickers placed ads on storefronts that had been plastered over. This inexpensive new wave of advertising is cheaper than outdoor boards, and the space is often donated by landlords.

Cinema

Digital cinema advertising, a form of specialty advertising long considered too expensive, too time consuming between production and airing, and not targetable enough to advertisers, has finally converted skeptics into users. Cinema advertising is now thought to be a great way to reach the elusive yet desirable 18- to 34-year-old target group. It is bigger than life and delivered to a captive audience. Theater lobbies are also a viable space for advertising; the high traffic space is a great place for posters, life-size die cut images, or kiosks. Concession stands are big business, so don't forget to use cups, popcorn tubs, wrappers, and napkins to extend the message seen during the premiere or in the lobby.

Movie Promotions

Major League Baseball (MLB) teamed with Walt Disney Pictures to promote the 2009 3-D movie *G-Force,* the first such pairing since the promotional arrangement with Sony Pictures to promote *Spider-Man 2* ended poorly. The misstep involved placing the movie's logo on every base in every ballpark the weekend before the movie opened. Fans immediately rebelled: They considered the idea too commercialized and the promotion was permanently benched.

Disney decided to go with a promotion that designated specific game days as *G-Force* days, featuring themed trading cards and movie ticket giveaways. Additionally, ballots for the All Star Game were sponsored by the movie, along with a contest titled "G-Force Grand Slam Sweepstakes." Before contestants could enter, a player had to hit a "grand slam" during the game, after which the first one million fans that registered on Disney.com would receive a complimentary ticket to the movie's premiere.

Coffee Cups/Sleeves

These functional vehicles are anything but dull. Some of the more colorful examples feature a picture of a nose on the side, mimicking the nose of the drinker that temporarily disappears from view with each sip. Other businesses have used the underside of the cup to mimic what the bottom of the cup sees when the drinker takes a sip; teeth, gums, tongue and tonsils. It may not promote coffee, but it does capture the attention of passersby.

Coffee cups and/or sleeves are a great way for the target to take a brand's message with them. The average drinker holds onto the cup for approximately 21 minutes. As the target moves about or has others move around them, the ad will be seen on average by six different people: This makes the carrier an active participant in the advertised message. Coffee cups and sleeves are an excellent way to extend the message seen in other traditional or alternative media vehicles and a great place to put a coupon or develop other types of cooperative ventures with area restaurants, donut shops, and so on.

More creative sleeves keep their message a secret until the hot liquid activates the heat-sensitive ink. Other interactive add-ons include sleeves with pull out handles that quickly and easily convert the cup into a mug. To give the drinker's hand even more protection from the hot coffee, some sleeves, when activated by the hot beverage, plump up into varied shapes.

Usually limited on space and money, sleeves showcase little more than a one- or two-color logo and a slogan or tagline. More expensive options can use full color visuals that are harder to miss, along with interactive options. To extend the message even further, use the wrapping or sleeves for sandwiches, cookies, or pastries in the same way.

Shopping Bags

Shopping bags can be very colorful, creative, and some can even be a little offensive depending on where the cutout for the handle appears. Let's take a look at a few creative examples.

One great bag has a color picture of a handgun on it. The cutout appears over the grip so it looks like the carrier is holding the gun down by his side. Sounds sinister, but the merchandiser was a bookstore. This creative bag was only available in Belgium with the purchase of a book by a popular local crime writer.

A beauty salon used real braided hair extensions as handles for their bags to promote the array of available colors.

Another creative bag placed a picture of a barbell at the top; when carriers placed their hands through the cutout, it looked like they were carrying the weight.

A magic shop created a black bag with a picture of white handles hanging down the side. The real handles were nearly invisible (they were made out of fishing line) so it looked like the bag was magically suspended in mid-air when carried.

Scaffolding

Construction scaffolding is a great cooperative advertising option that can help offset the cost of building or remodeling projects. Audi used scaffolding to advertise its A4 model. The advertising focused on the car's LED lights; to emphasize the point, working headlights were embedded into the advertising.

Branded Hand Stamp Advertising

Everybody has had their hand stamped at one point or another, allowing them to come and go from events and clubs. Instead of wasting a perfectly good surface, one great cooperative effort featured the message "Don't Drink and Drive," accompanied by the phone number of a local cab company. Most stamps are one color and measure around two inches by two inches. A typical stamp is a promotional vehicle that highlights a brand's logo and web address; many are tied to napkins, bar glasses, and even bathroom advertising for a more integrated and memorable approach.

Bathroom Advertising

Talk about a captive and targetable audience! Research has shown that 75 percent of people polled actually remembered specific advertisers by name when they saw them in a restroom advertisement.

Bathrooms where the target will be in and out quickly are great for small ads appearing on bathroom doors and above sinks and urinals. Larger framed or digital ads are better for restrooms that often have a waiting line. Most ads are simple, featuring a color visual, a little text, a logo, and contact information. Many of these ads can be very suggestive both visually and verbally; examples of some of the tamer ads follow.

One great example for drinking and driving featured a car with a crumpled front end that appears to have run into the top of the urinal. Some ads have little to say but are very interactive, such as the clever jewelry ad featured stickers of jewelry on the mirrors in women's restrooms. Women could align their bodies with the image to see how the piece would look on them.

Using the same alignment technique, a tattoo shop advertised its artistic prowess and think-before-you-buy philosophy when it placed stickers of tattoos on bathroom and locker room mirrors.

A large acne poster featured a close-up of a young women's face covered in real bubble wrap with copy that read: "ACNE. DON'T POP IT. STOP IT." Very visual.

New Zealand used bars of soap in public restrooms to promote the premiere of a television show called *Prison Break*. One side featured the logo embossed into the soap with the copy: "COMING SOON." The other side bore the impression of a key.

Other brands such as Carefree Pantiliners placed ads on toilet paper dispensers, Absolut Vodka used digital ads on bathroom mirrors, and DIRECTV used framed three-dimensional posters to showcase its sports programming.

Toilet paper has gone creative, as well. It is being used to promote movie and television premiers, products and services, and even some games.

Milk Carton Advertising

The 1980s promotions of missing children have moved to the Internet, leaving the surface clear for an array of products and services to promote an individual brand or participate in cooperative efforts between compatible brands. Most milk carton advertising is purchased by national brands. It is one of the few ways advertisers can still reach a mass audience with a relevant message and perhaps an instant redemption coupon (to help track results).

These ads can use the small cartons to reach school-age children and larger cartons to reach older adult shoppers. Brands that have used milk containers—both plastic and paper—include Stouffer's, Cheerios, and Honey Maid graham crackers. Duncan Hines cross-promoted the great taste of milk and brownies with an ad that read: "Cold Milk, Warm Brownies, mmmmmmmm."

Large carton or plastic ads can be either two or three colors, are printed on one side, and feature a single advertiser. Most ads feature a single visual, a small amount of text, a web address and/or a toll free number, a logo, and a slogan or tagline.

Small cartons use no more than one or two colors and feature a visual and a logo, slogan, or tagline. Some cartons can be interactive by including games kids can play while they eat and drink.

Grocery Cart Ads

These rolling billboards, often placed on the front of the cart, are meant to titillate your taste buds at the point of purchase with beautiful color photographs of delicious foods, cool refreshing drinks, or as a reminder, for instance, that mosquito weather is approaching, so protect yourself with this or that generic or national brand of bug spray. Companies like Procter & Gamble and Coke have long used this form of point of purchase advertising with good results.

Probably the most interesting grocery cart advertising is going digital. ShopRite is planning to test out a convenience shopping console that is mounted on the grocery cart. Shoppers who have a loyalty card can log on to the ShopRite website and input their shopping list. Once at the store, they will use the console to swipe their loyalty card, bringing up their shopping list and the locations of the items in the store. Like mobile, the technology can also send coupons to shoppers as they walk by certain products.

Added features allow consumers to scan each item before dropping it into the cart, successfully deleting it from the list. The ability to scan as they go also allows shoppers to pay from their cart, no longer requiring a long and often time-consuming stand in line.

Parking Meter Advertising

Basically, the label "parking meter ads" is a bit misleading, since the advertising is actually located on the pole holding the meter. These usually three-sided laminated ads feature one local or national brand in simple one- to four-color images. Readability and legibility are enhanced when a lot of white space surrounds the message. Ads are often limited to no more than one to two brands per block, allowing advertisers to sequentially deliver their message.

Drive-In Advertising

To promote Volvos in England, the upscale brand plans to hold a drive-in movie night. This is not all that spectacular until you find out there are no drive-ins in the UK. Even more unique, Volvo is supplying not only the location but the parked cars. The $40 tickets that sold out in 30 seconds provided moviegoers with a stylish place to sit, along with popcorn and a drink. Even the sound system was provided by Volvo—no old-fashioned speakers were attached to these upscale windows; instead, the talky could be heard through the car's radio. Surprisingly, concession items were allowed in the cars, and they were personally delivered by wait staff on roller skates.

Automated Shelf and Aisle Advertising

Forget traditional television: advertisers are now looking at producing 3GTV commercials that will air in stores at the point of purchase. Participating brands will use screens placed on shelves and above aisles.

Activated by the shopper, these ads use a mass-advertised message to reach the individual. Inventors are still working on ways to keep aisles and shelves from looking like a jumbled mess of technology adversely interrupting the shopping experience.

Three-Dimensional Advertising

Three-dimensional advertising is a great way to renew interest in brand advertising and reinvent how print and basic technology is used. Besides the rebirth of three-dimensional movies, look for three-dimensional ads in catalogs and magazines, on television, on the web, and on cell phones. Let's take a look at some very creative and innovative examples.

Three-Dimensional Catalogs

Consumers who opt in to receive their favorite catalogs enjoy a leisurely trip through their colorful pages. Capturing their attention is not difficult, but imagine how much easier it would be to sustain it if the ads were in 3-D? Barneys New York wants to find out. To promote its designer denim lines,

Barneys will use 3-D imagery complete with the glasses required to view them bound into the back cover of the catalog. Not only will the front and back covers bound off the page, but most of the featured items inside. Along with the catalog, Barneys will run a corresponding contest titled "Send Us Your Best Denim."

Three-Dimensional Commercials

Three-dimensional advertising has arrived, and it is every bit as creative as the technology currently employed in 3-D movies. To prove it, ESPN will be the first broadcaster to feature only 3-D ads on its new sports channel. The gutsy move is fraught with obstacles, the biggest being a lack of interest by many brands. Advertisers are hesitant to jump on the bandwagon because 3-D commercials cost about 30 to 40 percent more to produce than regular commercials. They are also time-consuming to develop due to the lack of production houses skilled enough to create them. ESPN is confident many brands will come to accept three-dimensional advertising in the same way they came to accept high definition. Still, many advertisers are taking a wait-and-see attitude to see how lucrative the sales of 3-D televisions will be before heavily investing in the new technology.

To get the ball rolling, ESPN offered a few of their regular advertisers a chance to air their 3-D ads for free. Procter & Gamble—always ready to try new technology—showcased a 3-D ad for its Fusion ProGlide razor, and Pixar and Disney also jumped on board with a spot for *Toy Story 3,* as did ESPN with a creative spot promoting its popular "Sports Center" program.

Three-dimensional advertising is still in its infancy. ESPN is hoping the format will help drive consumers to the sports channel and encourage more advertisers to invest in the newest technology.

Augmented Reality

Augmented reality (AR)–enhanced environments are one of the newest ways to engage and interact with the target both online and/or via their cell phones. The successor to virtual reality ads, this creative and interactive form of advertisement allows viewers to use the environment around an image to experience it in holographic and/or three-dimensional form.

Augmented reality is half reality and half virtual or computer-generated images. This point-and-inform technology can give consumers information on whatever they point it at. It works by overlaying images and sounds on the surrounding physical environment to create an enhanced computer-generated environment. On television, AR is most commonly seen during football

Figure 13.3 **Sample Ad: FAO Schwarz**

Source: Created by Stephanie Gilleran, The University of Tennessee, Knoxville.

broadcasts, with a yellow line representing a first down marker or sponsors' logos superimposed over the field in the lower right-hand corner of the screen. Augmented reality is:

1. A three-dimensional or holographic image.
2. A combination of real world and virtual experiences.
3. Immediately interactive and engaging.

Currently, AR is playing a largely promotional role in the media mix. Its job: Keep the target engaged a little longer in the brand. Advertisers hope the novelty will not wear off too soon, as they consider ways to integrate the AR experience into online advertising with an eye toward replacing traditional banner ads.

To see three-dimensional or holographic images, consumers must first own a computer with a webcam and/or a Smartphone.

When used with a webcam, users must first print out a two-dimensional coded number or graphic image and then hold it in front of their computer's webcam. This allows them to view a three-dimensional image on the monitor or a holographic image in the space immediately in front of their screens.

One of the first examples of this technique was a 3-D interactive *Popular Science* magazine cover for General Electric. When held up to a webcam, the cover became the base for a series of turning holographic wind turbines that emerge from the screen. To make it even more interactive, viewers could blow into the computer's microphone and make the turbines spin faster.

Topps, a sports collectables company, used AR to bring baseball cards to life by creating a miniature holographic image of each player. All viewers had to do was hold the special cards in front of a webcam and the holographic avatars took on an animated life of their own. To enhance the experience, figures could be moved by rotating the card or made to field, catch, and pitch by using the keyboard to control the action.

LEGO used AR to not only capture the kids' attention but moms and dads' as well. When special LEGO boxes were held up to an in-store AR camera, viewers were surprised to see a 3-D holographic image of a finished set materialize on top of the box right before their eyes.

Zugara, a California-based AR software company, made shopping for online clothes a little easier using AR technology. This ingenious retailer created the "Webcam Social Shopper," an app that lets shoppers see how they will look in the clothing by holding it up in front of them before purchasing. This type of shopping experience not only helps shoppers make an informed purchase but cuts down on the cost of returns.

Using face-mapping, Ray-Ban lets you try on different pairs of sunglasses while shopping online. The brand's nifty piece of software even allows viewers to move their heads so they can see how they look from various angles. If the shades are not too dark, viewers will be able to see their own eyes looking back at them.

To promote the latest 2009 *Star Trek* movie, Nokia and Verizon teamed up to help loyal fans receive a message from Starfleet. All viewers had to do was printout the required PDF and hold it up to their computer's webcam to get their individualized message. Other *Star Trek* movies that have gone on to DVD have codes printed on the front covers that give loyal fans a holographic tour of the USS Enterprise. These promotions got extra mileage when fans shared their AR experience with other enthusiasts online.

In a German campaign for the Mini Cooper Cabrio, a full-page AR magazine ad was placed in popular auto magazines. To interact with the car on their computer screens, viewers simply held up the ad in front of their webcams. The BMW Z4 was cross-promoted using television and electronic media. Interested consumers had to first download the required software, print out the required symbol, and show it to their webcam. Using key commands, viewers were then able to drive their own Z4 on screen.

Doritos printed a webcam code on the back of their package. Once entered online, the code reveals an image of a cartoon character that can be used as a player in an online game. Likewise, Burger King employed a relatively simplistic but creative way to promote their dollar menu. All viewers had to do was click on the ad and hold up a dollar to a webcam to see what it could buy off the Burger King value menu.

Rapper Eminem took AR one step further by including a competition. To enter, interested viewers had to print a special logo and hold it up in front of their webcams to produce a three-dimensional image and then design digital graffiti around it. The winning designer gets a trip to Detroit to attend a VIP album launch. This promotion adds more than just AR aspects; it also extends the interaction through the contest.

Papa John's Pizza is employing this very interactive and memorable advertising device to create their own buzz. The pizza shop adhered an AR image of a vintage Chevy Camaro to the back of millions of pizza boxes. Consumers with webcams were directed to a website where they were asked to hold up the image to the video camera, enabling them to use their keyboards to drive an animated version of the 1972 Camaro on their screens. Why a Camaro? The car plays a prominent role in the fast food franchise's current advertising campaign. In the future, Papa John's wants to place discount offers in its AR images to encourage purchase and better track ROI.

In a campaign for its flat rate Priority Mail service, the U.S. Postal Service directs consumers to prioritymail.com. Once there, visitors are introduced to a "virtual box simulator." They are asked to place the object to be mailed—perhaps a book or a vase—in front of their webcam so they can receive a three-dimensional image that helps them to determine the proper size box needed for shipping.

Burt's Bees used a more integrated approach to promote their participation in Earth Day activities. In addition to launching a website where consumers could get tips on how to be more eco-conscious, the company held Earth Day events in New York City's Union Square, where Burt look-alike street teams handed out Burt's Bees samples and "Burt" beards and hats. At the website, visitors could upload a picture or use their webcam to have their image "Burtified" with the addition of a hat and beard.

AR is an incredible interactive device, but designers must eliminate all glitches before distribution or launch to ensure consumers will not be disillusioned.

Mobile AR

AR advertising with Smartphones take a little less work. It can be activated by simply pointing the phone at whatever the viewer wants to interact with, whether it be the pages of a magazine, products on a shelf, a building, a train, or a subway station. The result allows viewers to see layers of text or animated content containing information that can be viewed on-screen, such as ingredients, scores, restaurants, time schedules and so on. On a more controversial level, there is even a facial recognition aspect that allows the shooter to obtain personal information about individuals at whom their phones are pointed.

On a more educational level, the World Wildlife Fund (WWF) used AR mobile to demonstrate how deforestation affects wildlife.

Mobile AR is helping Mattel modernize their decades-old Rock 'Em Sock 'Em Robots game. In the old days, a player had to use a joystick and buttons to punch their opponent's head off. The new augmented technology for Smartphones allows players to see the superimposed robot images rock 'em and sock 'em on their cell phones simply by pushing buttons on the phone.

Once only a gamer's device, augmented reality is now being picked up and used by companies such as Disney and Procter & Gamble. This technology, like many others we have already talked about, holds great promise because its 3-D, holographic, and interactive qualities give it the "wow" factor needed to hold the attention of a distracted, advertising-avoidant target.

Alternative Media Exercise 13.1

1. Now that you understand more about the different alternative media vehicles and how they work to reach their target, go back and review the first exercise in Chapter 3. Would you keep your choice of vehicles or change them for vehicles that better match the target's needs, wants, and lifestyle?
2. How will your choices change or strengthen the media plan? Adjust the plan as needed.
3. Resubmit both to the class for discussion. Be prepared to defend your choices and position.

Glossary

Advertising. A nonpersonal, paid form of one-way communication that uses persuasion to sell, entice, educate, remind, and/or entertain the target audience about one specific brand.

Alternative Media. Also called emerging media and new media; media vehicles that are used as an alternative to more traditional vehicles such as print (newspaper and magazine) and broadcast (radio and television). These creative and unusual vehicles deliver meaningful and memorable ads that are often more effective at reaching the target than traditional vehicles.

Astroturfing. The creation of artificial buzz.

Behavioristics. A research technique used to determine why the target buys.

Big Idea. A big idea is a creative way of promoting the key consumer benefit to make it stand out from other brands within its category.

Brand. Refers to a product or service's name and anything used to represent that name visually or verbally.

Brand Awareness. Awareness is achieved when the target uses a brand's visual/verbal identity to recognize it over other brands within the same product category.

Brand-Centric Media. Focuses on the use of traditional media.

Brand Equity. Equity is a brand's value in the mind of the consumer.

Brand Image. Refers to the perceived image of the product or service by the target.

Brand Loyalty. Refers to the customer who regularly repurchases the product or uses the service without the assistance of advertising or exposure to competing products.

Consumer-Centric Media. Focuses on the use of new or alternative media vehicles.

Continuity Media Schedule. A continuity schedule maintains a constant level of advertising during the year, dispersing media buys evenly across months.

Cooperative Advertising. A method of advertising in which local businesses combine advertising efforts with nationally advertised brands to defer some of the cost.

Creative Brief. Developed by the account manager, a creative brief defines the communications plan of attack.

Creative Strategy. The creative strategy defines how creative efforts will accomplish the stated objectives, promote the key consumer benefit, and talk to the target.

Customer Relationship Marketing. Also known as direct marketing, this form of personalized advertising builds and maintains a relationship between buyer and seller.

Database Marketing. The collection of a detailed list of customer names and contact information by an individual marketer.

Demographics. Deals with the target's personal characteristics such as gender, age, income, education level, and so on.

Die Cuts. A cutting method that can partially or completely cut out or around a specially designed shape.

Direct Response. A form of direct marketing that encourages the target to make a call, visit a website or brick-and-mortar store for more information, or make a purchase.

Emerging Media. See alternative media.

Experiential Marketing. Marketing that is both participatory and personally relevant to the target.

Exposure. This media term measures how many times targeted individuals see a specific program or ad.

Flighting Media Schedule. Alternates media buys across months.

Focus Groups. Usually these groups consist of 10 to 12 representative members of the target audience who will interact with the brand in a controlled environment.

Formal Surveys. Surveys that use closed-ended questions where participants choose from a predetermined set of responses.

Freestanding Insert (FSI). Coupons that are often reproduced in four-color and not physically attached to an ad.

Frequency. This media term refers to how many times the ad will need to be seen or heard by the intended target audience to be remembered and/or acted upon.

Geographics. Breaks down where the target lives by country, region, province, state, city, or zip code.

Gross Impressions. This term refers to the total number of people watching, reading, hearing, or just generally interacting with an ad or promotion.

Gross Rating Point. Refers to the total amount of ratings delivered by a single vehicle or mix of vehicles.

Guerrilla Marketing. A form of nontraditional advertising that uses unconventional means to attract attention, generate sales, and create memorable encounters.

Impression. An impression is the number of audience members exposed to a media schedule.

Influence Marketing. Pairs a brand with influential members within the target's life such as hairstylists, DJs, and so on to openly discuss the brand's perceived virtues.

Infomercials. A form of direct response, infomercials are long television commercials that last 30 to 60 minutes.

Key Consumer Benefit (KCB). The KCB refers to the one brand feature and consumer benefit that research has shown the defined target is interested in and will respond to. It becomes the single visual/verbal voice of a campaign.

Life Cycle Stages. Refers to a brand's length of time on the market. Most successful brands go through three separate stages in their lifetime: the new product launch, the mainstream or maintenance period, and the reinvention phase.

Logo. A logo is a recognizable emblem found on all advertised or promoted materials. Its job is to represent the company's brand (or the service's name), image, or use.

M-commerce. Mobile advertising.

Marketing Plan. This large document is the client's business plan that defines sales initiatives, usually for the coming year.

Media Buying. Deals with negotiating costs and determining the best vehicles or assortment of buys to promote the product or service.

Media Convergence. When alternative media and/or traditional vehicles successfully deliver a cohesive message.

Media Mix. A group of media vehicles that will be employed to reach the intended audience, such as magazines, newspapers, and so on.

Media Multitasking. Brands using a varied mix of media resources.

Media Plan. A document that outlines what media will be used, how long each one will be used, and where it will be used.

Media Planning. Involves creating a detailed timeline that defines what media vehicles or mix of vehicles it will take to deliver the message to the intended target.

Media Schedule. A chart that shows what media vehicles will be used in a campaign, when they will be used, and for how long, along with budget allocations for each.

Media Vehicle. Any surface, flat or otherwise, that can be used to deliver a message to the relevant target.

Message Impressions. Refers to the total number of exposures the target has to a single ad.

Message Weight. Message weight determines the total number of media vehicles that will make up a campaign media schedule.

Mixed Media Approach. A media term that refers to a campaign's use of multiple media vehicles.

Mobile Video. The ability to watch TV via mobile phone.

Multimedia Messaging Service (MMS). An extension of SMS, it allows users to send longer text messages and send and receive mobile photographs and audio and video clips.

Multiple Selling Propositions (MSP). A way to promote the key consumer benefit using multiple rotating messages in multiple media vehicles; the goal is to sell one feature/benefit combination to the target.

New Media. See alternative media.

Objectives. Objectives define what an ad or campaign needs to accomplish.

Observation Tactics. Involves watching the target in the place where the product or service is purchased or used to help determine ease of use, types of comparisons made, level of difficulty to assemble, and so on.

Piggybacking. When a brand purchases one 30-second television or radio spot and breaks it into two separate but related 15-second spots.

Podcast. A free or subscription-based audio or audio/video combination that can be downloaded to any mobile device such as an iPod or MP3 player.

Positioning. Positioning refers to how a brand is thought of or positioned in the mind of the consumer compared to competing brands.

Premium Short Message Service (PSMS). Allows consumers to use their mobile phones to purchase something (a ring tone, for example).

Primary Target Audience. That group of individuals currently using the brand, having used the brand in the past, or being targeted as most likely to use the product or service in the future.

Promotional Mix. The mix of media vehicles—such as advertising, direct marketing, outdoor, etc.—that are employed within a campaign.

Psychographics. Deals with lifestyle issues, attitudes, beliefs, activities, and personal interests of the target audience.

Pulsing Media Schedule. This media schedule is a combination of both flighting and continuity media schedules.

Qualitative Research. Secondary research that already exists or can be collected via open-ended surveys or farmed from focus groups.

Quantitative Research. Primary research that involves collecting new research in order to find an answer to a particular set of marketing needs.

RSS. An acronym for Rich Site Summary or Really Simple Syndication; a subscription-based group of web-based formats that deliver constantly changing audio and video web updates.

Reach. Reach determines the total number of people or households that will see or be exposed at least once to the visual/verbal message during a set period of time.

Relationship Marketing. A marketing strategy that is defined by the amount of one-on-one interaction that takes place between the brand and the target.

Secondary Target Audience. That group of individuals—typically family and friends—most likely to influence a purchase or those most likely to purchase a product on behalf of the primary audience.

Share of Voice. Refers to a brand's equity or dominance within its brand category based on the percentage of advertising dollars spent as compared to other competitors.

Short Message Service (SMS). A mobile text message that may or may not include a link to a sponsoring Internet site.

Slogans. Usually located by the logo, a slogan is a short statement of the company's mission statement or philosophy.

Stealth Marketing. Also known as word of mouth, buzz, or ambush marketing, this type of marketing often uses actors to talk about or use a product in social situations.

Support Statement. An additional feature/benefit combination found on the creative brief that will be pushed in advertising and promotional efforts.

Taglines. Usually located by the logo, a tagline has a shorter lifespan than a slogan and is typically no more than a short statement of the current campaign's theme or creative direction.

Tone. Gives the key consumer benefit a visual/verbal voice and defines the brand's personality and image through the use of humor, demonstrations, testimonials, and so on.

Transit Advertising. Any advertising that appears on the interior or exterior of buses, taxis, subway cars, commuter trains, or ferries, or at stations, on platforms, in terminals, at bus stops, or on benches.

Unique Selling Proposition (USP). If a brand is new or has a unique feature competitors do not have, the key consumer benefit can be promoted using a USP.

User Generated Content. Information on a brand that is passed along by consumers via e-mail, the Internet, or word of mouth.

Vidcast. Podcasts that have a video format.

Viral Marketing. Also called word-of-mouth marketing; an advertising message that is passed along between acquaintances on the Internet.

Webcasts. Deliver a one-way flow of information to the viewer.

Webinar. A web-based seminar that allows users to conduct live meetings, lectures, seminars, or workshops online either at a predetermined time or on demand.

Wireframe. A way of organizing a web page during the design stage.

Wireless Application Protocol (WAP). A wireless web connection.

Word-of-Mouth Marketing. See viral marketing.

Bibliography

Allen, Gemmy, and Georganna Zaba. *Internet Resources for Integrated Marketing Communication.* Orlando, FL: Harcourt, 2000.

Altstiel, Tom, and Jean Grow. *Advertising Strategy: Creative Tactics from the Outside/In.* Thousand Oaks, CA.: Sage Publications, 2006.

Altstiel, Tom, and Jean Grow. *Advertising Creative.* Thousand Oaks, CA: Sage Publications, 2010.

American Marketing Association. www.marketingpower.com/AboutAMA/Pages/Definition of Marketing.

American Marketing Association.www.marketingpower.com/Dictionary.aspx.

Asimov, Isaac. Wientzen, Robert H. "Direct to Dot,com . . . and Beyond" http://www.themarketingsite.com/live/content.php?Item_ID=420.

Avery, Jim. *Advertising Campaign Planning.* Chicago: Copy Workshop, 2000.

Bangs, David H. *The Market Planning Guide.* 5th ed. Chicago: Upstart Publishing, 1998.

Bendinger, Bruce. *The Copy Workshop Workbook.* Chicago: Copy Workshop, 1993.

Berman, Margo. *Street-Smart Advertising: How to Win the Battle of the Buzz.* Lanham, MD: Rowman & Littlefield Publishers, 2007.

Bernbach, William. *Bill Bernbach Said. . . .* New York: DDB Needham Worldwide Books, 1989, p. 87.

Bernstein, David. *Advertising Outdoors.* London: Phaidon Press, 1997.

Blake, Gary, and Robert W. Bly. *The Elements of Copywriting.* New York: Simon & Schuster, 1997.

Blakeman, Robyn. *The Bare Bones of Advertising Print Design.* Boulder, CO: Rowman & Littlefield Publishers, 2004.

———. *Integrated Marketing Communication: Creative Strategy, from Idea to Implementation.* Boulder, CO: Rowman & Littlefield Publishers, 2007.

———. *The Bare Bones Introduction to Integrated Marketing Communication.* Lanham, MD: Rowman & Littlefield Publishers, 2009.

Blanchard, Robert. "Parting Essay." July 1999. Excerpted on Brand I Cool Marketing: Resources, Brand Quotes. http://brandcool.com/node/21.

Book, Albert, C., and Dennis C. Schick. *Fundamentals of Copy and Layout.* 3d ed. Lincolnwood, IL: NTC Business Books, 1997.

Burnett, John, and Sandra Moriarty. *Introduction to Marketing Communication.* Upper Saddle River, NJ: Prentice Hall, 1998.

Burnett, Leo. *100 LEO's.* Lincolnwood, IL: NTC Business Books, 1995.

Burton, Philip Ward. *Advertising Copywriting.* 7th ed. Lincolnwood, IL: NTC Business Books, 1999.

Case, Tony, and AdweekMedia staff. Top Media & Marketing Innovations of 2008. Adweek.com, December 15, 2008. http://www.adweek.com/aw/content_display/special-reports/other-reports/e3if39d7edc6dfc96b523fd285ff204f7b4.

Chiat, Jay. Altstiel, Tom, and Jean Grow. *Advertising Strategy: Creative Tactics from the Outside/In.* Thousand Oaks, CA.: Sage Publications, 2006.

Clifford, Stephanie. "Bravo Shows Move Further into Licensing Products." *New York Times,* April 12, 2009. http://www.nytimes.com/2009/04/13/business/media/13bravo.html.

———. "As Storefronts Become Vacant, Ads Arrive." *New York Times,* May 11, 2009. http://www.nytimes.com/2009/05/12/business/media/12adco.html.

Clow, Kenneth A., and Donald Baack. *Integrated Advertising, Promotion and Marketing Communications.* Upper Saddle River, NJ: Prentice Hall, 2002.

Coyer, Kate, Tony Dowmunt, and Alan Fountain. *The Alternative Media Handbook.* New York: Routledge, 2008

Dalzell, Chet. "Building Relationships and Trust Online with E-Mail." TheMarketingSite.com, 2009. http://www.themarketingsite.com/live/content.php?Item_ID=1104.

Della Femina, Jerry. *From Those Wonderful Folks Who Gave You Pearl Harbor.* New York: Simon & Schuster, 1970.

Dolliver, Mark. "Tough Times Call for Reasons to Spend." Adweek.com, June 4, 2009. http://www.adweek.com/aw/content_display/news/agency/e3i573ed7d4bca6f9fc5ddf2bdcf5ae8aa1.

Duncan, Tom. *IMC: Using Advertising and Promotion to Build Brands.* Boston: McGraw-Hill, 2002.

Evans, Joel R., and Barry Berman. *Marketing.* 4th ed. New York: Macmillan, 1990.

Gelles, David. "Advertisers Brace for Online Viral Marketing Curbs." *Financial Times,* April 2, 2009. http://www.commercialfreechildhood.org/news/2009/04/advertisersbrace.html.

Giannini, Gaetan T. *Marketing Public Relations.* Upper Saddle River, NJ: Pearson, 2010.

Guth, David W., and Charles Marsh. *Public Relations: A Values-Driven Approach.* 2d ed. Boston: Allyn and Bacon, 2003.

Hafer, Keith W., and Gordon E. White. *Advertising Writing.* St. Paul, MN: West Publishing, 1977.

Hester, Edward L. *Successful Marketing Research.* New York: John Wiley & Sons, 1996.

Jaffe, Joseph. *Life After the 30-Second Spot: Energize Your Brand with a Bold Mix of Alternatives to Traditional Advertising.* New York: John Wiley & Sons, 2005.

Jakacki, Bernard C. *IMC: An Integrated Marketing Communications Exercise.* Cincinnati, OH: South-Western College Publishing, 2001.

Jay, Ros. *Marketing on a Budget.* Boston: International Thomson Business Press, 1998.

Jefferson, Thomas. "An Anecdote of Dr. Franklin." 1818. The Colonial Williamsburg Official History Site. http://www.history.org/almanack/resources/jeffersonanecdote.cfm.

Jewler, A. Jerome, and Bonnie L. Drewniany. *Creative Strategy in Advertising.* Belmont, CA: Thomson Wadsworth, 2005.

Jones, Susan K. *Creative Strategy in Direct Marketing.* 2d ed. Chicago: NTC Business Books, 1998.

Klara, Robert. http://brandweek.printthis.clickability.com. *Heard on the Street,* December 5, 2008.

Krugman, Dean M., Leonard N. Reid, S. Watson Dunn, and Arnold M. Barban. *Advertising: Its Role in Modern Marketing.* 8th ed. Fort Worth, TX: Dryden, 1994.

Levinson, Jay Conrad. *Guerrilla Creativity.* New York: Houghton Mifflin Company, 2001.

———. *Guerrilla Marketing.* 4th ed. New York: Houghton Mifflin Company, 2007.

Malickson, David L., and John W. Nason. *Advertising: How to Write the Kind That Works.* New York: Charles Scribner's Sons, 1977.

McDonald, William J. *Direct Marketing: An Integrated Approach.* Boston: Irwin/ McGraw-Hill, 1998.

McLuhan, Marshall. *Understanding Media: The Extensions of Man.* 1964. Reprinted. Cambridge, MA: MIT Press, 1994.

Mitchell, Alan. "Out of the Shadows." *Journal of Marketing Management* 15, no. 1–3 (January-April 1999): 25–42. www.brandcoolmarketing.com.

Mobile Marketing Association. www.mmaglobal.com/news/mma-definition-mobile marketing.

Monahan, Tom. *The Do It Yourself Lobotomy.* New York: John Wiley & Sons, 2002.

Moscardelli, Deborah M. *Advertising on the Internet.* Upper Saddle River, NJ: Prentice Hall, 1999.

National Bureau of Economic Research. Giles, Chris and Geoff Dyer. www.ft.com/ cms/s/edaeb336-bfdf-11dd-9222–0000779fd18c. December 1, 2008.

Ogden, James R. *Developing a Creative and Innovative Integrated Marketing Communication Plan: A Working Model.* Upper Saddle River, NJ: Prentice Hall, 1998.

Ogilvy, David. *Confessions of an Advertising Man.* New York: Ballantine Books, 1971.

———. *Ogilvy on Advertising.* New York: Vintage Books, 1985.

O'Guinn, Thomas C., Chris T. Allen, and Richard J. Semenik. *Advertising and Integrated Brand Promotion.* 3d ed. Mason, OH: Thomson South-Western, 2003.

O'Toole, John. *The Trouble with Advertising.* New York: Times Books, 1985.

Osborn, Alex. "Brainstorming—'Thought Showers!'" http://destech.wordpress. com/2009/03/25/brainstorming-thought-showers.com.

Parente, Donald, Bruce Vanden Bergh, Arnold Barban, and James Marra. *Advertising Campaign Strategy: A Guide to Marketing Communication Plans.* Orlando, FL: Dryden, 1996.

Percy, Larry. *Strategies for Implementing Integrated Marketing Communication.* Chicago: NTC Business Books, 1997.

Peterson, Robin T. *Principles of Marketing.* Orlando, FL: Harcourt Brace Jovanovich, 1989.

Porter, Michael. Adweek.com, Tony Case, 2008.

Reeves, Rosser. *Reality in Advertising.* New York: Alfred A Knopf, 1981.

Ries, Al, and Jack Trout. *Positioning: The Battle for Your Mind.* New York: McGraw-Hill, 2000.

Rothenberg, Randall. *Where the Suckers Moon: An Advertising Story.* New York: Alfred A. Knopf, 1994.

Schlage (press release). www.newsblaze.com, 2009.

Shimp, Terence A. *Advertising Promotion: Supplemental Aspects of Integrated Marketing Communications.* 5th ed. Orlando, FL: Dryden, 2000.

Sirgy, Joseph M. *Integrated Marketing Communication: A Systems Approach.* Upper Saddle River, NJ: Prentice Hall, 1998.

Thaler, Linda Kaplan, and Robin Koval. *Bang! Getting Your Message Heard in a Noisy World.* New York: Doubleday, 2003.

Throckmorton, Joan. *Winning Direct Response Advertising.* 2d ed. Lincolnwood, IL: NTC Business Books, 1997.

van Bel, Egbert Jan. "Want Loyalty? Buy a Dog!" TheMarketingSite.com, 2004. http://www.themarketingsite.com/live/content.php?Item_ID=3569&Revision=en%2F1&Start=0.

Vanden Bergh, Bruce, and Helen Katz. *Advertising Principles.* Lincolnwood, IL: NTC Business Books, 1999.

Vonk, Nancy, and Janet Kestin. *Pick Me: Breaking into Advertising and Staying There.* New York: John Wiley & Sons, 2005.

Wientzen, Robert H. "Direct to Dot,com . . . and Beyond" http://www.themarketingsite.com/live/content.php?Item_ID=420.

Wilcox, Dennis L., Glen T. Cameron, Philip H. Ault, and Warren K. Agee. *Public Relations Strategies and Tactics.* 7th ed. Boston: Allyn and Bacon, 2003.

Wright, Robert E. "Financial Crisis and Reform: Looking Back for Clues to the Future." *McKinsey Quarterly,* December 2008. http://www.mckinseyquarterly.com/Financial_crisis_and_reform_Looking_back_for_clues_to_the_future_2271.

York, Emily Bryson. "Denny's Grand Slam Giveaway a Hit with 2 Million Diners." *Advertising Age,* February 3, 2009. http://adage.com/article?article_id=134306.

Zucker, Jeff. Adweek staff. www.adweek.com, December 2008.

Index

Italic page references indicate illustrations and photographs.

About the Author

Robyn Blakeman received her bachelor's degree from the University of Nebraska in 1980 and her master's from Southern Methodist University in Dallas, Texas, in 1996.

In 1980, she moved to Texas, where she began her career as a designer for an architectural magazine. She then took a position as mechanical director for one of the top advertising agencies in Dallas before eventually leaving to work as a freelance designer.

Professor Blakeman began teaching advertising and graphic design in 1987, first with the Art Institutes and then as an Assistant Professor of Advertising, teaching both graphic and computer design at Southern Methodist University. As an Assistant Professor of Advertising at West Virginia University, she developed the creative track in layout and design and was also responsible for designing and developing the first Online Integrated Marketing Communication graduate program in the country.

Blakeman has been nominated five times for inclusion in *Who's Who Among America's Teachers,* is included in *Who's Who in America,* and is a member of Kappa Tau Alpha.

In addition, Blakeman is the author of six books: *The Bare Bones of Advertising Print Design, Integrated Marketing Communication: Creative Strategy from Idea to Implementation, The Bare Bones Introduction to Integrated Marketing Communication, The Brains Behind Great Ad Campaigns, Advertising Campaign Design: Just the Essentials,* and *Strategic Uses of Alternative Media: Just the Essentials.* Professor Blakeman currently teaches advertising design at the University of Tennessee, Knoxville.